*Swift
and the
Satirist's
Art*

EDWARD W. ROSENHEIM, Jr.

Swift and the Satirist's Art

THE UNIVERSITY OF CHICAGO PRESS

Library of Congress Catalog Card Number: 63-11400

The University of Chicago Press, Chicago & London
The University of Toronto Press, Toronto 5, Canada

For My Wife

Preface

IN THIS BOOK I have chiefly attempted to clarify the nature of Swift's achievement as a satirist. To do this, I have felt it necessary to suggest ways in which satire can be distinguished from other kinds of writing and to describe questions which, I think, are characteristically raised by the kind of works we call satiric. But it is the pursuit of these questions as they are uniquely reflected in Swift's satiric writings that has been my principal concern. If I can be said to have developed and applied a "method," I have done so not out of a desire to expound critical doctrine, but in the belief that a fairly systematic conception of the art which Swift practiced can augment our understanding of and admiration for his artistic accomplishment.

In the course of my discussion, I have conducted several close "analyses"—as I fear they must be called—of passages from Swift's writings, in particular *A Tale of a Tub*. These undertakings presume a reader who is rather familiar with the *Tale*—or at least willing to become so. I recognize with some chagrin the burden they place on my reader's attention. But it seems to me that criticism of a text inevitably presupposes close reading, that I can reveal the importance of particulars only by examining particulars, and that—as Swift above all men would insist—knowledge of a text is not a matter of master-keys and easy generalizations but of an energetic concern with what the author has actually said.

This book has made much use of the extraordinary accomplishments of Swift scholars, especially those of the last three decades. The labors of Sir Harold Williams, of D. Nichol Smith, and of Herbert Davis and his associates have brought us Swift's writings in a form which is unexcelled among editions of writers of any period. Professors Landa and Ehrenpreis have illuminated Swift's life, times, and work in ways that are profoundly and permanently helpful. Over a relatively short time, moreover, these and other gifted scholars have provided discoveries and interpretations which have tacitly become a part of even the common reader's understanding of many of Swift's individual writings. Thus, much of my own discussion has proceeded upon a substratum of Swiftian wisdom provided by such people as Professors Mohler, Nicolson, Starkman, Kathleen Williams, Case, Bullitt, Price, Elliott, and Harth—to name only some of those to whom I personally feel the greatest indebtedness. Above all, I think, my generation of Swift students has been aided by Professor Quintana and particularly *The Mind and Art of Jonathan Swift* which, in its rigor and sensitivity, remains a *vade mecum* for both the amateur and professional Swiftian. If my book succeeds in any way in adding to our understanding of Swift, my efforts must be viewed as a modest return on the prodigious investment of these scholarly predecessors.

Some of my ideas about satire and Swift were incorporated, in preliminary form, in a doctoral dissertation which I wrote over ten years ago. Since then, I have given these ideas a certain amount of ventilation in some lectures and papers, in an introduction to an anthology of Swift's writings, and particularly in my classes at the University of Chicago. Some passages in the third and fourth chapters of the present book have appeared in my article, "The Fifth Voyage of Lemuel Gulliver: A Footnote," in *Modern Philology*, LX (1962), and I am grateful for editorial permission to include them here. The responses I have had to such discussions of my views about Swift and satire have caused me to expand, modify, and sometimes to abandon many of my original notions. For these responses—including some very robust assaults—I can here give only omnibus but genuine thanks.

The sustained generosity with which I have been treated in other quarters can, however, be specifically if inadequately acknowledged here. I should, accordingly, note first that the completion of this book occurred during a period of release from academic duties, made possible by the kindness of Mr. Howard Willett, Sr., through a Willett Faculty Fellowship in the University of Chicago. I am indebted, too, to the interest and patience of my hosts during a recent visiting appointment to the English Department of Pennsylvania State University—and especially to the departmental chairman, Professor Henry W. Sams.

My adult introduction to Swift occurred in the classroom of Professor Louis Landa, and I am sure that I am only one of scores of students whose permanent enthusiasm for Swift's writings can be traced to Professor Landa's learned and humane approach to his subject. I am fortunate, too, in having studied with Professor R. S. Crane; although my views on Swift and satire can certainly not be assumed to coincide with those of Professor Crane, I have, I think, profited immeasurably by his training as well as by his illumination of many problems concerning Swift.

Among members of the English Department at the University of Chicago who have helped and encouraged me at various stages in my studies I am particularly grateful to Professors Donald F. Bond and Theodore Silverstein. My friend and colleague, Professor Gwin J. Kolb, has climaxed his continuing kindness by that most generous of acts—the careful reading and thoughtful criticism of my manuscript.

I can gratefully record the fact that Professor Arthur Friedman, who directed my dissertation, has read the manuscript of this book with great care and has offered suggestions so valuable that I have accepted all of them. Beyond this, neither the clichés of acknowledgment nor any graceful evasion of them can express my obligation to an admired friend who continues to be an admired teacher. In this preface I only venture the hope that my book does some small justice to Professor Friedman's friendship with its author.

Contents

NOTE ON COMMONLY USED EDITIONS

THE AUTHORITATIVE EDITIONS of which I have made the most frequent use, together with the abbreviated titles by which I regularly refer to them, are listed below.

Prose Works: *The Prose Works of Jonathan Swift*. Ed. HERBERT DAVIS. Oxford, 1937———. 14 volumes (Volumes V and XIV not yet published).

Poems: *The Poems of Jonathan Swift*. Ed. SIR HAROLD WILLIAMS. Oxford, 1937. 3 volumes.

Correspondence: *The Correspondence of Jonathan Swift*. Ed. F. ELRINGTON BALL. London, 1910–14. 6 volumes.

Tale: *A Tale of a Tub, To which is added The Battle of the Books and the Mechanical Operation of the Spirit.* Ed. A. C. GUTHKELCH and D. NICHOL SMITH. 2d ed. Oxford, 1958.

CHAPTER I

The Satiric Spectrum

No one who writes about Swift, I suspect, entirely forgets that satirist's genealogy, in *A Tale of a Tub,* of the "True Critick," whose lineal descent begins with Momus and Hybris and proceeds in a direct line to Etcaetera the Younger. Swift has, characteristically, engendered an uneasiness that persists into our own time. Among other things, he has pointed to the survival power of critical folly, and today's critic is made quite aware that he is not immune to the same vices that Swift assails.

But if pretentiousness and parasitism survive, so too does that more natural and laudable critical motive, curiosity. "When the eye or imagination is struck with an uncommon work," says Imlac to Rasselas, "the next transition of an active mind is to the means by which it was performed." Johnson's words are reassuring; when we stand, as did Imlac and his friends, beneath the dwarfing shadows of the pyramids, though we can build no monuments of our own, we can at least measure the monumental works of others.

The reassurance is welcome. To write about satire and to attempt to provide the term with explicit and limited meaning is to feel all the traditional critical misgivings with special acuteness. Satire is an ancient term, but as compared with tragedy or lyric poetry or rhetoric, it has prompted relatively little systematic discussion, at least in its generic aspects.[1] There are good reasons for this caution. The works which, at one time or another, have been called satiric represent an enormous diversity in substance, structure, style, and motive —covering, it is likely, as great a range as the literature which has, in any meaningful sense, been called tragic or comic. When in one age satire appears to be marked by certain identifying conventions, these often disappear or are altered in what is called satire in suc-

---

[1] Among the surprisingly few extended discussions of satire in general, one of the most notable continues to be David Worcester's *The Art of Satire* (Cambridge, Mass., 1940). Robert C. Elliott's *The Power of Satire: Magic, Ritual, Art* (Princeton, 1960) is a highly illuminating work, particularly as it considers the origins and continuing social and psychological role of satire. A lively and thoughtful discussion of "The Nature and Value of Satire" is provided by Edgar Johnson as an introductory essay to *A Treasury of Satire* (New York, 1945), pp. 3–37. Wyndham Lewis has a good deal to say about satire in general and about specific satirists, including himself, in *Rude Assignment* (London, 1950), pp. 45–58. And a most provocative section on "The Mythos of Winter: Irony and Satire" (in which the indispensable elements of satire are described at the outset in a manner rather like my own) appears in Northrop Frye's *Anatomy of Criticism: Four Essays* (Princeton, N.J., 1957), pp. 223–39. Certain studies of the satire of particular periods or individuals have also offered definitions of this species of writing. Among the most interesting of these discussions are those provided by the essentially historical account of John Peter in *Complaint and Satire in Early English Literature* (Oxford, 1956), the "Theory of Satire" in Alvin Kernan's *The Cankered Muse: Satire of the English Renaissance* (New Haven, 1959), and, of particular relevance for the present essays, John M. Bullitt's *Jonathan Swift and the Anatomy of Satire* (Cambridge, Mass., 1953). As should shortly become clear, the approach to satire suggested by the present study differs quite fundamentally from what is offered by these and other scholars of the subject. On the other hand, A. R. Heiserman's *Skelton and Satire* (Chicago, 1961) takes into generous account some of my basic ideas about satire as well as making clear the points on which Professor Heiserman and I are in sharp though amiable disagreement.

ceeding ages. No mode of writing is more frequently identified with terms applied to other literary species; the achievements of satire are, more often than not, assessed by standards appropriate to rhetoric, comedy, or even moral philosophy. And in its particularity, its "topicality," satire seems to resist our attempts to establish principles by which, over the ages, the art of the satirist can be regularly recognized and described.

Doubts concerning the usefulness of literary definitions—doubts perhaps expressed more frequently than ever in our own time—are particularly troublesome when it comes to defining satire. We are properly inhibited by the image of the satirist himself as a peculiarly hard-boiled individualist, whose talent for derision can be employed to advantage upon those who strive to reduce his art to rules and who plod in his wake with solemn explanations of what it is that he has done. When the satirist discusses his own art, he is seldom very thorough or convincing: Swift's statements about satire are oblique and fragmentary, Dryden's pedantic and sanctimonious, Pope's of doubtful applicability to his own work. It does not help the student to realize that, quite indifferent to what has been said or left unsaid about the nature of satire, these writers have affected us as powerfully and permanently as have the practitioners of the most-discussed and best-defined literary *genres*.

Yet, as the words of Imlac suggest, the more uncommon the work of art, the more natural are the questions which it raises. In these essays I am concerned, above all, with questions raised by memorable literary art in minds which, whether active or not, are curious. We admire the great satirists for the practice of an art to which we are prepared to give a name and which we must thus presumably be prepared to understand. In other words, it is natural to ask just what it is that the successful satirist does well. And when we feel that a particular satirist does his job superlatively well, our question assumes added urgency. This, I believe, is true about Jonathan Swift, whose particular art raises the questions with which these essays are concerned.

Swift's claim to greatness rests to a considerable extent upon his achievements as a satirist. His strange and tragic life, the lively times during which he wrote, and his proximity to vital currents of contemporary thought are not, despite their strong fascination, the chief reason for his permanent stature. His complex personality, however engaged in the issues of his own day, has attained its peculiar robust immortality because of the literature he produced—and the most famous of that literature is almost universally regarded as satiric.

Even within his own lifetime, and certainly ever afterward, Swift's admirers have been virtually united in their conclusions about his success as a satiric artist. About the nature of his art, however, they have been divided, uncertain, or, more often than not, entirely silent. For almost exactly two centuries after Swift's death, the hundreds of people who wrote, usually with vast care and respect, about England's greatest satirist had very little to say about satire itself or the way in which Swift created it. Many of their studies invaluably illuminate Swift's life and times, the vexed problems of text and canon, the sources and consequences of Swift's ideas, and his stature as a clergyman, moralist, correspondent, historian, and pamphleteer. To the great majority of such undertakings any student of Swift is deeply indebted. Beyond such scholarly contributions, moreover, those who love Swift can find abundant stimulation in various specialized interpretive writings which, while they profess to illuminate Swift's personality and beliefs, employ his literary accomplishments as means to such ends. The egregious strictures of Thackeray against Swift long ago appeared in a lecture which openly purported to speak of "men and their lives, rather than of books";[2] an equally candid profession of emphasis might well become the authors of many more recent studies, among them the interesting attempts to probe Swift's emotional life with the methods of modern psychiatry or to "exhume," with whatever resources of art or scholarship come to hand, that compelling personality whom, it must be admitted, most of us really would like to have known.

The only disturbing aspect of this preoccupation with Swift's personality is its implicit neglect of his art. Until the last ten or fifteen years, what seems most to have interested those who wrote about the great satirist is not his satire but rather his madness, his "marriage," his friends and enemies, habits and beliefs, and a dozen similar matters. Paradoxically, perhaps, it is in the best of the biographies of Swift that this emphasis upon the personal and historical yields, in some measure, to a concern for the nature of Swift's work itself.

[2] W. M. Thackeray, *The English Humorists of the Eighteenth Century* (New York, 1853), p. 5.

Forster, Craik, Quintana, and, most recently, Ehrenpreis[3] have not hesitated to reverse the ordinary priority and employ historical and biographical research in the illumination of Swift's writings, moving from events to ideas and their embodiment in books, and producing, for better or for worse, unabashed, explicit judgments.

To the extent that these biographers have also performed as critics, they have adumbrated the emphasis upon analysis, explication, and assessment which, rather surprisingly, marks the most influential books about Swift which have appeared since the end of World War II. At least eight books and a large number of scholarly articles have been frankly addressed to the analysis and criticism of Swift's writing. For the first time in over two centuries, one feels that the admirers of Swift's work are deliberately and directly contemplating "the means by which it was performed."

Each of the major studies which have recently appeared has, in its own way, shed light upon Swift's literary performances. Our "understanding" of Swift has been augmented on a variety of levels, ranging from the acquisition of "meanings" which have hitherto been elusive to a new and important recognition of the astonishing diversity of literary arts which he practiced with almost uniform brilliance.

The present essays are in no sense intended to call into question the conclusions advanced by recent criticism and scholarship. Clearly, for example, Swift was a brilliant rhetorician—in a very practical sense, perhaps a more successful one than any other "man of letters" in English history—and it is of obvious importance to note, within the context of rhetorical tradition, those respects in which his virtuosity is unique.[4] We have also been invited to recognize (at a sur-

---

[3] John Forster, *The Life of Jonathan Swift* (London, 1875); Sir Henry Craik, *The Life of Jonathan Swift* (London, 1882); Ricardo Quintana, *The Mind and Art of Jonathan Swift* (London and New York, 1936); Irvin Ehrenpreis, *The Personality of Jonathan Swift* (London, 1958).

[4] This is, I think, the principal achievement of Martin Price in *Swift's Rhetorical Art: A Study in Structure and Meaning* (New Haven, 1953). Swift's familiarity with and attitudes toward traditional rhetoric are made clear by Harold D. Kelling in "Reason in Madness: *A Tale of a Tub*," *PMLA*, LXIX (1954), 198–222; the *persona* of the *Tale*, it is argued, is employed to exemplify bad rhetoric, a process of exposure which the article treats essentially as successful rhetorical strategy. A recent, very systematic rhetorical analysis of four of Swift's essays will be found in Charles Allen Beaumont's *Swift's Classical Rhetoric* (Athens, Ga., 1961). The author is convincing in his argument for Swift's wide knowledge and use of rhetorical principles; his ulti-

prisingly late date in the history of Swift studies) the singular flexibility with which Swift can employ such a common device as the literary *persona,* and William Ewald's study, by stressing the diversely imaginative character of Swift's "masks," reminds us—as we need to be reminded—that Swift's greatest writings are as notable for artifice as for argument.[5] We have, likewise, been aided through textual analysis and interpretation to see with renewed clarity the normative values from which Swift's attacks proceed and, by assuming the satirist's office to be chiefly moral, to discover within his philosophic principles much which explains both his choice of victims and his method of attack.[6]

Despite these contributions, however, it is difficult to find either in recent or in older studies a satisfactory definition of satire—and hence a firm assertion that the art which Swift practices most brilliantly is not truly that of the rhetorician or the comedian or an amalgam of the two. It is true that we find descriptions of devices and procedures which, implicitly or explicitly, are considered satiric, but we are not told whether the listing of such devices is exhaustive or, indeed, by what standards, if any, they can be judged intrinsically satiric.[7] Where the relationship between satire and comedy is not ignored, the two terms are often indifferently employed to modify one another.[8] And where the major object of examination is Swift's

---

mate recognition that Swift did not hesitate to "burst beyond the bounds of rules" (p. 148) is welcome, however.

[5] William Bragg Ewald, Jr., *The Masks of Jonathan Swift* (Cambridge, Mass., 1954).

[6] Bullitt's wide-ranging discussion of Swift's satiric methods asks ultimately, as I understand it, that we view his literary achievement as the reflection of "an outraged conviction subdued and controlled by a sustained artistic intention" (p. 191). Though Bullitt distinguishes clearly and profitably between Swift's techniques and his motives or "vision of life," it is in the latter area that, it seems to me, he finally locates the peculiarly satiric character of Swift's art. J. Middleton Murry's *Jonathan Swift: A Critical Biography* (London, 1954) provides a more flamboyant and far less responsible specimen of analysis by "personal vision," in which the special quality of Swift's writing is regularly equated with the problems and peculiarities of the author.

[7] Price, for example, considers Swift's style or diction, his wit, his satiric "masks" and his "symbolic works," ultimately moving to "patterns of meaning" in a discussion of the beliefs which seem to have motivated Swift.

[8] Bullitt refers, apparently indifferently, to "comic satire" and "satiric comedy" (e.g., p. 7) as well as to the possibility that, in such writing as the fourth book of *Gulliver's Travels,* Swift's art verges upon tragedy but "without the grandeur which is a necessary quality for the true tragic *catharsis*" (p. 15).

rhetorical power, we are led, in the absence of any firm distinction between satire and rhetoric as a whole, to infer that most of the procedures which may be called satiric are species of the more general art of persuasion.[9]

In effect, most of the studies of Swift's writings tend to *assume* that what Swift produced can often be called satiric and either to ignore or to take for granted the precise nature of his performance qua satire. There have, on the other hand, been recent attempts to "read out" of such a work as *Gulliver's Travels* the satiric element and to argue that the book must primarily be considered as a specimen of comic narrative.[10] Clearly, the absence of a workable definition of satire leaves in a state of embarrassing disarmament those students for whom such a view is, at the most, fragmentary. Such a definition is needed, one suspects, as an antidote not only to uneasiness among the critics of Swift's art but to actual error as well.

In some instances, indeed, critics have overtly abdicated the responsibility for dealing with Swift's work as satire and have approached it instead in terms of the author's philosophic belief, the general qualities of literary style which it displays, or the singularity of the character it reflects. In such an analysis, of course, the term "satire" becomes a mere cipher, whose loss of meaning is explained

[9] Price distinguishes between the "new rhetoric" and older traditions of an essentially Aristotelian character, but, as an example of the "new," Swift's writing is largely examined for its resemblance to rather than its distinction from the work of Swift's non-satirist contemporaries. This is a valuable and convincing account, but it is obviously not designed to shed much light on the problem which concerns us —the establishment of Swift's unique satiric achievement.

[10] Harold D. Kelling's *The Appeal to Reason: A Study of Jonathan Swift's Critical Theory and Its Relation to His Writings* (unpublished doctoral dissertation, Yale University, 1948) seems to have begun the "comic" approach to the *Travels*. He asserts, for example, that "the effects of [Swift's] individual works range from that of political propaganda to that of pure comedy" and he equates the latter with *Gulliver's Travels*. Two studies which reach similar conclusions are John F. Ross, "The Final Comedy of Lemuel Gulliver," in *Studies in the Comic* ("University of California Publications in English," VIII, 1941), pp. 175–96, and Edward Stone, "Swift and the Horses: Misanthropy or Comedy?" *Modern Language Quarterly*, X (1949), 367–76. Both of these articles urge that the "misanthropic" condition to which Gulliver attains in Book IV is the experience of Swift's comic protagonist. Neither these studies nor that of Kelling attempt to distinguish between the comic and the satiric. Thus Kelling includes even "pure comedy" in the category of satire and later refers to the *Travels* as "laughing satire or comedy." And Ross, having vigorously argued that Gulliver's misanthropy is not his creator's, concludes that "Swift is above him in the realm of comic satire" (p. 196).

away upon historical grounds.[11] What results from such procedures is not, as a rule, demonstrably erroneous, but only inadequate. It is entirely possible to limit one's discussion of the Voyage to the Houyhnhnms to its extraordinary vision of the human condition or to rejoice in the dynamic prose of the *Drapier's Letters* without raising questions about the satiric quality of either.

More often than not, however, the word "satire" does appear in discussions of Swift and, as a rule, some meaning is implicitly attached to the term. These definitions tacitly tend to be essentially traditional and to have as their basis some concept of the historical development of satire as a literary type. The conventions which form the core of such concepts have, as a rule, one principal referent: "form" (in the sense of actual disposition of parts, etc.); substance or "topic" (such as vice or folly, a particular order of mankind, etc.), or the less tangible matters of motive (anger, jest, and the like) or effect (contempt, moral enlightenment, and many more). As we have seen, however, such views of satire are rarely employed in any very sustained way for the analysis of Swift's writing—and for rather obvious reasons. To define satire in this "unitary" fashion— by its form or substance or purpose alone—is to offer relatively slight guidance to the reading of a particular satiric work. In consequence, when most discussions of Swift's writings descend to detailed analysis, they proceed in substantial indifference to the character of the work as satire, and the distinction between satire and other literary modes becomes obscured. Style is assessed in generic terms, the beliefs sought become those of the philosopher, politician, or other theorist, and whatever is observed about structure or method is seldom intrinsically satiric.[12]

---

[11] Thus, for example, a popular biography of Swift asserts: "Yet, when all is said, nothing preserves *A Tale of a Tub* but its style, which is a pickle more trustworthy than that which a passage in it attributes to Lord Peter" (Stephen Gwynn, *The Life and Friendships of Dean Swift* [New York, 1933], p. 92); yet of this "style" we are told only that it is "the prose of a master . . . a poet's prose" (p. 91). John Hayward, too, in his conscientious anthology, *Gulliver's Travels and Selected Writings* (New York, 1934), remarks that "it is perhaps Swift's greatest gift and a measure of his genius that even now his style can knit together the dry bones of forgotten controversies and make them live again" (p. xiii).

[12] The best of the more recent studies—notably those of Price and Bullitt—are somewhat exceptional in this respect. While I am not certain that they ever clearly distinguish the satirist's art from other kinds of writing with which it can be confused, their emphasis is upon goals and procedures which are characteristically Swiftian, if not generically satiric.

To the extent that implicit conceptions of satire rest upon historic classifications, they are almost doomed to inadequacy. For the art of satire itself is, in David Worcester's term, protean.[13] Even in its Roman origins, Jebb tells us, satire "is the only [form] which has a continuous development extending from the vigorous age of the Commonwealth into the second century of the Empire"—from the innocuous farrago of the *lanx satura* to the fierce nationalist diatribes of Juvenal.[14] The briefest glance at the history of what has been regarded as satiric writing—the early and late Roman, the convention-laden medieval, the Augustan, the neglected but vigorous tracts of early nineteenth-century England, the social criticism which today's assortment of communications media sporadically provides—reveals the impossibility of finding in a single source, whether form, substance, or function, the common denominator which will bring uniformity to the entire field. The notion, indeed, of arriving at a definition of a literary kind through purely historical scrutiny of its origin or development seems paradoxical; for such examination requires precisely that prior definition which history cannot supply.

Yet one historical fact has real bearing upon our task and suggests a workable approach to a definition of satire. This fact is simply the persistence of a common tendency to regard certain kinds of writing as satiric. And this tendency is no mere matter of textbook classifications or the categories of literary historians. Most of us are surely aware of those moments when, in the book or the performance before us, we recognize something which we are prepared to call satiric. At that moment of recognition, the words we read or hear acquire new dimensions and lose familiar ones. We are conscious that the possession of explicit sorts of knowledge or belief is indispensable to an understanding of the author's intention; our conceptions of what the work "means," of its mode of conveying "truth," of the way in which we are expected to respond to it are all clearly altered. We are, as it were, in a new frame of mind. And because we detect in this new attitude much that has been previously elicited by works traditionally regarded as satiric, we are ready to describe as "satire" the art with which we are currently confronted.

[13] Worcester, *The Art of Satire*, p. 3.

[14] Sir Richard Jebb, *Essays and Addresses* (Cambridge, 1907), p. 152.

The ideas about satire which this study seeks to bring to the work of Swift have their basis primarily in this sort of recognition—in the expectations and demands which we commonly feel upon being exposed to works which are called satiric. The definition of satire which will be proposed is not derived from a concern for absolute principles with their sources in immutable qualities of human nature or of art, nor is satire here classified by location within a system of strictly logical categories. On the other hand, I have already implied the futility of seeking an "empirical" definition by attempting to take into account whatever has been regarded as satiric by any society at any time.

The most dogmatic feature of the argument which will be offered is its insistence that, if we apply the term "satire" to elements in the writings of Swift or any other author, we do so meaningfully and usefully. To put it in another way, we shall only be content to designate as satiric those kinds of writing which—in their procedures or in the demands or effects which they produce on audiences—can properly and profitably be *distinguished* from other literary species. The propriety of such distinctions rests, one suspects, upon our willingness to agree that satire does, indeed, provide a special kind of experience for its audience and that this experience has its source in identifiable procedures undertaken by the artist. The usefulness of these distinctions, on the other hand, rests ultimately upon the questions to which they lead in the scrutiny of satiric works. These are the questions which are the peculiar accompaniment to satire; upon our awareness of them depends our full appreciation of the satirist's achievement.

II

We have spoken of the "moments" in which we recognize satire within a particular work. To speak in this fashion implies an initial fact about our experience with satire, namely that it *can* be a matter of moments, of brief, transitory significance within literary products whose total nature, though generally affected by whatever satire they contain, is of itself by no means satiric. This fact, in turn, points to the resolution of a preliminary question. Must satire be considered as an "element," an ingredient which subserves goals describable only in other, broader terms? Are we, that is, confined to speaking about satiric "touches" or passages or satiric "coloring" in works

which, in their entirety, must be described as comedies or arguments
or allegories? Or is satire, on the contrary, a genuine literary form,
possessing, like the literary species established by Aristotle, its own
"peculiar power" or (in terms other than those of the *Poetics*) some
hallmark of its own—in structure, substance, style, or motive—
which allows us to classify the work in its entirety as "a satire"? The
answer again lies, I think, in our experience with satire. It is simply
that satire may be either of these things.

There are works which we think of as essentially satiric, and the
recognition that we have described informs our entire reaction to
them and must be sustained throughout. On the other hand, there
are the "moments" in other works—the passing remarks, brief
scenes, single passages—which we stamp as satiric before passing on
to other elements to which we respond in very different ways. Between the satire which is incorporated in a work of another species
such as comedy and that which is sufficiently dominant so that the
work itself is largely satiric, there is a difference which is one of
degree. If the total work demands from us that frame of mind peculiarly required by satire—sets us to asking certain kinds of questions and seeking certain kinds of satisfaction—then we are in the
presence of writing which is predominantly, though seldom exclusively, satiric. If, on the contrary, the satiric elements are quantita-
tively subordinate in the work (and hence as a rule qualitatively
subordinate in our response to it), we must seek elsewhere to explain the kind of total literary product with which we are dealing.

This question and its answer seem self-evident. They must be understood at the outset, however, for, in the first place, they indicate
that we shall not be advancing what is ordinarily regarded as a theory of literary "form"; we shall, that is, be discussing a species of
writing but not necessarily a species of complete written work. If
satire, moreover, is found in a quality or group of qualities which
may subserve or dominate, augment or order the work as a whole,
we must be alert for the non-satiric as well as the satiric constituents
of the writings we are considering. Thus, when confronted with a
particular writing by Swift, we cannot be misled by either its reputation as "satire" or its authentic satiric qualities, notable though
they may be, into the assumption that it is entirely or even predominantly "a satire." And this fact imposes upon us the obligation to
determine, with respect to every significant part of the work, the

presence or absence of satire. It reveals the possibility that satire may be juxtaposed to, or proceed concurrently with, other kinds of writing and the likelihood that these other kinds will be precisely those which, because of their frequent identification with satire, must be distinguished from it. It should be added, however, that this view relieves us of the burden under which certain analysts of satire have at times labored unnecessarily, namely the explication of all parts of a work in order to show their contribution to a purely satiric end. If a book accomplishes ends other than those of satire, we must be aware of these accomplishments; we must, furthermore, not confuse these other accomplishments, whatever their nature or importance, with those of satire itself.

To return to the sources of our common feeling that we are in the presence of satire, there is one general quality which, although it has been given various names, seems most readily and widely recognized. This is the quality which, although the term may seem rather loose, we shall describe as *attack*. For in one way or another, satire seems always to treat an object of some kind in an unfavorable way. To speak of "unfavorable" treatment is inexact, yet the difficulty is that a more limited definition ("criticism," "ridicule," or "exposure," for instance) will not do justice to the full range of writing which merits description as satire.

It is evident that a considerable number of satiric works strive for goals which are substantially the same as those of polemic rhetoric, and to such works the term "attack" seems readily applicable. Here the classic rhetorical categories can be illuminating: satire may truly "expose" evils or infirmities hitherto unrecognized by its audience; it may elicit blame, employing any of countless intellectual or emotional strategies, for individuals, groups, institutions, or ideas; it may urge its audience to future action, in some measure hostile, against the object under attack. And these rhetorical modes may be combined in various proportions to achieve various persuasive ends. Thus the traditional categories of rhetoric—forensic, epideictic, and deliberative—may often be imposed upon satire, although always in their "negative" aspect; i.e., the forensic exposure of past folly or evil, the epideictic incitement to blame rather than praise, and the deliberative exhortation to hostile action.

Many generalizations about satire imply that its characteristic effect is inevitably persuasive. Of this sort are the assertions, often advanced apologetically by satirists themselves, concerning the moral power of the art. And it is quite true that the concept of satire as a kind of uniquely effective rhetorical weapon is entirely just in many cases—including some of Swift's most notable writings.

At the same time, there are many works which we are prepared to regard as satiric but which, if we are to be candid, do not seem to "persuade" us, in any reasonable sense of the term. In such works, the object under satiric treatment emerges, to be sure, in an unfavorable light, but it is a light which is accepted a priori by the audience. No new judgment is invited; no course of action is urged; no novel information is produced. The audience, rather, is asked chiefly to rejoice in the heaping of opprobrium, ridicule, or fancied punishment upon an object of whose culpability they are *already* thoroughly convinced.

If the reader considers, for example, poems such as Dryden's *Mac Flecknoe* or Pope's *Dunciad,* he should see how difficult it is to assign any genuinely rhetorical function to these works, even though they are traditionally discussed and acclaimed as satiric productions. In *Mac Flecknoe,* Shadwell's dulness is entirely taken for granted. The apt humor of his accession to the throne vacated by Flecknoe, with all of its attendant devices, is effective only if one *assumes* from the beginning that Shadwell is an inferior poet, worthy of comparison to Heywood, Shirley, Ogleby, and his own Sir Formal. Neither the plot nor the details of diction, however ingenious they may be, are directed to altering our opinion, providing new grounds for scorn, or presenting any systematic argument against the historical Shadwell. The character of the protagonist is assumed to be familiar to the reader, whose part is solely to delight in the just abuse of an accepted figure of fun. The same may be said of virtually the entire *dramatis personae* of *The Dunciad.* Indeed, it may be precisely because we are required, from the outset, uncritically to accept far too much about the deficiencies of these hapless scribblers that *The Dunciad* is viewed with distaste by certain modern critics.[15] Pope's

[15] See in particular Gilbert Highet, "The Dunciad," *Modern Language Review,* XXXVI (July, 1941), 320–43. Professor Highet's hostile re-examination of the poem proceeds upon several grounds, none of which explicitly stresses the particular interpretation I have suggested. But, in his strictures against Pope's "subject" and in his assertion that "Pope has made his enemies into criminals" (p. 321), Highet in effect reveals his unwillingness to accept Pope's original, unsupported assumption that the punishment he will mete out fits the crimes of his victims.

dunces are "punished," violently and often wittily, but it is the exceptional passage in the poem which truly exposes or even exploits their actual sins. If we delight in the treatment they receive, it is chiefly because we are prepared to believe, for reasons largely unrelated to what Pope actually says in the poem, that the treatment is deserved. Over the centuries, it is true the historical figures of Theobald and Cibber have suffered (in the former case at least most unjustly) because Pope singled them out as monarchs of dulness, but this is not attributable to any demonstration on Pope's part. He has "persuaded" posterity, if at all, only by erecting an impressive monument to his own hostility. And, indeed, with the passing of time we lose most of our awareness of the historical figures against whom satire of this order is directed. The Shadwell of Dryden's verses and the Cibber of Pope's have become, for the common reader, little more than characters of fiction, whose relationship to their historical counterparts is now scarcely more significant than that of Falstaff to the misty figure of John Oldcastle.

There appears, then, to be a kind of satire which does not truly seek to be "persuasive" and to which a term like "punitive" may be more aptly applied. We should be at no loss to discover specimens of this kind of satiric procedure. It crops up repeatedly in various forms of popular entertainment in our own day—most commonly, perhaps, in the performances of those comedians who specialize in what is "good for a laugh" and, by ringing changes on the same well-established foibles of public men and institutions, produce a kind of humorous satire of derision. It is not difficult, if we are honest in considering our own responses, to distinguish between the most plainly representative works of persuasive and of punitive satire. Clearly there is a difference between, for example, the occurrences in *The Dunciad,* Book II (with its chain of ribald indignities which might have been inflicted upon any victims whom the reader was willing to accept as suitably culpable) and the bill of particulars which supports the critical assaults in Pope's *Peri Bathous.* In the former instance, most of us are amused without being induced at any point in the course of our reading to change our opinions of anything. In the latter case, Pope provides us with a special kind of proof—fragmentary, to be sure, and distorted as is proper to satire—which, for all its playfulness, reveals the authentic presence and badness of the writing which he calls bathetic.

But like most of the distinctions which will be suggested in this essay, that between persuasive and punitive satire is not always easy to make, and many instances can be cited, in satiric passages and entire satiric works, in which the reader may purport to find *both* persuasive and punitive effects. To take, as an example, a famous passage from Swift, it has always been agreed that Gulliver's account of the rope-dancing agility of Flimnap, the Lilliputian Treasurer in *Gulliver's Travels,* is a satiric thrust against Sir Robert Walpole. Now from one point of view, the passage does not seem calculated to alter opinions about the historical Walpole: one assumes that, for an audience already convinced that the Lord Treasurer was a slippery opportunist, the rope-dancing appeared only as an appropriately debasing image—and thus a kind of artistic castigation—for vices firmly recognized by readers before the book was ever opened. On the other hand, it may be argued that the rope-dancing episode sheds new light on a questionable faculty of Walpole's—one which might previously have passed muster as facile statesmanship but is now revealed only as a kind of low agility, subject to the caprice of fortune and the king's mistresses. To call Walpole a "rope-dancer" becomes, in the latter case, no mere epithet but an apt epitome, capable of disclosing to readers in a novel way the questionable character of the gifts on which the man's eminence chiefly rests. In this instance, therefore, we seem to be confronted with a "borderline" situation—with an effect which may be described either as punitive or persuasive, depending upon several variables, of which the most important is the previous knowledge and attitude of the reader.

What should be seen, however, is that if we truly seek to judge the satirist's art, our assumptions as to its persuasive or punitive character may lead to very different conclusions. And if we are unwilling to commit ourselves to the view that writing like the rope-dancing passage is exclusively one or the other, we should be prepared to see that the satirist achieves at least two very different things, according to the approach which we select. For the distinction between persuasive and punitive discourages a quest for rhetorical accomplishment in works which, while genuinely and often superlatively satiric, do not necessarily seek to persuade us of anything. If, for example, there is satiric brilliance in *The Rape of the Lock,* it does not lie (despite Pope's jocularly didactic claims in the introductory epistle) in the power of the poem to implant conviction in the reader's mind. The converse is equally true: the work which seeks seriously to persuade, expose, or exhort may often conspicuously lack the pleasurable characteristics—and notably the humor—of the more purely punitive kinds of satire. American readers probably derived very little amusement from George Orwell's *1984;* it seems safe to say, however, that many of them received new, disturbing opinions from that book. And when a work is less plainly a specimen of the punitive or the persuasive, the distinction remains equally important to acknowledge. *The Battle of the Books* has often been seen as a highly effective satiric weapon, employed in the cause of the Ancients against the Moderns and constituting an authentic development in that famous controversy. For some readers, however (and the present writer is among them), it is chiefly a humorous, immensely ingenious exploitation of convictions, long held by those sympathetic to the Ancient cause, concerning the personalities, issues, and occurrences of the affair. The two approaches, each quite defensible, have very different consequences for the judgment of Swift's satiric achievement, since, for example, they would regard in two very different lights Swift's obvious failure to join issue with Bentley and Wotton on the substantive, scholarly points which had been made in defense of "modernity."

Although this distinction calls for commitment to the view that a satiric work or passage be regarded as either punitive or persuasive, it would be wrong to regard these categories as inviolable compartments into which, because of some intrinsic quality, all satire can be firmly thrust. It may prove more useful to regard these kinds of satire as areas in what a contemporary scholar has called—although with a somewhat different intent from mine—the "satiric spectrum."[16] If we say that one portion (let us call it the lower half) of this spectrum is occupied by persuasive satire, then, in turn, at the lowest point in this area would be that work which is most plainly and exclusively persuasive. To works which can be placed at such a point, the modes of analysis appropriate to rhetoric should be profitably applicable, and the work may well be judged ultimately by the

---

[16] Arthur Melville Clark, "The Art of Satire and the Satiric Spectrum," in *Studies in Literary Modes* (Edinburgh and London, 1946), pp. 31–49. Although the views expressed in this study coincide with those of Clark in certain particulars—notably the "occasional" quality of satire, its essential hostility, and, to some extent, the relation of satire and humor—his definition of the satiric spectrum is not the same as mine nor does he employ this figure for the purpose it serves here.

degree to which it achieves one or another of the traditional rhetorical ends. Questions of humor, of imaginative artistry, or of absolute intellectual merit would, in such instances, be relevant only in their relationship to the more basic question of persuasive effect.

The remaining, "upper," half of the spectrum in such a scheme will represent punitive satire, and at its extreme upper limit will be located the kind of work which, with no discernible attempt at persuasion, seeks to delight the reader by the indignities to which a pre-established victim or dupe is exposed. From this kind of satire the categories of rhetoric are remote, for we are here confronted with imaginative artifice, and our delight determines the measure of the artist's success.

Midway between the areas of the persuasive and the punitive, we may place the intangible line which separates the two, and near it, on one side or the other, will lie writing which, like the passage we noted from *Gulliver's Travels,* may be legitimately described in terms appropriate to either area. The possibility of employing either approach to such writing should make clear what is characteristic of the entire view of satire which is here suggested. The problem is not to determine conclusively whether a given piece of literature *is* unqualifiedly punitive or persuasive; it is to recognize that, though in many instances elements of both are present, we need to ask the most profitable and relevant questions and hence to assume, at least temporarily, that one effect or the other is paramount.

The device of the satiric spectrum can thus be employed to suggest the scope and the broadest divisions of what is meant by the satiric attack. Obviously, however, I have not yet offered a definition of satire which will distinguish it from other literary kinds. It will be noted, for example, that as yet nothing has been said to distinguish between persuasive satire and rhetoric itself. If, we may ask, the satirist's effect can in many instances be described in the traditional terms of rhetorical analysis, in what respects, if any, does what we call persuasive satire differ from ordinary polemic rhetoric?

In answering this query, we encounter the first of two qualities which, for our purposes, set apart the satiric from the non-satiric and apply, although in greatly varying degrees, to the entire satiric spectrum. For all satire involves, to some extent, *a departure from literal truth* and, in place of literal truth, a reliance upon what may be called a *satiric fiction*. The true rhetorician is assumed to proceed in a literal manner. His evidence is presumably susceptible of objective scrutiny; his emotional appeals are taken to rise from and be directed to authentic emotions; his logic should withstand the rigors of logical examination. The satirist, on the other hand, depends, to the extent that his procedure is actually satiric, upon a *recognized* departure from truth and upon the ability of his audience to assert, "What you say cannot be taken literally, but I am aware of the true meaning which, in your non-literal fashion, you seek to convey."

To be sure, the rhetorician himself often fails in his obligations to truth. Hyperbole, distortion, and suppression are all devices which are familiar to us, largely because of their rhetorical employment. But if such devices really succeed, it is because the rhetorician "brings off" his falsehood and is rhetorically successful precisely because the audience has accepted fiction for truth. If, on the other hand, the audience detects falsehood in the rhetoric which purports to be true, the attempted deception is plainly a failure. And if the rhetorician departs at any point from literal truth into a deliberate fiction which he intends the audience to recognize for what it is, if this fiction is a means for conveying or augmenting his literal argument, and if that argument involves an "attack" as we have been using the term, then the rhetoric assumes, however transiently and transparently, the character of satire!

As the central, indispensable element in the satirist's "method," the satiric fiction can assume an infinite number of forms. It may appear as a slight but patent exaggeration, a brisk derisive metaphor, a manifest sarcasm—constituting, it may well be, the kind of "wit" which for most of us marks the satiric "touches" imbedded in writing whose general nature is not satiric at all. At the opposite extreme, the term "fiction" applies equally well to book-length narrative structures which are fictional in every detail. Although not always recognized as such, the satiric fiction has been the subject of considerable critical discussion and of various attempts at classification, professing to impose categories upon what have been variously described as "devices," "situations," and "stages" of satire itself.[17] The

---

[17] Thus, for example, since Worcester attempts "to construct a simple rhetoric of satire" (*The Art of Satire*, p. 9), it is natural that the various kinds of satiric procedure he considers be viewed as "devices" of an essentially persuasive sort. A. M. Clark's "spectrum" on the other hand is composed of "stages" which mark the satirist's progress from the benignity of the humorist to the mirthless malignity of in-

discussion of "high" and "low" satire recognizes, implicitly at least, a fictional construction which either directly debases or mockingly elevates the non-fictional object which is its counterpart in the world of reality.[18] Once the satiric fiction is isolated, it is entirely possible, if one wishes, to impose upon it virtually any kind of classification. For, in the construction of the fiction, the satirist is a literary artist at whose disposal lies the entire range of imaginative creations.

The earnest classification of possible satiric fictions, however, seems to be of limited usefulness, particularly when one is confronted by a writer like Swift, who moves without warning and with incredible nimbleness among fictions of enormously varied kinds and degrees. Such classifications do little to aid us in meeting the fundamental question of determining, in any satiric writing, what precisely *is* fictional and the nature of the truth, or alleged truth, which the fiction has been constructed to convey or exploit. Once the fiction has been thus identified, it may, of course, be analyzed, classified, and compared with other fictions, and it is obvious that, from such examination, useful generalizations concerning the habits of the satirist may often be formed.

Generalizations concerning the satiric fiction, however, can be misleading, especially when they are either too broad or too narrow to do justice to the *particular* fiction in a specific satiric work. An example of this sort of danger can be seen in the overworked term,

vective (pp. 45–49). In both these instances, the categories of satire established could be—although they are not—distinguished from each other in terms of the nature and purpose of the satiric fiction. To the best of my knowledge, the only study which deliberately sets out, albeit in terms of a rather limited problem, explicitly to classify satiric writings in terms of the fictions they employ is Ricardo Quintana's "Situational Satire: A Commentary on the Method of Swift," *University of Toronto Quarterly*, XVII (1948), 130–36. Although Quintana's discussion is very brief, he clearly recognizes the crucial importance of the satiric fiction and is able, moreover, to show that differences in kind among fictions (or, as he calls them, "situations") account for basic differences in kinds of satire.

[18] The "high-low" gambit is manifestly susceptible of many mutations. The difficulties this approach involves can be seen even when it is applied to the very limited area of satire on literary works (conventionally described as "parody," "burlesque," and the like). Richmond P. Bond's *English Burlesque Poetry, 1700–75* (Cambridge, Mass., 1932) works within the two simple variables of "form" and "content" yet emerges with a series of terms which are highly complex and extremely difficult (at best) to apply in analyzing individual works of "literary" satire.

"irony."[19] A very general definition of the word is offered by Worcester, who suggests that irony is, as much as anything, "a grand artistic lie."[20] Professor Bullitt, while recognizing the range of meanings which have been applied to the term, asserts that its "very essence . . . whether considered as a rhetorical trope (along with synechdoche, metonomy, and hyperbole) or as a whole way of life, is *dissimulation:* the ironist appears to say or to be one thing while making it apparent to his audience that he means or is something quite different."[21] But what has thus been described as a "lie" or "dissimulation" appears to be nothing other than the "fiction" which, we have argued, is to some extent the mark of all satire; and to seize, for example, upon a debasing allegory—which plainly says one thing but means another—as "ironic" would be to obscure rather than to illuminate the distinction between kinds of satiric fiction, presumably sought by the introduction of such a term as "irony." At the other extreme, the meaning of irony is often confined to "inversion," a term which, on analysis, means no more than simple sarcasm or the statement of a position so antithetical to the truth that authentic meaning can be attained by pure negative inference. This narrow definition is grossly inadequate as an explanation of many, if not most of the false positions deliberately assumed by such a satirist as Swift. If, like some critics, we are tempted, for example, to assume that the *persona* who serves as Swift's satiric spokesman represents the opposite of the author's actual position, a moment's reflection should reveal the strange consequences of such an approach. For if *A Modest Proposal* is an "ironic" argument in this sense, then it appears that Swift has written the tract to prove that Irish babies should not be eaten; or, again, we should be forced to infer, from this position, that

[19] The range of uses to which, historically, the word has been put is made elaborately evident in Norman Knox's *The Word "Irony" and Its Context, 1500–1755* (Durham, North Carolina, 1961). Although this careful study establishes the limits of the very ample variety of meanings which the term assumed during the period under discussion, it confirms one's doubts as to the utility of the concept of irony for analytical purposes. It is also interesting to note that the simple notion of "inversion" (praise-by-blame or blame-by-praise) dominates the historic employment of the term.

[20] Worcester, *The Art of Satire*, p. 80.

[21] Bullitt, *Jonathan Swift and the Anatomy of Satire*, pp. 49–50. Both Bullitt and Norman Knox rely considerably on G. G. Sedgewick, *Of Irony Especially in Drama* (Toronto, 1948), whose emphasis on the Socratic origins of the concept of irony serves to expand rather than confine the range of its meanings.

the famous *Argument* is truly intended to advocate the abolition of Christianity!

"Irony," as a term applied to situations in which a "speaker" professes a position which is patently not his own, is doubtless an innocuous term. At the same time, except in those instances in which it describes a patently sarcastic, "inversional" situation, the use of the term does little to disclose the precise nature of the fictional posture, the degree to which it departs from the satirist's authentic position, or the nature of the authentic position itself. And discoveries of this character are, inevitably, unique with respect to any single piece of satiric writing. The familiar practice of describing as "ironic" whatever pose or invention or obliquity makes more salient the truth from which it appears to depart serves, indeed, to enforce our view that a manifest fiction is an indispensable element of satire, but it does little or nothing to indicate the manner in which such a fiction appears.

Despite the difficulty of imposing classifications upon the huge range of fictional procedures open to the satirist, it is possible to note certain broad distinctions among the methods which he may undertake. To generalize upon our common experience with satiric works, it would appear that their fictional components may be seen as *distortions, analogies,* or "pure" *fabrications.*

These general terms, like others I have introduced, may be useful in reminding us of the several fundamentally different kinds of achievements attributable to the satirist and in discouraging confusion or unprofitable comparison between widely disparate sorts of satire. Excessive reliance upon them for analytic purposes, however, is imprudent, for a writer like Swift can employ these distinct procedures in close conjunction—and even concurrently. These terms, moreover, must not be regarded as descriptive of satiric "devices," since beneath each of these rubrics are subsumed almost infinite possibilities for the actual conduct of the satiric attack.

We may call "distortion," for example, any kind of description, assertion, or argument in which an authentic state of affairs or a sincerely held conviction undergoes palpable alteration. Thus it will be seen that the term can apply to all modes of partial and unflattering selection: a degrading synechdoche, relentless emphasis upon infirmities alone, disregard for natural contexts and associations, suppression of mitigating facts, and the like. It can apply, too, to the very different form of attack involved in "mock elevation," of which sarcastic praise and overstatement provide familiar examples. What seems common, however, to all forms of distortion is that an authentic position or state of affairs, no matter how fragmented, warped, elaborated, or partially concealed, is ultimately discernible by our taking into account the character and purpose of the distortion. And thus, when the satirist's method is distortion, his reader's method is that of "restoration," of grasping the literal meaning which is, as it were, the inception of the satiric procedure.

The analogical fiction, on the other hand, provides us with some kind of independent construction—narrative, character, description, or argument—which ordinarily possesses an autonomous capacity to interest us yet relies, for its proper satiric effect, upon our recognition of salient resemblances between the fictional artifice and the truth. Distortion is, in a sense, frequently involved in the satiric analogy—a living person or institution may appear, for instance, in a new, palpably debased identity—but in other instances, notably in some satiric allegory, the fictional "transformation" is not in itself degrading, and we are required to draw, from the narration of events for example, the inferences which provide fundamental satiric meaning. In either case, the satirist has not merely manipulated the truth but has engaged in a novel creation, and the reader's task is not only to restore a distorted truth to its proper proportions but to find correspondences and draw inferences.

In the "pure" satiric fabrication, we are in the presence of a myth, recognizable neither as analogy nor as mere distortion, but acceptable, presumably, because we are convinced that there is something apt about the humiliation or degradation which, entirely fictitiously, the satiric victim undergoes. When such a fabrication, inhabited by authentic figures, exposes its victims to abuses that do not appear appropriate or, at the least, intrinsically amusing, it will represent little more than a piece of bad-tempered wishful thinking. And the greater the role played by fabrication alone—that is, the greater the departure from the facts and issues of reality—the less persuasive the attack is likely to be. Pure satiric fabrications are, to turn Marianne Moore's phrase to our own use, "imaginary gardens with real toads in them." And the imagined indignities to which real toads or rogues or fools are exposed may provide us with a good deal of satisfaction but very little in the way of enlightenment or conviction.

But, however we may choose to classify or describe the satiric fiction, what is important is that we recognize it *as* fiction. The case of Defoe's *Shortest Way with the Dissenters,* in which Defoe's mocking assumption of a fiercely militant Anglican position was not immediately noted and hence failed entirely to produce the intended effect, is only one dramatic example of the unrecognized fiction. As we shall point out later in greater detail, even such a widely admired work as Swift's *Argument against Abolishing Christianity* has been misinterpreted in some quarters because of a failure to identify the satiric fiction from which Swift's entire attack proceeds. In fact, every commonplace instance in which sarcasm "misfires" plainly represents a failure to recognize the fiction which, in this simple form of abuse as in the most elaborate artifice, is the central element by which the direct expression of hostility or criticism is transformed.

The presence of a satiric fiction, then, distinguishes the kind of satire which we have assigned to the "lower," persuasive range of the satiric spectrum from the art which is purely rhetorical. At the very bottom of this area there lie those works or parts of works whose reliance upon the satiric fiction is minimal and whose essential procedure is by the literal methods of true polemic. Such writings or speeches may rely fleetingly upon an obvious figure or analogy, upon a manifestly false or distorted characterization, and so on; to that extent alone, they partake of the nature of satire. But in the absence of some kind of manifest fiction, as we have defined the term, the attack lies beyond the satiric spectrum altogether. Thus, in our scheme, the lower limits of that spectrum coincide with the boundary of true polemic rhetoric.

When we consider the punitive kind of satire, which we have assigned to the upper portion of the spectrum, a new distinction is called for. We have already noted that the presence of the satiric fiction is necessary to both persuasive and punitive satire. But if the persuasive quality disappears—if, that is, we are exposed in punitive satire to neither argument nor exhortation, however obliquely couched, but to the abuse of a victim of whose culpability we are already properly convinced—we appear to be dealing with something very like comedy. Among most traditional attempts to define the comic, there is wide agreement that comedy represents humiliation, discomfort, frustration, or some similarly defined experience on the part of agents who fail in some way to adhere to normally expected standards of conduct.[22] The comic victim, that is, ordinarily tends to be duped or discountenanced, to undergo some form of distress which pleases us pretty much to the degree that it seems just and relevant to his character, as previously established. Seen in such general terms, the comic formula seems entirely applicable to what we have described as punitive satire. It reveals what occurs to the protagonists of both *Mac Flecknoe* and *Volpone,* to the dunces of Pope as well as to the enchanted innocents of *A Midsummer Night's Dream.*

The relationship of comedy and satire almost inevitably receives attention in discussions of the satirist's art—and often, as well, in systematic treatments of the comic. Interest in this relationship stems, it can be supposed, from nothing more complicated than our tendency to discover what is laughable in many satires or, conversely, to suspect that many of the things we ordinarily laugh at have their satiric aspects. Students of this relationship have rarely gone so far as to equate the two species, yet have, for the most part, remained fairly indifferent to the need for a distinction between them. We can discover passages which tacitly assume that satire is a class or an ingredient of comedy, that the comic is a category or a tool of satire, and hence that "satiric comedy" or "comic satire" are terms which can be legitimately employed, presumably in the description of writings which make us laugh and do something else as well.[23] Here,

[22] Aristotle's famous observation that comedy involves a form of painless suffering on the part of men worse than ourselves (*Poetics,* 1448a and 1449a) subsumes —or is at least compatible with—the most familiar attempts to define comedy in later times, with a few such benign exceptions as Meredith. Thus, for example, Bergson's view of the comic as the "mechanical encrusted upon the living" derives essentially from the notion of man's inability to perform, physically, morally, and socially as man should (see Henri Bergson, *Laughter: An Essay on the Meaning of the Comic,* trans. Cloudesley Brereton and Fred Rothwell [London, 1911], esp. pp. 1–66). The ultimate moral function assigned to comedy by Bergson (and by such frankly moralistic arguments as those of Molière and Fielding) rests, as does the more sophisticated functional account of Freud (*Wit and Its Relation to the Unconscious,* trans. A. A. Brill [New York, 1917]), upon the exposure or discovery of human qualities in some measure shameful.

[23] Bullitt's treatment of "exposure by ridicule," for example, discusses seventeenth- and eighteenth-century notions of the ridiculous, of contempt, of the "comic attitude" and of satire without, it seems to me, making clear how the satiric exploitation of the ridiculous differs from that of comedy. He points out, however, that the "defense and

however, it is urged that the presence of satire elicits special awarenesses, invites particular questions, and accomplishes particular effects, and it follows that these must, in some way, be distinguished
from those we regard as comic. Moreover, most of us would agree
that some comedy is clearly without satiric impact, however we may
define the latter, and—a previously made point in which any student
of Swift should concur—satire of a persuasive kind can affect us in
ways which are very far from comic.

The distinction which we are seeking—that between punitive
satire and comedy—requires a further general description of satire,
one which, once more, applies in some measure to all writing which
falls within the limits of the satiric spectrum. All satire is not only
an attack; it is an attack upon *discernible, historically authentic
particulars*. The "dupes" or victims of punitive satire are not mere
fictions. They, or the objects which they represent, must be, or have
been, plainly existent in the world of reality; they must, that is,
possess genuine historic identity. The reader must be capable of
pointing to the world of reality, past or present, and identifying the
individual or group, institution, custom, belief, or idea which is under
attack by the satirist. *Mac Flecknoe* acquires its satiric dimension
not only by the punishment which its "hero" undergoes but also by
the fact that a historical Shadwell lived and can be identified with
the dullard protagonist of Dryden's poem. And, indeed, when—as
I have suggested sometimes happens—the historical identity of a
satiric victim pales or disappears with time, the satiric quality of
the work diminishes accordingly and its continued survival comes
to depend upon facts, whether accidental or artistic, which are ex-
trinsic to its original satiric character.

I have said that persuasive satire moves toward rhetoric as the
fictional quality becomes subordinate to literal polemic and that,
when the fiction is no longer apparent and operative, the bottom
limit of the satiric spectrum is crossed. In an analogous fashion, as
the tie to the historic particular becomes less important, punitive
satire "ascends" in the satiric spectrum until it ceases to be satiric
in any way. Just as "truth" dominates and destroys the fictional in

---

justification of satire urged by Swift and supported by a sizable number of the writers
and critics of his day is . . . an appeal to the moral usefulness of this minor genre"
(*Jonathan Swift and the Anatomy of Satire,* p. 37).

those persuasive works which tend to lose their satiric quality, so the fictional element tends to dominate literal significance in those punitive writings which approach the upper limit of the satiric spectrum. At that limit lies the region of the genuine comic, of plots and speeches and poses which may resemble in their structure and language those of many satires but which, in the absence of reference to the authentic and the particular, make no claim to satiric effect.

Punitive satire is distinguished from the comic by the presence of *both* the historically authentic and the historically particular; in the absence of either, the satiric quality disappears. In other words, the satiric is lost when the object of attack is entirely imaginary (or "false" with respect to historical reality) or when, as a phenomenon so persistently recurrent and widespread as to be regarded as "universal," it cannot, without further qualification, be assigned specific historical identity. The first condition is easy enough to understand. Falstaff, Tony Lumpkin, and Donald Duck are, for all their appealing "humanity," manifest fabrications, composites of qualities which, though each may be very familiar to us, are here joined in synthetic combination. It is sometimes said that each of these figures inhabits his own "world" of fantasy; if true, this suggests how very far from satiric is the appeal which they have for us. If, in their presence, our world and our preoccupations tend to slip away from us for the time, then, in a frame of mind which is almost the antithesis of that invited by satire, we rejoice in our escape from the issues and problems and "significance" of ordinary existence.

But aside from these rare and, in a sense, "unlikely" creations, most comic characters may be said to have a crucial correspondence with reality and to derive verisimilitude from our worldly familiarity with the most important qualities they display. The moralistic critic of comedy, moreover, often insists that it is precisely because basic human weaknesses and the dilemmas to which they lead are represented by the comic artist that his work deserves our serious attention. If, therefore, the great majority of comedies can be said to expose very real and familiar human frailties, why are they not, for this reason, satiric? And if this is true, is there not, at the least, a satiric element in most of the literature which moves us to laughter?

To these questions, the answer appears to be that between sheer comedy and those satires which produce laughter by the employment of comic formulas the difference is one of *particularity* in the object of attack. It is true that the most common sort of comic dupe is the character who, we suggest as we look around at our neighbors, might well have been Smith or Jones or Robinson. This is, indeed, an appropriate reaction, for the credibility and interest of such figures depend heavily upon thair conforming to our own knowledge of human nature. But in such statements, the "might have been" is of central importance. In satire, the victim *is* Smith, Jones, or Robinson —or, if not, belongs to a particular group or embraces a particular view which can be isolated, for the purpose of receiving our un-flattering attention, from the rest of the world about us.

Of the several assertions which are here made about satire, it is likely that this insistence upon the particularity of the satiric object will prove most controversial. Traditionally, satire has more often than not been discussed as though its principal function were to oppose vice and folly, if not in the abstract, then at least in terms sufficiently general to admit wide and profitable application to com-mon human problems. Satirists themselves (Swift among them, at times) have tended to insist that their assaults are prompted not by limited and specific aversions but by a hatred of evil, however and in whomever manifested. This is a position with which it is easy to sympathize; a serious writer cannot be expected to relish the role of a mere controversialist. It is similarly understandable that audi-ences conspire in this lofty view of the satiric mission, since most of us find gratification in the belief that our entertainment can provide us with "insights" into profound questions of human conduct.

Insistence upon the particularity of satire raises, moreover, a further formidable difficulty in the fact that "particular" is itself an elusive and relative term. Distinctions are, again, quite clear if one cites extremes. Thus, sin and folly—or such aspects of them as avarice, cruelty, or imprudence—are subject to no temporal or geo-graphic restrictions, and an attack upon them, rather than upon the authentic, particular individuals in whom they may be embodied, can be readily discerned. At the opposite extreme, we should have little difficulty in sensing how the overt identification of, let us say, a specific living person with the dupe or villain of a literary per-formance is a signal of satiric intent.

The difficulty again lies in a middle region, in determining whether phenomena of major historical magnitude—intellectual abstractions, beliefs held by millions, institutions embracing similar millions, or pervasive habits of behavior—are objects of satiric attack. Is religion or man's religious instinct a "particular" object? Is organized religion, in all its forms? Is Protestantism—or Puritanism? If an attack upon foppishness as a general human foible is not satiric, what shall we say about an attack upon *women's* preoccupation with fashion—or upon a vogue for sword-knots or Ivy League trousers? How "particular" is the concept of democracy, or the conviction that it is a noble concept? Does the degree to which a work may be regarded as satiric increase in direct proportion to the particularity of the object which it assails? Or is it possible that strictures against womankind, American women, American "career" women, and American female psychiatrists may all be conducted in equally satiric fashion?

I have already said that the object of satiric attack must have an authentic historical identity. In effect, such an object may be vast or small, abstract or concrete, yet it must yield meaningfully to historical predications and descriptions and should do so without the need for further refinement and specification. In effect, then, the "particularity" with which we are concerned is found in any phenomenon whose temporal or geographic confinement permits the kind of description which is characteristic of the historian. A doctrine is a phenomenon about which it is generally possible to make many firm historical propositions; a human trait, in its abstract or universal aspects, is not. It is difficult to make any meaningful historical assertion about all of womankind; it is, on the other hand, perfectly possible to speak in conventional historical terms of modern American women—and hence to satirize them. To the extent, of course, that what is originally generic and not historically specified becomes manifested within particulars which permit historical identification, it will yield to satiric attack. Thus the "spirit" of faction and controversy is, doubtless, always with us and, in this timeless aspect, not an appropriate target for the satirist; when, however, it becomes, in the eyes of Swift, a positive social and political force, operating within a clear historical context to produce certain specific consequences, it is an object for satiric attention.

From the standpoint of the satirist himself, the particularity of the satiric object is a matter of selectivity. Whether he is viewed as a controversialist, moralist, or mere tease, the satirist must be successful in his choice of opponent or victim, and he must accordingly seek a target which is identifiable and vulnerable. In truth, the satire which, in Swift's famous words, "is a sort of Glass, wherein Beholders do generally discover every body's Face but their Own" is ineffectual, if it is satire at all. The victims of true satire must "suffer," whether through their own injured awareness of assault or in the ridicule or hostility which the satirist produces in the minds of others. The ultimate wellspring of the satiric spirit is perhaps benign, and sin itself, rather than the sinner, may be the true object of the satirist's wrath. But the essence of the satiric procedure is attack, and the attack launched impartially against everyone is no attack at all.

In the distinction between the satiric and the comic, as in that between satire and rhetoric, since it is difficult, of course, to draw absolute divisions, it is prudent to speak rather of tendencies toward one or the other of the species. Yet the difference between satire and comedy becomes the more crucial when we are confronted by works which may lay claim to being either. In Molière's *Tartuffe,* for example, we are shown the machinations and the ultimate discomfiture of the hypocrite. Now, as a stereotype of the sanctimonious dissembler, known to all ages and nations, Tartuffe remains a comic character, with a didactic capacity to "make clear" in Molière's own phrase, "the distinction between your hypocrite and your man of true devotion."[24] But Tartuffe may also readily be taken to represent a highly particular, historically authentic manifestation of religious hypocrisy; and so he was taken by Molière's enemies. These, insisting in effect that the play was satiric rather than purely comic, read it as an attack upon the power and practices of the French Jesuits under Louis XIV. The repressions, banning, deletions, and revisions which form the history of *Tartuffe* in print and on the stage may well be said to revolve about the presence or absence of *satire* within the work.[25] For the crux of the controversy lies in the question as to whether the evils Molière is assailing are limited and historically identifiable or timeless and universal.

An example of this kind suggests anew the extent to which the identity of a satiric victim must be established if we are to speak

24 The quotation is from Molière's preface to the first edition of the play. I have used the translation of Curtiss Hidden Page (New York, 1908), p. 8.

25 For a history of the vicissitudes of *Tartuffe* during the lifetime of Molière, see Henri d'Almeras, *Le Tartuffe de Molière* (Amiens, 1928).

about true satiric achievement. When, either by calculation or inadvertence, the historically authentic object of attack is obscure, the
satiric impact of the work is plainly weakened—although often we
properly find our chief satisfaction in other literary qualities it
possesses. There are works of fiction which provide us with a delight
that is little affected by our belated recognition of individualized
attacks which may accompany their purely inventive elements. Students who have long admired such novels as *Bleak House* or Huxley's
Point Counter Point may, at some time, discover that Harold
Skimpole, in the former, represents the hapless Leigh Hunt or that
many of the characters of the latter were drawn by Huxley with
specific contemporaries in mind. In such instances, a satiric element
is established and a satiric "reading" is possible; yet these characters,
compounded as they are of familiar follies and infirmities, continue
to delight as essentially fictional dupes and villains, and analysis of
the novels as predominantly satiric does scant justice to their stature
as products of the creative imagination.

Not all critical or hostile literary treatment of universal phenomena is, of course, comic or entertaining. It is clearly possible to
deal, through the use of some kind of fiction, with problems that
are grave, generic, and recurrent. Here the sources of the author's
uneasiness, skepticism, or hostility transcend time and place and are
rooted in the changeless facts of the human condition. Such works
are distinguishable from satire by their ultimate effect, which is
basically didactic—and, in fact, philosophic. For they consider, albeit
unfavorably, the timeless nature of man and his world.

Plato, for example, is largely critical and even destructive, and he
employs obliquities, understatements, and myths, which can all be
regarded as satiric fictions. We do not generally regard his dialogues
as satire (although to the degree that they attack such historical particulars as the Sophists or Athenian leadership, they *are* satiric), because the errors of thought to which they are addressed are generic
and timeless—because they become the objects of an attention which,
however unfavorable, is essentially philosophic. Indeed, to consider
universal propositions, in whatever light, is not mere "attack," but,
if it is to be effective, philosophic inquiry. A true "satire against
mankind"—on the assumption that it transcends particular men or
groups of men yet strives to speak the truth—would lie beyond our
definition of satire. If it were frivolously or insincerely conceived,

of course, it would become, if not philosophy *manqué,* then a
species of imaginative writing in which a fictional pose domina
rather than subserved the truth. If, more significantly, it sought
provide us with authentic and meaningful propositions about ma
and the universe, such propositions, however hostile, would be those
of philosophy itself.

III

This is, perhaps, the moment for summary. It has been urged that
the principal achievement of satiric writing may always be described
as, in some measure, "attack," this attack being directed either to
persuading us to look or act unfavorably toward the satiric victim
or to pleasing us by the representation in a degrading manner of an
object which, we already assume, deserves such treatment. I have
further asserted that the attack in satire proceeds by the use of a
"recognizable fiction," a departure in some way or other from a
literal truth of which the audience must be in possession. Finally, it
has been argued that the objects attacked by either persuasive or
punitive satire must constitute historically authentic particulars,
recognized as such by the audience. To gather these observations
into a single sentence, we may say that *satire consists of an attack by
means of a manifest fiction upon discernible historic particulars.*

In describing this view of satire, I have employed the figure of a
"spectrum" to suggest that satire begins, on one hand, at a point
where traditional polemic rhetoric discards literal argument in favor
of manifest fiction; that within the area of attack by the use of fiction
we find works whose purpose is to persuade as well as those which
seek only to deride objects which are plainly culpable; that at the
limit of satire which lies farthest from rhetoric we approach comedy,
in which objects of attack or ridicule are either without meaningful
historic reality or so general as to prevent our finding in them any
significant particulars.

It must be pointed out once more that this conception of satire
does not have as its object a classificatory system of absolute validity
or a "key" to secrets which have hitherto eluded readers of satire.
Still less does it offer criteria of excellence which will enable critical
readers to tell good satire from bad. We are here concerned with
modes of inquiry, with questions that may be profitably asked in
our reading of works we are prepared to call satiric. The "responsi-

bilities" implicit in such modes of inquiry are, in the last analysis, suggestions as to the kinds of questions which will make our use of the term "satire" most meaningful and increase our awareness of the special achievements of the satiric artist.

In the actual scrutiny of allegedly satiric works, therefore, we must, in the first place, determine the possibility of viewing the total work as satiric and, in the absence of such a possibility, identify as precisely as possible the nature and magnitude of its non-satiric as well as its satiric elements. It seems difficult, moreover, to advance any useful assertions about whatever satire the work contains without establishing the precise object or objects which are under satiric attack. This discovery inevitably requires a recognition of the method by which the attack proceeds, and, since the satirist's method crucial-ly depends upon a fiction of some kind, the location and description of the satiric fiction are equally necessary. Further, since we have indicated that the satiric attack may be of two basically different sorts, we should, as a preliminary to any judgment of the satirist's art, consider how his antagonist is treated. In an awareness that the pleasure afforded by punitive satire differs sharply from our response to persuasive procedures, that is, we must consider the satirist's means in terms appropriate to the end he appears to be seeking. Finally, we must remain alert to the fact that whatever distinctions we make also imply relationships; for example, that the non-satiric elements— comic, rhetorical, etc.—may justify, enforce, or heavily depend upon the satiric, or that the discrete objects of attack we isolate may bear a significant relationship to each other.

No laws, of course, require the satiric writer to adhere to satire throughout, to maintain a single mode of satiric assault, to limit in any special way the objects of his attention, or to strive for the kind of "unity" which many other species of literature lead us to expect. In the case of a writer like Swift particularly, the reader must proceed in an awareness that a single paragraph—or a single sentence—may contain abrupt changes in method, and even in purpose. The un-predictable flexibility of such an artist will inevitably elude narrow analytical procedures. If it appears that certain questions may be use-fully regarded as paramount, there is still no limit upon the sources to be consulted in answering them.

Thus it is often impossible to establish, through inspection of the text alone, the precise objects of the satirist's attack or the essential truth by which the identification of the satiric fiction proceeds. The popular distinction between "criticism" and "historical scholarship," the insistence that rigorously "autotelic" analyses of texts are necessary preliminaries to judgment, tend to break down in the presence of genuine satire. We have stressed the indispensable relationship between satire and historic fact. Whatever can disclose relevant historic fact is accordingly a legitimate—and usually an indispensable—source for the student of satire. The search within the canon of the author, through the contemporary materials which may prove germane, and into more remote sources which have conceivable bearing upon the satirist's intention is, of course, a formidable task with results that are rarely definitive. In such searches, however, the student may find one principle of considerable value.

This principle is simply that the satirist presumably writes to be understood. His attack is designed to persuade or delight. In consequence, the objects of his attacks must be discernible to his audience; the fiction which he constructs must be recognizable as fiction; the true position which he wishes, however obliquely, to convey must emerge clearly if his satire is to be successful. These facts are heartening, for they imply that men, documents, ideas, and events which were obscure for the satirist's original audience are far less likely to be importantly reflected in the work than those which the audience found clear, familiar, and immediate. As a result, our search for the satiric object may ordinarily proceed on the assumption that what must be recaptured was once intelligible and interesting to an audience not very different from ourselves. Even here, of course, the task may be difficult, perhaps impossible, yet the maxim that satire which has once been successful must, at the same time, have been intelligible may lend order and economy to our extra-textual researches.

One of the persistent questions raised about satire concerns its power of survival—the capacity of a satiric work to engage our interest long after the issues to which it is addressed have lost all claim upon our attention. Admittedly, the principles I have proposed do not seem very helpful in answering this question. By discouraging the view that satire is addressed to general and timeless problems, we have destroyed a traditional explanation of the satirist's lasting appeal. If we insist that Swift's chief target is the Royal Society rather than vanity in general, Walpole rather than man's venal tendencies, Puritan Enthusiasm rather than the vice of affectation, the task of recapturing and sharing the conviction and delight of Swift's original readers seems difficult.

In subsequent essays, I shall offer some views about the lasting appeal of Swift's writing and shall even, in certain instances, suggest that the appeal may well have changed over the centuries. Here, however, I shall initially urge that we lay the groundwork for an understanding of his art by becoming vicarious members of his original audience. Hume's prescription for the appreciation of rhetoric applies very well to the understanding of satire. We must, that is, suspend what Hume calls our "prejudices," those habits and attitudes which would keep us forever and inelastically our twentieth-century selves. As preacher, jester, or poet, Swift may have written for "Prince Posterity." As satirist, he wrote for those to whom his assaults on men, ideas, and institutions had immediacy of meaning and effect. The artist whose audience is particularized, whose mission is limited by historical circumstances, and whose motives are of the same genuine but ephemeral sort which most of us share most of the time is probably harder to understand and admire than is the writer whose "message" is transparently intended for posterity. But he is none the less an artist, for all that. If we are prepared to understand, if not necessarily to admire him, let us begin on his own terms. As for the admiration—wit, imagination, and verbal artistry can compel it on grounds quite other than the merit of the goals they are employed to serve. If we understand what Swift is doing, it is likely that we can sense the intrinsic power of his gifts to make themselves felt in any cause and any context.

CHAPTER II

The Satiric Victim

*T*HE SEARCH FOR a precise object of the satirist's attack can be an uncomfortable procedure. It is flattering neither to the satirist nor to his admiring readers to pursue the likelihood that particular men or institutions are the primary targets of satiric assault and so to imply that the author's hostility is directed more against the sinner than against the sin. In the case of Swift, such an inquiry appears to reject the writer's own profession and to insist that underlying his strictures is an aversion to "John, Peter, and Thomas" greater than his distaste for the general vices and follies which they share with mankind.

Moreover, the view that particular satiric victims are to be sought before proceeding to more general ideas about the satirist's achievement may impede the operations of the "unity-seekers," those earnest critics for whom the establishment of a unifying principle within a given work is the ultimate, triumphant step in literary analysis. As we shall discover shortly, the absence of a literary "form" peculiar to all satire or to its principal kinds may lead the analyst, naturally enough, to attempt the establishment of a single "goal" (and hence of a single, readily definable target) as the source of unity within a satiric writing. Unhappily for many such enterprises, the search for particular objects of satiric attack often yields a mixed bag; and while from such diversity it is often possible to re-create a pervasive attitude or intellectual position which lends strength to each individual assault, the "unity" is here discovered belatedly and does little to explain the character of individual thrusts or their relationship in a total structure.

The previous chapter defended my insistence upon the particularity of the satirist's victims largely in theoretical terms, urging that only this quality served to distinguish satire from such other forms as comedy or the philosophic myth. As I have suggested, however, definitions and the distinctions which accompany them are of little value save as they illuminate the character of individual literary works. Such illumination is, I believe, still needed in the case of a number of Swift's most famous writings, and particularly in the identification of the precise objects of Swift's attacks. In some instances, this identification can be achieved only at the sacrifice of easy generalizations concerning the structure and motivation of the work. In other instances—and we shall begin with these—the establishment of a precise object of attack can help to resolve views which have been confused and controversial and can provide for the work, if not a formal "unity," then a reasonable explanation of what the satirist is seeking to accomplish.

Lest our initial inquiries become complicated by the problem—and as I have suggested, it is an important and very common problem—of isolating satiric from non-satiric qualities in a work which, according to our definition, contains both, let us begin our discussion with a work which, it is commonly agreed, is satiric throughout.

Swift's *Argument against Abolishing Christianity*[1] is such a work, although more than one student of Swift has shown a strange reluctance to admit the fact.[2] Its structure can be described quite readily: the author, characterizing himself as a defender of "nominal" Christianity, seeks to refute the arguments put forward by those who wish to abolish his professed religion; following these refutations he goes on to point out certain additional "Inconveniencies" which "may possibly happen by such an Innovation, in the present Posture of our Affairs" (p. 28).

Among the majority of critics, there is some sort of tacit recognition that what we have specified as the qualities of satire are all present in the work; through the use of such terms as "irony"[3] these critics convey the suggestion that the *Argument* is not to be taken literally, and in their various conjectures there is always the implicit recognition that something or somebody is being satirized and hence attacked. With respect, however, both to the identity of Swift's victim and to the nature of his satiric procedure, there is wide disagreement—and some frank admission of bewilderment.[4]

[1] The complete title is *An Argument to Prove that the Abolishing of Christianity in England, May, as Things Now Stand, Be Attended with Some Inconveniencies and Perhaps Not Produce Those Many Good Effects Proposed Thereby.* My references are to the text as it is printed in *Prose Works*, II, 26–39.

[2] Leslie Stephen, in explaining the "serious meaning" underlying the work, finds in it the belief that "religion, however little regard is paid to it in practice, is in fact the one great security for a decent degree of social order; and the rash fools who venture to reject what they do not understand, are public enemies as well as ignorant sciolists" (*Swift*, "English Men of Letters"; pocket edition [London, 1927], p. 47). Sophie Shilleto Smith, in *Dean Swift* (London, 1910), p. 83, concludes that the *Argument*, like Swift's other religious tracts of the same period, "was written in support of Christianity, laying down the tenet that, from the point of view of common-sense alone, religion as embodying an element of stability, was for the advantage of the nation."

[3] "Irony," not further defined, is used to describe the *Argument* by, among others, Deane Swift in his *Essay upon the Life, Writings, and Character of Dr. Jonathan Swift* (London, 1755), p. 135; Dr. Johnson in *Lives of the English Poets*, ed. G. B. Hill (Oxford, 1905), III, 12; Rossi and Hone, *Swift; or, The Egotist* (London and New York, 1934), p. 149; and Robert W. Jackson, *Jonathan Swift, Dean and Pastor* (London, 1939), p. 71. J. Middleton Murry, in his *Jonathan Swift: A Critical Biography*, begins (p. 139) by noting the "irony" which distinguishes the *Argument* from the *Sentiments of a Church-of-England Man* but then proceeds, rather astonishingly, to conclude that "the defence of nominal Christianity, however comical it may be in detail, is very close to a position which Swift actually did hold . . ." (p. 143).

[4] In *The Mind and Art of Jonathan Swift* (pp. 145–46), Quintana says that Swift's "intellectual sleight of hand . . . is not to be analyzed," going on to assert that "the

In terms of the system we have suggested, the primary task of the student is to establish, by whatever means he can employ, the explicit object under attack, the precise nature of the satiric fiction, and, correspondingly, the true position from which the attack proceeds. Among these three tasks there is no necessary logical priority; it should be clear, furthermore, that their pursuit may proceed concurrently and that discoveries at any point regarding one of these major questions may illuminate the others. Where one "begins," in point of fact, is with what appear to be the most pressing problems raised by the individual text itself. And certainly the question of who or what is being attacked, where these are not evident, appears to be a natural point of departure.

In the case of the *Argument,* the most arresting feature of the document also seems to be the most perplexing. It is clear that the author's "refutations" and his anticipated "inconveniencies" proceed

---

arguments of the deists against religion and the church are turned inside out and drolly tossed back at the enemy." In a review of Quintana's book in *Modern Philology,* XXV (November, 1937), 202–4, Louis Landa rejects this view and holds that Swift is urging his readers "to recognize the dangers which would result from any attack on the Church of England, as by Law established." "Swift's method," Professor Landa argues, "is characteristic: by assuming the identity of the Test and Christianity, he proves that those who are enemies of the Test are enemies of the Christian religion. . . . In their pamphlets the dissenters argue to the point of tiresome iteration that removal of the disabilities would enlarge liberty of conscience, unite the protestants, eliminate factions, improve trade, and strengthen the state by permitting dissenters to take their rightful places in civil and military employments. Swift simply parrots these arguments and reduces them to absurdity. His reading public could not have missed the real purport of his argument." Herbert Davis, in his Introduction to *Prose Works,* II, appears to align himself with those who fail to find a satiric fiction in the *Argument* (p. xix). He maintains that Swift "was only concerned with the advantages of preserving *Nominal* Christianity, and proving that that was preferable to open infidelity." Attributing to Swift a kind of expediential cynicism, he proceeds, "On that firm foundation of skepticism and common sense, he could then indulge in Bickerstaffian gaiety and wit, rallying all groups of the 'low party,' and almost without arousing any suspicions, pursue his main intention of meeting all criticisms put forward by those whose design was to destroy the power and influence of the Church by the repeal of the Test Act."

More recently, in *The Satire of Jonathan Swift* (New York, 1947), p. 50, Davis has appeared less certain of Swift's "main intention" and of his success in achieving it: "I would almost say," he writes, "that [the *Argument*] is written with such enjoyment of the play of irony, and of the ways of the world, and occasionally with such double-edged scorn, that it hardly succeeds in its defence of the Establishment or in its support of the dignity of the clergy. . . ." This unusual divergence among the opinions offered by three senior Swiftians suggests that the problems of interpretation posed by the *Argument* are by no means trifling!

upon grounds that are variously expediential, venal, impious, non-sensical, or immoral; without exception they are far removed from the principles of any devout and thoughtful Anglican. It is also clear that most of the alleged "advantages" urged for the abolition of Christianity are shocking and dangerous-looking distortions of tendencies and doctrines which Swift purports to discover in the words and deeds of freethinkers and dissenters as well as in the common practices of the godless.

Swift's genuine apprehensions concerning the real dangers which are here distorted, as well as the firmly orthodox position from which he actually regarded them, are generally quite possible to discover. At about the same time as he wrote the *Argument* he also produced several serious tracts dealing with questions of religion and morality. It seems safe to say that three other pieces—*The Sentiments of a Church of England Man, A Project for the Advancement of Religion,* and *A Letter from a Member of the House of Commons in Ireland to a Member of the House of Commons in England Concerning the Sacramental Test*—were all written within a short time of the *Argument.*[5] Moreover, by the latter part of 1708, the *Argument,* the *Sentiments,* and the *Project* were all designed, whether completed at the time or not, for inclusion in a single volume of Swift's writings.[6] In addition, there should be grouped with these discussions of religious issues the *Remarks upon a Book Entitled "The Rights of the Chris-*

[5] All four of the works in question appeared in the *Miscellanies* of 1711. The *Project* and the *Letter* had each appeared as a separate pamphlet in 1709. Temple Scott's conjecture—in his edition of the *Prose Works* (London, 1898), III, 4 and 50 —that the *Argument* and the *Sentiments* were likewise separately published at an earlier date lacks all support. Irwin Ehrenpreis, in "The Date of Swift's 'Sentiments,' " *Review of English Studies,* III (1952), 272–74, argues that the *Sentiments* was composed in 1704. He points out that Swift's allusions to various speeches, documents, and events would have been highly topical in that year and that his neglect of Tindal's *Rights of the Christian Church* would be most uncharacteristic in any discussion of freethinking produced in 1707—or for many years after. Swift's own date for the piece (1708) is dismissed by Ehrenpreis, who offers, as the most likely explanation, that "Swift's tricky memory, which was amazingly fallible, simply played him false" (p. 274). Amazement borders on incredulity at the notion of Swift's confusing in 1711 (the date of the *Miscellanies*) the years 1704 and 1708! I should concur with Ehrenpreis in doubting the precise date assigned to the *Sentiments* by Swift, but I am skeptical about firmly attributing it to as early a year as 1704.

[6] *Correspondence,* I, 111. Ball reports, but does not reproduce, a list of "Subjects for a Volume" in Swift's hand, written on the back of an envelope dated October, 1708. The *Letter,* the only one of the works in question not thus listed, appeared in December, 1708.

tian Church," which was not published until after Swift's death but which can, with certainty, be assigned to either 1707 or 1708.[7]

From these records of Swift's immediate concerns at the time of the *Argument*—and also, in some instances, from views which emerge clearly in various of his writings over a period of many years—it should be apparent that the "case" for the abolition of Christianity, however distorted and exaggerated, has its origin in manifestations which Swift considered authentic and formidable. These manifestations range from the pervasive intellectual skepticism of freethinking writers to the profanation of the sabbath, from militant anticlericalism to fashionable secularism. The "extra-textual" facts would strongly suggest this abundant catalogue of evils as the primary object of Swift's satire in the *Argument.*

But within the text, the "proposals," representing alarming distortions of dangers which, in themselves, should give the devout Anglican cause for distress, are in no way discredited by the preposterous rejoinders of the nominal Christian. If, in some measure, they may be said to be "exposed" through Swift's representation of them in an exaggerated light, what are we to make of the author's complacent and ineffectual responses to them? Swift's rejoinders have been spoken of as "ironic," and it is sometimes implied that his grotesquely frail defense is in some way a contemptuous dismissal of his antagonists. But besides the difficulty of explaining how, precisely, a feeble answer to a dangerous proposition can operate "ironically," this view fails to account for the concluding pages of the *Argument,* in which Swift deliberately assigns new "disadvantages" to the abolition of Christianity, rather than confining himself to "refutation." He ceases, that is, his catalogue of distorted "anti-Christian" proposals in order to produce "a few Inconveniencies that may happen, if the Gospel should be repealed," thereby abandoning the pretense of give-and-take between the spokesman and his enemies in favor of a display of the nominal Christian's own gratuitous apprehensions (p. 35).

If we establish the primary object of Swift's satire in the *Argument,* we simultaneously reveal the fiction by which it is executed.

[7] References within the *Remarks* to refutations of Tindal by Hicks, Potter, and Wotton (all published in 1707) and to the Battle of Almanza (March, 1707) suggest a date no earlier than June of 1707 (Defoe's *Review* reports the news of Almanza in its issue of May 29, 1707). By March 8, 1708, Swift writes to Ford that his plans for replying to Tindal are "long layd aside" (*Letters to Ford,* p. 5).

Swift's chief satiric victim has been named by Professor Eddy and has received greater emphasis from William Ewald,[8] but I should go beyond them and insist that only if we see this victim as primary and consistent throughout the satire do the ambiguities and shifts in the document disappear. The victim can only be the nominal Christian himself, the lip service church member, tilting misguidedly and compromisingly with the overt enemies of his professed faith and abetting, the while, vicious kinds of religion and immorality. And the essential satiric fiction of the entire satire is nothing more than its author's putative adoption of the nominal Christian position.

Though I have not the space to analyze the *Argument* point by point, I am confident that the object of attack and the fictional device by which the attack proceeds remain substantially the same throughout. Thus, for instance, the *persona* begins his argument by accepting the equation of liberty of conscience with liberty to blaspheme; he proudly asserts that, in general, this "liberty is widely preserved," and deplores the single instance in which it has been violated (p. 28). One need hardly consult evidence in Swift's other writings of his views on blasphemy[9] to recognize in this position a muddle-headedness and impiety which are the grotesque antithesis of Swift's views and habits.

And even in the final "refutation," we discover the author entirely resigned to the inevitability of religious dissent, believing that religion provides the safest "stuffed dog" for the ineradicable spirit of opposition (p. 35). In this argument it is clear that, for the writer, the laws of the land and the public peace are institutions which are quite separate from the church and that he values their security more highly than that of Christianity. Here there are, to be sure, mocking echoes of the logic by which the opponents of the Test Act defended their views. But are the foes of the Test Act the chief targets here? Are Swift's spokesman and his position mere caricatures of

[8] William A. Eddy (ed.), *Swift's Satires and Personal Writings* (New York, 1939), p. 2, and Ewald, *The Masks of Jonathan Swift,* pp. 47–51. The latter notes the importance of the nominal Christian as a *persona,* but fails to establish any priority among "at least six results, all of them interrelated" which the essay is said to accomplish. In aptness and force, the attack upon anti-Christians (for which Ewald, following Landa, suggests we can read the opponents of the Test) seems decidedly secondary.

[9] For Swift's literal sentiments regarding blasphemy, particularly in the military establishment, see the *Project for the Advancement of Religion* in *Prose Works,* II, especially pp. 45, 47, and 50.

those who sought to abolish the Test? If so, the satire appears neither very startling nor very effective, for the fundamental position taken by the spokesman is no very great distortion of that assumed by enemies of the Test; for such controversialists, one supposes, the principles of justice and national welfare were to be adhered to in considerable indifference to the doctrines and prosperity of the Established Church. These views, like most of the other sentiments advanced on either side of the *Argument,* are deeply shocking, not when voiced by deists or dissenters, but only when expressed by those who call themselves Christians, who allegedly embrace the true embodiment of Christianity provided by the Church of England!

From Swift's readily established true point of view, the nominal Christian of the *Argument* is a false Christian. We need go no further than the early pages of *The Sentiments of a Church of England Man* to find Swift's forthright and literal statement of the position which is *sine qua non* for the true believer and which, incidentally, exposes the complete character of the *Argument*'s bogus spokesman:

And here, although it makes an odd Sound, yet it is necessary to say, that whoever professeth himself a Member of the Church of *England,* ought to believe a God and his Providence, together with revealed Religion, and the Divinity of *Christ.* For beside those many Thousands, who (to speak in the Phrase of Divines) do practically deny all this by the Immorality of their Lives; there is no small Number, who in their Conversation and Writings directly or by consequence endeavour to overthrow it: Yet all these place themselves in the List of the National Church; although at the same Time (as it is highly reasonable) they are great Sticklers for Liberty of Conscience.[10]

The morals of the nominal Christian are those of the "many Thousands"; the consequences of his "Conversation and Writings" are plain.

The nominal Christian, whose views are the basis for the position taken by Swift's *persona,* is, therefore, a very real and very important phenomenon for Swift. His identity as the principal victim of satiric attack in the *Argument* can be established not only by the evidence provided when one moves beyond the text to Swift's preoccupations at the time the work was written, but by examination of the text itself. For assuredly, far more than a refutation of the arguments

10 *Prose Works,* II, 4.

advanced against the Established Church, against the Test, or against Christianity itself, the *Argument* is a persuasive satire, designed to reveal the shocking implications of casual lip service to the Church of England.

Swift's procedure, viewed in this light, is actually very simple. He has constructed the figure of a nominal Christian, endowed him with a representative selection of mundane and materialistic values, de- picted him as a servile defender of a lamentable status quo, and justified the appellation of "Christian" only by providing his puppet with a shaky and superficial loyalty to the name of the Church. But this exaggeration of the weaknesses of nominal Christianity is only the beginning of the satiric artifice. Swift has taken this feeble specimen of popular "piety" and brought him face-to-face with the dangers which in 1708 most immediately and drastically threaten his professed religion. These dangers, we recognize, are found in the sophistries of deists and dissenters as well as in the widespread weakness of ordinary men who bear no such opprobrious labels. Swift, however, has not been content to introduce these dangers in their usual context, disguised as wisdom, wit, or common sense and allegedly proposed for the attainment of socially useful goals. Re- ducing all such proposals, usually at the patent sacrifice of accuracy and logic, to the basest, most alarming terms, he has lumped them together as elements in a single fictional project—the abolition of Christianity. Thus to distort his enemies' views is to call attention to their dangerous essence, but this procedure is but a step in our progress to the final and crucial question.

Faced with such formidable threats (threats which, while exag- gerations, are by no means entirely fanciful), what can the ordinary Christian-in-name do in the defense of his faith? The answer is the *Argument*. Without meaningful conviction, with only a few catch- words and the materialistic values to which he has succumbed for guides, the nominal Christian can produce only the feeblest of "prac- tical" reasonings, which in their very premises deliver him into the hands of those who would destroy him. The speaker is doubtless a debasing caricature, and yet, through this device, Swift relentlessly drives his readers to one compelling question: When a man's Chris- tianity, belied by his opinions and deeds, lies only in a name, what stronger defense than that of the *Argument* can he produce against its destruction?

The *Argument,* therefore, is not a document primarily intended for the refutation or discrediting of deists, dissenters, or enemies of the Test Act. Indeed, to reveal the flimsy foundations of so much "Christian" faith could very well be construed as lending aid and comfort to the foes of the Establishment. The demonstration produced by the *Argument* can only be intended for the very audience whose weakness is so mercilessly exposed. The improvement of morality, the enforcement of piety, the suppression of heresy and license can only be accomplished by those who have hitherto been weak, selfish, and shortsighted in these respects.

Thus the *Argument* is not only persuasive satire, but persuasion of a sort which is largely "homiletic." Swift's audience is, as it were, a huge congregation whose errors and vices are isolated and excoriated. We may, if we wish, particularize further upon the identity of the "nominal Christian," speculating that the position he has taken upon such explicit issues as the Test has been, for Swift, the chief manifestation of his weakness and the occasion for the *Argument* itself. If this is true, however, such a person remains a professed member of the Church of England, for, as we have seen, in this tract Swift's concern is for the weakness which lies within the Establishment itself.

To convince an audience of its own frailty is as imposing a task as the satirist can undertake. It is natural, therefore, that within the limits of a short document, Swift does not venture beyond the satiric spectrum. Here there are none of the excursions into pure comedy which we shall note in many of Swift's longer works. We today find amusement in the virtuosity with which the satiric task in the *Argument* is pursued, but the pre-eminently comic is largely lacking. So too is the element of punitive satire, for Swift's audience, who must be convinced of their own culpability, are not invited to laugh at the weakness of others. In structure and content, the work is governed throughout by considerations of persuasive strategy. And accordingly, when we have located Swift's satiric object and the central fiction by which his attack proceeds, we have the key to his total accomplishment within the work.

II

Strangely enough, *A Modest Proposal*[11] presents the reader with some of the same difficulties that are encountered in the *Argument*.

[11] Textual references to *A Modest Proposal* can be found in *Prose Works,* XII, 107–18.

With the exception of *Gulliver's Travels,* Swift's grotesque argument for infant cannibalism as a solution to the problems of Ireland is certainly the most widely read of his works. And it may be argued that the ordinary reader has little difficulty in understanding *A Modest Proposal* or in responding with shocked fascination to the incomparably outrageous method by which Swift suggests that a tragic human problem be overcome.

In subsequent discussion, we shall note the importance of Swift's uniquely memorable fiction, in itself, as a source of the appeal which *A Modest Proposal* has retained through the centuries. For the moment, however, let us concern ourselves with the work as a satiric attack and again raise the question which is primary for the analysis of satire. What is the object of Swift's attack in this famous document?

It may, of course, be argued that Swift's chief purpose is to reveal, in the most arresting possible terms, the full horror of the Irish economic situation. And certainly this is one of the achievements of the tract since, in effect, the "proposer" adopts a posture in which he implies that cannibalism is a reasonable alternative to an unspeakable status quo. When, however, we assert that the chief effect of the tract is to underscore the lamentable condition of the Irish peasantry, we court difficulties. It is true that, as a preliminary to the proposal itself, Swift is able to provide an appalling—and, one judges, not excessively distorted—view of the hopeless squalor and suffering which afflict his countrymen. Yet how does the "proposal" itself serve to reinforce this distressing picture? The answer one is tempted to give is that the proposal is no more shocking than the state of affairs which actually exists. Yet this implies that the proposal is therefore authentic, that the document is an affirmative, literal argument, that we are to take the author's position seriously—and that, in short, we are dealing not with satire but with a straightforward advocacy of the most revolting economic project ever to occur to a Western mind.

That such an interpretation is unthinkable need not, I hope, be argued. It is clear, from the scrutiny of all that has been written about *A Modest Proposal,* that thoughtful readers of the tract refuse to accept its argument literally, seek beyond Swift's apparent attitude for some essential object of attack, and, in effect, regard the work as satiric in substantially the terms which we have been employing to define this species of writing. Such responses have led to a number of illuminating suggestions concerning the true direction which is taken by the work. One of the most common conclusions to be offered is that the ultimate object of satiric attack is the English—and sometimes more specifically, English legislators, landlords, or economic apologists. From such an approach, Swift's *persona* can be seen—as he is in the *Argument*—to represent his satiric victim; the extravagant inhumanity of his proposal is thus construed as a distortion (or perhaps merely a *reductio ad absurdum*) of English indifference to the most basic matters of human need when they are manifested in Ireland. The acceptance of such an interpretation, however, is difficult for several reasons, The *persona* is not identified in any way with a position that might be characteristic of the English. Indeed, throughout the text he is clearly addressing his Irish countrymen and regards the nation as his own.[12] Moreover, we have, in the *Drapier's Letters* and elsewhere, abundant evidence of the kind of viciousness in practice and policy with which Swift is willing to tax the English nation; in *A Modest Proposal,* however, we are allowed to see, at most, the consequences of English evil, and it is Irish policy, or lack thereof, in the face of these consequences which occupies the writer.

Efforts to locate the object of satiric attack with greater precision have also led to the view that the *Modest Proposal* is largely a parody or derisive caricature of writings which have preceded it. And certainly in the glib and pseudo-systematic working-out of particulars and anticipation of objections there are mocking echoes of what must have been familiar discussions of Irish problems.[13] There is likewise, without doubt, a derisive distortion of influential economic theories, particularly, as Professor Landa has pointed out, those of the mercantilists.[14] The question remains, however, whether the

[12] E.g., "this great Town" (p. 109); "For we can neither employ them . . ." (p. 110); "this one individual Kingdom of Ireland" (p. 116); "by advancing our Trade" (p. 118).

[13] See Davis' Introduction, *Prose Works,* XII, xx–xxi.

[14] *"A Modest Proposal* and Populousness," *Modern Philology,* XL (1942), 161–70, and "Swift's Economic Views and Mercantilism," *ELH,* X (1943), 310–35. See also George Wittkowsky, "Swift's *Modest Proposal:* The Biography of an Early Georgian Pamphlet," *Journal of the History of Ideas,* IV (1943), 75–104. Wittkowsky points to rather clear analogies between Swift's style and putative purpose and the writings of those economic projectors who practiced "political arithmetic"; his case might, indeed, have been strengthened by noting the association of such a founder of the

bleak clarity with which the Irish plight is represented, the savage resentment which it has engendered, and the repellant solution which is offered can be satisfactorily explained as assaults upon either the substance or the language of previously published attempts to deal with the problems of the Irish.

As is so often true in Swift's satire, there are several victims against whom, by a single comprehensive satiric fiction, appropriate thrusts are delivered. But at the same time, only one end can account for all of the means which the writer has employed in the *Modest Proposal*, and one candidate alone qualifies as the principal goal of Swift's attack. The central satiric victim in this tract, as in the *Argument against Abolishing Christianity*, is the audience for whom the work is primarily intended. The audience—and satiric target—are the Irish people themselves; or, more explicitly, that part of the people of Ireland which determines the country's policies. Swift here is again the angry preacher, bent upon the exposure of the lethargy and obtuseness of his congregation. The "melancholly Object" which is the spectacle of Irish poverty is, after all, the occasion for the tract, but the plain facts about Irish populousness must have been lamentably familiar to Swift's original readers. The elaborate, systematic advocacy of the proposal, with its resemblance to the manner in which other "projects" have been couched, strikes passing satiric blows at victims ranging from absentee Anglo-Irish Protestants to the prolific Irish peasantry. But the crucial impact of the satire becomes unmistakable only belatedly, in the famous passage which asserts that this remedy is calculated "for this one individual Kingdom of IRELAND, and for no other that ever was, is, or I think ever can be upon Earth."

Therefore, [*Swift goes on*] let no man talk to me of other Expedients: *of taxing our Absentees at five Shillings a Pound: of using neither Cloaths, nor Household Furniture except what is of our own Growth and Manufacture: Of utterly rejecting the Materials and Instruments that promote*

---

new economic science as Sir William Petty with the Royal Society (and particularly its Irish correspondents) during the period (1682–85) when the *Philosophical Transactions* furnished abundant material for Swift's future attacks on the projectors. To imply, however, that even "from the point of view of the student of political economy" (p. 104) the tract is a parody of mercantilist theories, is to ignore the facts—largely economic—of Irish wretchedness and apathy which, in 1729, were Swift's most passionate concern.

foreign luxury: Of curing the Expensiveness of Pride, Vanity, Idleness, and Gaming in our Women: Of introducing a Vein of Parsimony, Prudence, and Temperance: Of learning to love our Country, wherein we differ even from LAPLANDERS, and the Inhabitants of TOPINAMBOO: Of quitting our Animosities, and Factions; nor act any longer like the Jews, *who were murdering one another at the very Moment their City was taken: Of being a little cautious not to sell our Country and Consciences for nothing: Of teaching Landlords to have, at least, one Degree of Mercy towards their Tenants. Lastly, Of putting a Spirit of Honesty, Industry, and Skill into our Shop-keepers; who, if a Resolution could now be taken to buy only our native Goods, would immediately unite to cheat and exact upon us in the Price, the Measure, and the Goodness; nor could ever yet be brought to make one fair Proposal of just Dealing, though often and earnestly invited to it* (pp. 116–17).

What is immediately clear about these "other Expedients" is that they represent the precise steps which Swift has long advocated.[15] And when this fact is recognized, the entire context of the *Modest Proposal* becomes clear. Writing to Pope in the year previous to the publication of this tract, Swift denies all motives of disinterested altruism in his concern for Irish affairs. "I do profess," he says, "without affectation, that your kind opinion of me as a patriot, since you call it so, is what I do not deserve; because what I do is owing to perfect rage and resentment, and the mortifying sight of slavery, folly, and baseness about me, among which I am forced to live."[16]

In the light of this kind of statement, *A Modest Proposal* is very close to a direct expression of Swift's rage and disgust, and the *persona*, driven by the obdurate rejection of every reasonable "other expedient" into the advocacy of a final, outrageous solution, is not very different from the historic figure of the bitterly frustrated Dean of St. Patrick's.

We are bound to discover in this document the sort of conceit which, for many readers, is memorable because of its unique Swiftian amalgam of wild fancy and perverse logic. We likewise recognize a variety of satiric assaults which find their mark in such diversified phenomena as anti-Catholicism, sexual irregularity, the follies of people of fashion, and, as we have suggested, most notably the

[15] See earlier "Irish Tracts" in *Prose Works*, XII, 1–90 *passim*, including *Intelligencer*, No. 19 (pp. 54–61).

[16] *Correspondence*, IV, 34.

economic projectors, among them those who had offered prescriptions for Irish problems. The principal satiric achievement, however, must be seen as persuasive and, indeed, once more a "homiletic" one. Swift is concerned with providing, for an audience whom he regards as lethargic and foolish, the most devastating assessment of their own condition and with arguing, almost literally, that as they have rejected all reasonable courses of action, the incredibly repellent proposal he advances is at least better than doing nothing.

This is, in truth, an address to and an assault upon "this one individual Kingdom of Ireland," for, whatever Swift may have felt about the English conduct of Irish affairs, within this document it is the Irish who are plainly taxed with bringing about their own deplorable condition. The so-called "paradox" of Swift's furious nationalism is illuminated rather than complicated by *A Modest Proposal.* For a people who should, he believes, truthfully "think it a great happiness to have been sold for Food at a Year old," Swift offers, in his anger, a prescription for virtual race suicide which is no more shocking than the state of affairs at which, through the folly of their own national policy, they have already arrived.

III

In both the *Argument* and *A Modest Proposal,* the identification of a principal satiric victim allows, us, I think, to answer all the chief questions raised by the presence of satiric writing. When we know the victim's identity, we can feel rather confident about the fictional dimension of the argument as well as the assumptions, the "truth," from which it proceeds, and we should be able, too, to describe quite precisely how that victim is exposed, is refuted, or otherwise "suffers" in the course of the satiric performance. In the *Argument* we have seen that the position of the *persona* is the position which Swift is attacking and that, moreover, the follies with which he taxes his spokesman-victim are those of which his immediate audience is guilty. In *A Modest Proposal,* the *persona* adopts a posture which differs only in its extravagance from the actual position which we can attribute to Swift himself. Here again, even more patently than in the *Argument,* the audience itself is the object of satiric assault. But in this case, Swift has constructed no fictional surrogate by which the follies of his true victim can be disclosed and distorted. His artifice consists entirely in the outrageously cruel course of action which the obtuseness and lethargy of the Irish have endowed with a kind of hideous logic.

Both of these relatively brief works acquire a kind of "unity" through this approach. For each is almost exclusively addressed to the attainment of a single satiric end; each sustains a consistent satiric fiction throughout; in neither is there any save the most transient digression from the systematic pursuit of the satiric enterprise. But it is obvious that the clarity which can be discovered in such brief and orderly works must not mislead us into expecting comparable simplicity from writings, however consistently "satiric," which are patently longer and more complex. As we have pointed out earlier, no rule requires the satirist ex officio to select a single object of attack, adhere to a single fiction, or, indeed, regard his artistic purpose as satiric throughout.

The difficulties presented by a relatively lengthy and patently diffuse work have been notoriously apparent in critical discussions of *A Tale of a Tub*. The puzzling complexity of the work is plain on even the most superficial inspection. Swift himself makes clear the plurality of his satiric goals and the modes in which they are pursued in the "Apology" with which he begins the fifth edition of the book:

> Thus prepared, he thought the numerous and gross Corruptions in Religion and Learning might furnish Matter for a Satyr, that would be useful and diverting: He resolved to proceed in a manner, that should be altogether new, the World having been already too long nauseated with endless Repetitions upon every Subject. The abuses in Religion he proposed to set forth in the Allegory of the Coats, and the three Brothers, which was to make up the Body of the Discourse. Those in Learning he chose to introduce by way of Digressions.[17]

Thus in substance and structure the *Tale* avowedly proceeds along two courses, however closely they may be related. And the casual reader is bound to be struck by the exuberant disregard for formal order with which Swift exploits the latitude he has allowed himself. The "tale" proper, the allegorical account of Christianity's decline through schism which ultimately focuses largely on the follies of the Puritans, is the nominal *raison d'être* for the work, yet it does not

---

[17] Unless otherwise noted, all my references to *A Tale of a Tub, The Battle of the Books,* and the *Mechanical Operation of the Spirit* are to the single-volume edition of A. C. Guthkelch and D. Nichol Smith (2d ed.; Oxford, 1958). The present quotation is found on p. 4.

begin until more than a third of the book has been devoted to prefatory materials of a plainly facetious sort. The "tale," moreover, is regularly interlarded with the "Digressions," and even its own slender narrative thread (the story of the three brothers actually occupies only about a quarter of the volume) is interrupted by the accounts of the clothes-philosophy and the Aeolists, which depart quite obviously from the general allegorical history to which the tale-teller is presumably committed. Within the prefatory materials and digressions, it is plain that the abuses in "Learning" cover a multitude of sins: the pedantry and arrogance of scholars, the vulgarity and poverty of hacks, the vapidity of satirists, the venom of critics, the nonsense of hermetic philosophers, the self-pity of poets—to name only a few.

To these self-apparent difficulties, the casual reader will be bound to add the perplexing matter of the satirist's "position." At times, it is clear, Swift is engaged in frank parody, but many other passages appear to be relatively forthright statements of sincere belief. The sentiments of the tale-teller toward his materials manifestly shift—from patronizing amusement to fatuous admiration, from pride in his ignorance and vulgarity to apology and equivocation, from the urbanity of the dedication to Lord Somers to the naïve self-revelation in the Preface.

In the face of difficulties which are thus apparent, critics have regularly attempted to confer on *A Tale of a Tub* the respectability which presumably inheres in a unified work of a recognizable genre. Something of the spirit which, in 1710, prompted Edmund Curll to offer a "Complete Key" to the *Tale* has found its way into many—if not most—of the investigations into the work which have gone on ever since. Accepting the *Tale* as a "problem," many of its students seem to believe that it should be "solved," and solved, moreover, by some formula of structural unity, dealing with Swift's writing throughout as a single organic undertaking.

Perhaps it is this desire to lend a single principle of order to a manifestly complicated work that has led many students into the whole realm of traditions, trends, habits, and doctrines which were presumably distasteful to Swift. Valuable as these researches have been as studies into the attitudes and traditions reflected in the *Tale*, they seem to have slighted the immediate objects of Swift's scorn, possibly since the latter, in their very immediacy, tend to defy generalization.[18]

The tendency to stress the relatively remote and generic sources of Swift's satire in recent studies of the *Tale* may be a reaction to the narrow and fragmentary treatment of an earlier day. To William Wotton the responsibility should probably attach for originally shifting the issues treated in the work from the arena of learned controversy to that of religion. When he asserted that in the *Tale* "God and Religion, Truth and Moral Honesty, Learning and Industry are made a May-Game,"[19] Wotton imposed upon future critics—both attackers and defenders—congenial grounds for controversy. As a result, it is not until Craik's *Life* of Swift, in 1882, that the insistence upon the narrative allegory and its religious attitudes as the core of the *Tale* is plainly repudiated. In a careful pursuit of "the broad foundations upon which the superstructure is raised," Craik concludes, as any sensible reader surely must, that "satire such as this reaches far beyond the accidents of ecclesiastical controversies."[20]

Certainly within our own century the traditional view of the *Tale* as a work primarily about religion seems largely to have been discarded.[21] There remains, however, an understandable, if not entirely

[18] Of the studies which deal with the "general" position taken by Swift in the *Tale*, particular attention should be given to Miriam K. Starkman's *Swift's Satire on Learning in "A Tale of a Tub"* (Princeton, 1950) and Phillip Harth's *Swift and Anglican Rationalism: The Religious Background of "A Tale of a Tub"* (Chicago, 1961). As their titles suggest, the two works explore, respectively, the two major areas in which Swift professes to locate the abuses he assaults. My debt to each of these superlative studies—as well as the points at which my own approach to the *Tale* departs from those of their authors—will be made at least partially apparent in the ensuing discussion.

[19] William Wotton, *A Defense of the Reflections upon Ancient and Modern Learning in Answer to the Objections of Sir W. Temple and Others with Observations upon a Tale of a Tub* (London, 1705). The *Defense* appeared in 1705 both as a separate volume and as an addition, with continuous pagination, to the third edition of Wotton's *Reflections upon Ancient and Modern Learning*. For this and future references I have used the latter volume (hereafter referred to as *Reflections*), in which the quoted passage appears at p. 520.

[20] Henry Craik, *The Life of Jonathan Swift* (London, 1882), p. 103. The emphasis on the religious issue by Swift's nineteenth-century biographers may be seen by consulting, *inter alia*, Sir Walter Scott's "Memoir" in his edition of Swift's *Works* (2d ed.; London, 1883), I, 75–76; William Monck Mason, *The History and Antiquities of the Collegiate and Cathedral Church of Saint Patrick* (Dublin, 1819), pp. 237–38; and John Forster, *The Life of Jonathan Swift* (London, 1875), pp. 144–58.

[21] The great pioneer was Émile Pons, *Swift: Les années de jeunesse et "Le Conte du Tonneau"* (Strasbourg, 1925), which, though superseded in many particular respects,

profitable tendency to offer a single, comprehensive definition of Swift's satiric intention.[22] For those who admire Swift, such efforts are naturally congenial. The quest for subsuming principles and unifying terms with which to describe Swift's aversions suggests that the *Tale* proceeds from broad and intelligent moral convictions, and this is certainly a more sympathetic assumption than is the notion of a series of highly personal, truculent, and sometimes inexplicable assaults.

For the historian or biographer, the assignment of all of Swift's aversions to a single, significant position is obviously desirable. If, as Mrs. Starkman's invaluable study concludes, it is possible to regard all of Swift's attacks as directed against "Modernity," we are able not only to align him with the Temples and Boyles against the Bentleys and Wottons, but to hail the special achievement of the *Tale* as that of a central document in the struggle against "Modern" innovations, claims, and doubts. The search for highly particularized satiric victims, the implicit suggestion that Swift's hostility could be the product of occasions and accidents as well as of firmly held principle, may place us in some danger of neglecting the most permanently important and moving elements in the *Tale*. We may tend to ignore total phenomena which he hated for transient attacks on mere manifestations; we may likewise, as is sometimes argued, yield to a pedantic exploration of particulars, ignoring, meanwhile, the ebulliently playful fancy of a work which is largely humorous. Moreover, the quest for particular satiric victims may produce re-

---

remains a highly illuminating work. Pons, in an older tradition, continues to place major emphasis upon "la satire religieuse qui est l'objet essentiel du Conte," although he recognizes that madness "s'étende à tous les domaines de la pensée et de l'activité humaine" (p. 377). The work of Richard F. Jones in *Ancients and Moderns: A Study of the Background of the Battle of the Books* (St. Louis, 1936) recognizes that Temple's and Swift's entry into the Ancient-Modern quarrel was a "hopeless effort to revive a dead controversy" (p. viii), yet clearly suggests that Swift's objects of attack lie as much in learned as in religious areas. The Guthkelch–Nichol Smith edition itself, first appearing in 1920, revealed the extent to which Swift's satiric victims were guilty of literary or learned offenses, rather than religious error. And Quintana, quite as much as Mrs. Starkman herself, has directed our attention to the thesis that "the two themes of zeal in religion and of enthusiasm in learning have been inextricably woven into one" (*The Mind and Art of Jonathan Swift*, p. 96). Thanks to these enterprises, more recent studies have not found it necessary to labor the importance of Swift's assaults against non-religious victims.

22 For an ambitious specimen of the effort to establish "unity" in the *Tale* see Ronald Paulson, *Theme and Structure in Swift's "Tale of a Tub"* (New Haven, 1960).

sults precisely the opposite of those yielded by this procedure in our scrutiny of the *Argument* and *A Modest Proposal*. Instead of a sustained principle of order and wholeness, we are likely to discover greater diffuseness, fragmentation, and even contradiction than the *Tale* presents at first sight. Our search for particulars may illuminate crannies and corners but leave the great structure of the *Tale* in relative darkness.

The search, I feel, must be undertaken nonetheless. It is not prompted by my own notion of what satire ought to be or a conviction that this elusive book must be brought into conformity with a priori principles. It is invited by several facts about the *Tale* itself. For, in the first place, the general formulas which have been advanced about the work do not eliminate from its enigmatic pages the nagging suggestions of purely personal malice, the hints of hidden animosities, or the puzzling bits of irreverence which, after two and a half centuries, continue to lend some small support to Wotton's angry protests at the work's impiety. Nor are the outlines of Swift's feigned literary personality ever sustained for very long at a purely general level; his habits may be those of Grub-street or Modernity in general, but from the beginning Swift's notes and the knowledge of the common reader have shown how frequently they are also those of particular men.

Swift, moreover, regarded the *Tale* as a satiric undertaking,[23] and I think he commits himself to a conception of the satiric attack which is not substantially different from the one that is offered in this study. For the volume which contains the *Tale* includes most of the observations which Swift ever offered about the satirist's art and these, in my opinion, point strongly to the view that satire succeeds only when there is punishing impact upon specific victims.

In the "Preface" to the *Tale*, one of the protracted introductory pieces in which Swift mockingly assumes the identity of various of his literary victims, he facetiously dissociates himself from his contemporaries on the "sole point" of his "refusal" to write satire.[24]

[23] "Thus prepared, he thought the numerous and gross Corruptions in Religion and Learning might furnish Matter for a Satyr . . ." (*Tale*, p. 4).

[24] "'Tis a great Ease to my Conscience that I have writ so elaborate and useful a Discourse without one grain of Satyr intermixt; which is the sole point wherein I have taken leave to dissent from the famous Originals of our Age and Country" (p. 48).

What is quite apparent in the ensuing discussion is that if satire is defined according to the practice of "the famous Originals of our Age and Country," Swift quite literally will have no traffic with it and it is proper to say, of the *Tale,* that it has been written "without one grain of Satyr intermixt." The grounds for this rejection, advanced chiefly in the guise of well-meant advice to writers, reflect what Swift authentically feels is wrong with contemporary satire and imply, as well, a view of the proper satiric function. The satirists whom he assails

use the Publick much at the Rate that Pedants do a naughty Boy ready Hors'd for Discipline: First expostulate the Case, then plead the Necessity of the Rod, from great Provocations, and conclude every Period with a Lash. Now, if I know any thing of Mankind, these Gentlemen might very well spare their Reproof and Correction: For there is not, through all Nature, another so callous and insensible a Member as the *World's Posteriors,* whether you apply to it the *Toe* or the *Birch* (p. 48).

From this passage alone, it is possible to construct the bill of particulars with which Swift charges his satirist contemporaries. There is nothing to be gained in an assault upon a supine but incorrigible victim. Such gestures are doubly ridiculous when accompanied by pious explanations and pleas of "Necessity." The "World's Posteriors" is a Swiftian image to sum up precisely the wrong kind of object for satiric attack—the universal and hence impervious target. An attack on all mankind, whatever its professed moral purpose and however actually malicious, is an attack on nothing!

The rejection of satire, as popularly practiced, continues throughout all of Swift's mocking advice to contemporary writers. This advice—which urges that the writer will do well to shun panegyric and to write "satyr"—is based on the fact that the former art, since it is designed to praise "one or a few Persons at a time," creates envy on the part of others. "But Satyr being levelled at all, is never resented for an offence by any, since every individual Person makes bold to understand it of others, and very wisely removes his particular Part of the Burthen upon the shoulders of the World, which are broad enough, and able to bear it" (p. 51).

The explication of this actual passage on satire depends (since the passage *is* satiric in its attack and its obliquity) on our recognizing the precise identity of the satire which, through his derisive advocacy, Swift holds up to scorn. That it is satire as practiced in contemporary England is made entirely clear by Swift's comparison of the present state of affairs with that of the ancient Athenian state. In the Greek society, personal vituperation prevailed and blanket attack upon the "people" was seditious, in contrast to the current situation —described by Swift in a passage which deserves particular attention:

Here, you may securely display your utmost *Rhetorick* against Mankind, in the Face of the World; tell them, *"That all are gone astray; That there is none that doth good, no not one; That we live in the very Dregs of Time; That Knavery and Atheism are Epidemick as the Pox; That Honesty is fled with Astræa;* with any other common places *equally* new and eloquent, which are furnished by the *Splendida bilis.* And when you have done, the whole Audience, far from being offended, shall return you thanks as a Deliverer of precious and useful Truths. Nay farther; It is but to venture your Lungs, and you may preach in *Convent-Garden* against Foppery and Fornication, and *something else:* Against Pride, and Dissimulation, and Bribery, at *White-Hall:* You may expose Rapine and Injustice in the *Inns* of *Court* Chappel: And in a *City* Pulpit be as fierce as you please, against Avarice, Hypocrisie and Extortion. 'Tis but a *Ball* bandied to and fro, and every Man carries a *Racket* about Him to strike it from himself among the rest of the Company. But on the other side, whoever should mistake the Nature of things so far, as to drop but a single Hint in publick, How *such a one,* starved half the Fleet, and half-poison'd the rest: How *such a one,* from a true Principle of *Love* and *Honour,* pays no Debts but for *Wenches* and *Play:* How *such a one* has got a Clap and runs out of his Estate: How *Paris* bribed by *Juno* and *Venus,* loath to offend either Party, slept out the whole Cause on the Bench: Or, how *such an Orator* makes long Speeches in the Senate with much Thought, little Sense, and to no Purpose: whoever, I say, should venture to be thus particular, must expect to be imprisoned for *Scandalum Magnatum:* to have *Challenges* sent him; to be sued for *Defamation;* and to be *brought before the Bar of the House* (pp. 51–53).

Swift leaves us in no doubt as to the kind of satire he will not engage in or his grounds for rejecting it. His most basic premise may concern the inalterable obtuseness of modern man, but from this assumption there proceeds an equally firm conviction about effective satire. Assaults upon sins in general, however violent, cannot succeed, even when addressed to the most patently culpable audience. True satire—imprudent, unpopular, indeed obsolete as it may be—must be directed to "such a one," unequivocally leveling its particular charge against its particular victim.

The passage anticipates and, in fact, reinforces the more famous observation in the Preface to *The Battle of the Books:* "Satyr is a sort of *Glass,* wherein Beholders do generally discover every body's Face but their Own" (p. 215). And although the latter statement seems largely to reflect Swift's despair at the power of satire to affect its victims, the lines which follow suggest that he himself is not resigned to the frailty of his art.

But if it should happen otherwise, the Danger is not great; and, I have learned from long Experience, never to apprehend Mischief from those Understandings, I have been able to provoke; For Anger and Fury, though they add Strength to the Sinews of the Body, *yet are found to relax those of the* Mind, *and to render all its Efforts feeble and impotent.*

The satire which fails to meet its mark is the "glass" as it is the "ball bandied to and fro," and in the passages in which the figures appear, there is the powerful implication that such satire is not for Swift. Years later, in his spirited defense of Gay in the *Intelligencer,* No. 3, he again reveals the particularized nature of his own satire. Recognizing that a public spirit may prompt "men of genius and virtue, to mend the world as far as they are able," he implicitly commits himself to a form of writing which yields only personal satisfaction. "If I ridicule the Follies and Corruptions of a *Court,* a *Ministry,* or a *Senate,*" he asks, "are they not amply paid by *Pensions, Titles,* and *Power;* while I expect, and desire no other Reward, than that of laughing with a few Friends in a Corner?"[25]

In the act of attacking contemporary satirists and of defending his own practice, as well as John Gay's, Swift reveals his commitment to a brand of satire which refuses to profess lofty motivations or to equivocate in its punishing assault upon particular men and institutions. (Against this evidence for Swift's conception of the satiric office, one can, of course, always offer the mellow sentiments of the lines in the *Verses on the Death of Dr. Swift:*

> Yet, Malice never was his Aim;
> He lash'd the Vice but spared the Name
> No Individual could resent,
> Where Thousands equally were meant.[26]

[25] *Prose Works,* XII, 34. [26] *Poems,* II, 571.

Yet one need not move beyond the context of the *Verses* themselves for a plain refutation, from Swift's own practice, of the precept he professes in this uncharacteristic posture of mellow benevolence.)

Thus, Swift's discussion of satire in the *Tale* and elsewhere makes it quite clear that unabashed attack upon particular satiric victims is, for him, a proper function of the satirist. It would be more than strange if this vigorously stated principle were not plainly embodied in Swift's satiric performance—and particularly in that performance of which the statement of theory is a part.

Of course the particularized attacks are abundantly present in the *Tale*—and have always been recognized, if only tacitly, by its critics. Where, I think, many students have tended to err is in hastily expanding upon, generalizing, and departing from these particulars in an effort to explain the general or entire achievement of *A Tale of a Tub*. The "explanation" which the work still most urgently requires is in the explication of vexed passages and in the recognition of facts which enforce rather than minimize the truly satiric dimension of the book. Swift is often at pains to let us know the precise identity of his victims. And it is the knowledge of these particular identities which, I would suggest, can best shed light on areas of the work which remain relatively obscure.

Consider one example. Sir Roger L'Estrange, the notorious politician and journalist of the later seventeenth century, is one of the men among Swift's contemporaries who are named explicitly and unsympathetically in both the *Tale* proper and its prefatory apparatus.[27] Here (for reasons which cannot be established precisely but which appear entirely compatible with Swift's views on literary and political decorum) is a specific object of Swift's hostility—far more immediate, one would judge, than the philosophic roots of "Modernity" or Cartesianism or even Puritanism. It would seem probable that in this particular man, quite as much as in general habits or tendencies, one can find the model for some of Swift's parody, the object of some of his pointed jests.

It is, therefore, interesting to note that near the end of the Preface to his edition of the *Fables of Aesop,* L'Estrange remarks, "An Emblem without a Key to't, is no more than a *Tale of a Tub;* and that Tale Sillily told too, is but one Folly Grafted upon Another."[28] Al-

---

[27] *Tale,* pp. 7, 70, 183.

[28] Roger L'Estrange, *Fables of Aesop and Other Eminent Mythologists with Morals and Reflections* (2d ed.; London, 1694), Sig. A4ᵛ.

though it seems highly likely that Swift was familiar with L'Estrange's edition of Aesop, I hesitate to offer more than a conjecture that Swift had L'Estrange's phrase in mind when he named his own book. Yet it is a precedent which seems unusually apposite: Swift's aversion to self-conscious fables and to the unlocking of "mysteries" with easy "Keys" emerges plainly in the *Tale;*[29] the air of capricious mystification, the solemn presentation of a "tale" in which the tale is the least part, can certainly be described as an attempt, whether deliberate or not, to produce precisely the kind of writing for which the despised L'Estrange expresses aversion. L'Estrange's passage, moreover, is closer in time to the publication of Swift's book than any prior use of the phrase "a tale of a tub" which annotators have thus far reported. More than Swift's own account of the tub used to divert whales, more even than the obvious allusion to the dissenters' uncovered pulpits, L'Estrange's assertion serves to describe the general nature of Swift's undertaking. In his title, Swift has blithely flaunted L'Estrange's dictum, and in his book he has produced an "emblem" whose key is far subtler than the threadbare aphorisms which L'Estrange supplied for Aesop. One cannot prove that L'Estrange prompted Swift's choice of a title. One can assert, however, that a knowledge of Sir Roger's writings lends a particular and novel dimension to the title as a satiric device. And the probability of this added interpretation is increased by at least two other satiric assaults which—in addition to the overt identifications already mentioned—seem to apply to L'Estrange with a particularity which has not previously been suspected.

The extended introductory sections to the *Tale* which delay the beginning of the narrative proper until well over one-third of the physical volume has been completed are obviously a deliberate tease. This ludicrous proliferation of apparatus can be viewed as a general mockery of literary practice, directed against learned prefaces and annotations as well as fulsome dedications, apologia, and various species of personal self-advertisement. It has long been noted that Swift seems to have had in mind, within the particulars of his prefatory materials, certain performances of Dryden.[30] The sheer *multiplicity* of these materials, however, is harder to explain as the parody of a particular writer. And here, again, the most vulnerable target is

[29] *Tale,* pp. 61, 66–69, 167, 185–87, 190.
[30] See text and notes in *Tale,* pp. 70–71, 131.

L'Estrange. For the latter's *Brief History of the Times* (1687) is actually a *preface* to the third volume of the collected *Observators,* whose preface to the *History* itself is self-consciously admitted to be "A Preface upon a Preface." The parallel between Swift's jestingly multiplied introductions and this egregious procedure of L'Estrange is so close that it is hard to believe that Swift's joke is directed merely against a common literary practice. Inordinately long and compounded introductory materials were not so common in Swift's day as to appear a "general" folly. It seems far more likely that a characteristic habit of a widely read (if not devoutly admired) author would occur to Swift's contemporaries as the "original" from which Swift's mocking caricature proceeds.

An even more striking parallel, however, is found between the writings of L'Estrange and Swift's delightful "Epistle Dedicatory to His Royal Highness, Prince Posterity" (pp. 30–38). Within this dedication we discover a single idea, not inherently satiric, which serves as the framework for a complex argument, multiple in its satiric ends and shifting in its method. Suspending inquiry into the numerous directions, satiric and otherwise, taken by Swift's argument in this section, I think we can find that the basic notion of an appeal to posterity acquires satiric meaning if, once again, we turn to L'Estrange. Swift himself supplies a fifth edition note which shows some reluctance to name names:

It is the usual style of decry'd Writers to appeal to *Posterity,* who is here represented as a Prince in his Nonage, and *Time* as his Governour, and the Author begins in a way very frequent with him, by personating other Writers, who sometimes offer such Reasons and Excuses for publishing their Works as they ought chiefly to conceal and be asham'd of (p. 30).

Again there is little evidence that an appeal to posterity constituted, in Swift's day, the "usual style" of writers, decried or otherwise. The phrase "other writers who sometimes offer" carries a guarded suggestion that Swift has in mind something other than mere widespread custom. And of those "decry'd Writers" for whom his posture has relevance, L'Estrange appears to be the leading candidate. His *A Brief History of the Times &c. in a Preface to the Third Volume of the Observators* was published separately in three sections, the first in 1687, the second and third in 1688. Each of these sections contains a preface, and *each* of the prefaces is headed "To Posterity":

in fact, the first section contains the "Preface on a Preface" already mentioned, and *both* of these prefaces are addressed "To Posterity." Whatever deeper significance may be read in Swift's derisive appeal to unborn generations, he seems quite clearly to have borrowed for satiric ends from a writer whose work he certainly knew and just as certainly disliked.

But the "Epistle Dedicatory" may remind us of L'Estrange in more respects than the basic device of an address to posterity. The curious quality of its syntax, in which lumpish and ill-mated clauses are loosely strung together, and the peculiar mixture of a pontifical air with mean sentiments, inflated banality with shameless triviality in diction are strongly suggestive of stylistic parody. This, assuredly, is not Swift's usual manner of writing. The prose in the section has led Mrs. Miriam K. Starkman, for one, to conclude that the "Epistle," while substantively an assault on Modern faith in progress, "is also a parody on style." In her study of the *Tale,* she writes of the "Epistle":

It is a parody on the style which we now call the "baroque" or the "anti-Ciceronian"; a style which in the hands of Sir Thomas Browne and John Milton achieved a complex imaginative power; a style which in the hands of less able writers became merely a heavy, digressive, asyntactical morass. The aspect of the baroque style which Swift parodies chiefly in the "Epistle" is the loose structure of the sentence, composed of many separate and digressive members only loosely tied together. Note the five separate members of the opening sentence of the "Epistle," its sententious weight, as Swift, the mock Modern, makes his disingenuous plea to Posterity's regard.[31]

The opening sentence confirms Mrs. Starkman's account of it:

I Here present *Your Highness* with the Fruits of a very few leisure Hours, stollen from the short Intervals of a World of Business, and of an Employment quite alien from such Amusements as this: The poor Production of that Refuse of Time which has lain heavy upon my Hands, during a long Prorogation of Parliament, a great Dearth of Forein News, and a tedious Fit of rainy Weather: For which, and other Reasons, it cannot chuse extreamly to deserve such a Patronage as that of *Your Highness,* whose numberless Virtues in so few Years, make the World look upon You as the future Example to all Princes: For altho' *Your Highness* is hardly got clear of Infancy, yet has the universal learned World already resolv'd

[31] Starkman, pp. 119–20.

upon appealing to Your future Dictates with the lowest and most resigned
Submission: Fate having decreed You sole Arbiter of the Productions of
human Wit, in this polite and most accomplish'd Age (pp. 30–31).

The need for verbal ligature, the plethora of colons standing between clauses which are variously independent or mere appositions,
and the almost conversational arrangement and vocabulary which,
despite the apparent complexity of the entire period, mark each of
its members are essentially "Senecan." Mrs. Starkman has been content to describe this as a parody on mere "Modernity" (although in
the substantive profession that the letter is a product of idle moments she finds echoes of Blackmore and of certain scientific writers,
including Robert Boyle). But of the "less able writers," in whose
hands the "baroque" became, indeed, a morass, L'Estrange furnishes
a conspicuous and familiar example. He had published Seneca's
Morals in 1678 and had brought to that work, as to all of his writings, so egregious a specimen of "the familiar, the facetious and
jocular Style," that his contemporaries and immediate successors
considered him, whether in praise or detraction, the exemplification
of the "pertness" of the period.[32]

We need only turn to one of L'Estrange's multiple prefaces addressed to Posterity to discover, in its very opening sentence, the
qualities which have gained for his prose its dubious reputation:

These papers are the *True History* and bear the *Lively Image* of the Lewd
Times they were *written* in, and Consequently, not for the *Palate* of the
Present Age: For a *Wicked Generation* will no more bear *Truth,* in a
Book, than an *Ill-Favour'd Woman* will bear it, in her *Picture,* or in her
Looking-Glass: and though the Fault be manifestly in the *Face,* or in the
People; 'tis the Poor Innocent *Painter,* that is to be *Curs'd* for't, and the
Glass Broken; because her *Ladyships Nose stands awry* perhaps, or that
the *Manners* of the *Age* will not endure the *Light.*[33]

[32] Applying the descriptions offered by Morris W. Croll, "The Baroque Style in
Prose," *Studies in English Philology . . . in Honor of Frederick Klaeber,* ed. Malone
and Ruud (Minneapolis, 1929), pp. 427–65, one may identify L'Estrange's style as
the "loose" variety of "Senecan." In George Williamson's *The Senecan Amble* (Chicago and London, 1951), chap. xi, "Pert Style in Neo-Classic Times" is particularly useful in suggesting egregious aspects of L'Estrange's prose. Evidence for
regarding L'Estrange specifically as a prime representative of this tendency can be
seen in *The Senecan Amble* at pp. 345–46, 354, 363, 364–65, 367. Explicit assaults on
L'Estrange's "corrupting" influences on the language are not uncommon in the
eighteenth century. For a well-known specimen, see *Spectator,* No. 135.

[33] L'Estrange, *A Brief History of the Times* (London, 1687), p. 1.

I cannot discover that Sir Roger ever departs from this kind of writing unless it is in the direction of greater vulgarity and ineptness. Real passion seems only to drive him to formless and repetitive diatribes or shameless self-pity, and when he professes to serve the cause of piety or learning, it is with a prose whose pretentiousness only underscores its essential poverty of invention. If, as I believe, Swift was chronically sensitive to sins against the canons of style, then, in the latter years of the seventeenth century, he could find no more familiar or abundant display of these sins than the writings of L'Estrange.

Although by identifying L'Estrange as a satiric victim, we can clarify certain passages and devices in the *Tale,* the procedure effects no magic falling-together of other pieces. On the contrary, the more emphasis we place on the particularity of the assaults in a work of this magnitude and elusiveness, the more we confirm the impossibility of encompassing its achievement within a single formula. But while the analysis of satiric writing may not produce a principle of total unity, it clearly requires more than the explication of fragments. Satiric attacks are not, as a rule, the captious expressions of "motiveless malignity," nor is it likely that a book the size of the *Tale* is a mere compendium of dissociated snipings. When the satirist plainly addresses himself to "abuses" in such general areas of human life as religion or learning, his various attacks are likely to proceed from grounds which are compatible if not demonstrably common. In the absence of overt statement of principle, however (and the obliquity of the satiric art discourages this), these grounds can be established only by the examination of particular attacks. We are obliged, that is, to recognize the specific aspects of the satiric victim which the satirist finds offensive and vulnerable in each instance. We naturally expect these grounds to be individually intelligible and mutually compatible (although not necessarily "unified" or even significantly related). If, beyond this, we can discern a meaningful pattern of conviction or attitude which these grounds collectively reflect, then —and only then—we can attempt some observations about the kinds of phenomena, the general customs and beliefs, to which the satirist addresses his assault. Even at this stage, we may have shed no light on the satirist's most fundamental convictions or on his actual motives. Swift's inveterate hostility toward Dryden has yet to be satisfactorily explained in biographical terms, yet in the *Tale* Dryden is repeatedly taxed, justly or not, with the same literary vices which Swift plainly finds offensive in other contemporary writers.

So, too, with a victim like L'Estrange, it is possible to point out the grounds on which Swift bases his aversion. It is clear that Swift is concerned neither with the dubious morality nor the fanatic political commitments of Sir Roger.[34] It is the literary and journalistic practice of his victim which prompts Swift's derision in the "Epistle to Posterity" and elsewhere. If the multiplication of prefatory apparatus is an echo of L'Estrange, it is directed against that "unexhausted copiousness in writing" which Burnet derisively notes.[35] The arrogance and silliness of L'Estrange's addresses to Posterity, the ineffectual disorder and vulgarity of his style, and, quite possibly, the insistence that learning without "emblems" and accompanying "keys" is merely "a tale of a tub" are the aspects of L'Estrange to which Swift addresses his scornful attention. These choices, among the abundance of follies and infirmities which L'Estrange's enemies could—and did—select for their assaults upon him, must be remembered if we are to interpret Swift's treatment of L'Estrange as anything more than an attack upon an individual man. The fact that such an attack has been launched against an identifiable victim serves to establish the satiric character of the writing. If, as we are certainly prompted to do in the case of Swift, we seek for the principles which lend authority to such assaults, the single instance remains, as it were, our point of departure. From the sum of such instances alone can we draw our inferences as to the *kind* of victim the satirist has selected and the general convictions, if any, from which his attacks proceed.

IV

In a work as complicated as *A Tale of a Tub,* the identification of particular satiric victims is a piecemeal procedure, during which, if anything, whatever satiric "unity" the work may claim tends to dis-

[34] Political satire, of course, plays a negligible part in the *Tale.* Its youthful author (who dedicates his book to the Whig Somers) would probably not have found L'Estrange's virulent brand of Toryism particularly attractive in any case. The contrast between L'Estrange's fanaticism and the moderately loyalist position of such a man as Temple can be seen in discussions by George Kitchin, *Sir Roger L'Estrange* (London, 1913), pp. 222–59, and Homer E. Woodbridge, *Sir William Temple* (London and New York, 1940), pp. 193–209.

[35] *Bishop Burnet's History of His Own Time* (London, 1753), II, 90.

appear. The specific targets unearthed in this sort of search may
so widely dissociated that the umbrella-terms under which we try t
subsume them become inadequate or meaningless. A further difficulty with the *Tale* may lie in the fact that in this work—as in *Gulliver's Travels*—many passages are difficult to construe as attack on
particular victims, or perhaps attack of any sort. This means that we
can anticipate a frequent conjunction of satiric and non-satiric elements or, at the least, interruptions and diffusions of the satiric assault. One wonders, accordingly, how it is possible to take even a
single section of the *Tale*, define its satiric achievement in terms
which take account of widely diversified victims, note those elements
which may not even be satiric in our sense of the word, and still
preserve a sense of its wholeness as a literary structure.

I believe, however, that many of the most bewildering and apparently shapeless parts of the *Tale*—and notably the "digressive"
sections—can be seen as effective and fundamentally orderly satire if
we consider three broad levels or classes of question. In the first
place, despite his deliberate discursiveness, the pseudo-author invariably *purports* to be offering an argument addressed to some
topic. In its bare outlines, the professed purpose offers a fictional
raison d'être for the section and provides, despite the countless subtleties it inevitably masks, an overt, intelligible structure. Moreover,
at this level, there are usually superficial but genuine satiric results.
We can advance general, although by no means exhaustive, observations about the egregiously vulnerable aspects of the posture assumed by the *persona*. To the extent that he assumes and loosely
sustains the role of one of Swift's victims, engaged in a palpably preposterous enterprise, we should have little difficulty in sensing the
direction of the satiric attack. Thus to "digress" in defense of criticism or of "digressions" themselves or "in the modern kind" is an
undertaking which almost automatically proclaims its own folly
and that of the author who pursues it.

The countless departures from these professed roles, however, severely limit their usefulness as "keys" to the entire satire of any
section. It is these departures—the apparent suspensions of the alleged arguments—that call into play the second kind of awareness
which is necessary for a satisfactory understanding of the *Tale*. The
persona rarely sustains his style and his sentiments for long; his arguments are constantly interrupted by apparently irrelevant excur-

sions; where one sentence courts only our derision, the next compels our surprised concurrence. These are the points at which, quite naturally, we intensify our search for a particular satiric victim. Some of the *persona*'s gestures must finally be appreciated as largely comic, without discernible satiric impact. But before this happens, we remain alert to signals of parodic intention, to allusions, to the displays of apparent nonsense which acquire sense when we locate the authentic styles or habits or doctrines of which they are a mockery.

In our pursuit of the particulars by which alone such satire becomes meaningful, the unity of style and structure which our more superficial scrutiny has produced is likely to disintegrate. The broad movement of the chapter is interrupted and the *persona* loses his significance as surrogate-victim. But at this point, a third kind of recognition may help to recover the order and responsibility which, in some measure, underly all of Swift's playfulness and diffuseness. This kind of recognition involves a careful consideration of emphases and relationships, distinctions and resemblances among the objects of satiric attack. It produces an ultimate, pointed awareness of the *kinds* of victims Swift has singled out for attention in a given section—and, more important, the *grounds* on which he finds them culpable. It does not, I should insist, substitute a general for a particular object of attack, any more than it necessarily involves an affirmative—or even a normative—statement of overt belief. It tends, however, to indicate a selective principle, to suggest what was in Swift's mind, to dictate his particular collocation of satiric victims, and to imply that, for all their appearance of diversity, his attacks follow from consistent conviction. Ultimately, moreover, such principles can lend new significance to elements within the section that have hitherto seemed merely playful, very broadly satiric, or, in some instances, quite inexplicable.

This theoretical account of our developing response to the individual sections in the *Tale* can only be supported by illustration. I should like, therefore, to examine as a specimen a section of that work, the first chapter of the "tale" proper, which Swift calls "The Introduction." Since it further delays the beginning of Swift's actual narrative, it is, in a sense, the last of the prefatory materials, yet it can also be classed with the digressive chapters by which Swift deliberately impedes the unfolding of his allegorical fable. In any case, we approach it with an awareness of the challenges which Swift imposes in his non-narrative role.

"The Introduction" (pp. 55-72) appears to be singularly discursive, even within the loose context of the *Tale*. It digresses, perhaps, more than any of the frankly labeled digressions. Actually, however, like the prefatory pieces, it is contained within a very simple outward plan, dictated entirely by the task to which the spokesman addresses himself. He wishes to make clear and to apologize for his identity and the character of his literary undertaking. And his argument is a pseudo-defense and hence an "exposure" of his entire enterprise along with whatever genuine phenomena we are invited to associate with it.

"Whoever hath an Ambition to be heard in a Crowd," begins the section and the entire *Tale* proper, "must press, and squeeze, and thrust, and climb with indefatigable Pains, till he has exalted himself to a certain Degree of Altitude above them" (p. 55). The statement is a kind of leitmotif for the entire *Tale,* a commitment, at the very outset, to the purpose which (as I shall try to show in a subsequent chapter) is the single fiction which sustains the total work. For the moment, we note that the author is concerned with no goal more lofty than that of "being heard," no emotion nobler than "ambition," no means for securing attention other than mechanical ones, to which the importance of his message is quite irrelevant.

These means, he indicates, are the pulpit, the ladder (from which the "gallows-orations" of condemned men are traditionally delivered), and the stage-itinerant (the platform of the mountebank-player). But, he goes on to confess, this scientifically expounded problem and its solutions are mere analogies, employed to suggest the occupations by which writers can achieve eminence—fanatic religious writing, factional pamphleteering and verse, and the popular productions of Grub-street. It is to the last that the author is committed, and he feels obliged to defend the brotherhood of which he is a member—particularly since it is threatened by its rebellious offspring, the scientists of Gresham College and the poets of Will's coffee-house. To this end, he offers a catalogue of the "Prime Productions of our Society," a ludicrous list of folk legends to which are added the works of Wotton and Dryden as well as his present undertaking (i.e., the *Tale*), a ripe Grub-street specimen even to its titles and sub-titles. The author concludes his "Introduction" with the defense of his book by thus invoking the practice of his "brethren."

This pedestrian summary of a notably brilliant chapter is offered chiefly to suggest that the unobtrusive pursuit of a simple purpose actually lends order to an apparently wild collection of techniques and ideas. That is, the chapter—like all those in the *Tale*—openly addresses itself to a literary task; and while this putative undertaking never coincides with the true accomplishment of the section, the alleged purpose provides, at the least, an adequate principle of progression. If, moreover, we are willing to settle for a single "basic" effect (which will, admittedly, not comprehend the many divergent postures within the section), it is probably safe to say that the *persona* clearly stigmatizes himself, his enterprise, and the various kinds of contemporary writing with which he associates it.

Yet the chapter fairly bristles with satiric reflections which are, at most, very indirectly related to the infirmities which its mock-author displays. As he expounds his "Physico-logical Scheme of Oratorial Receptacles or Machines"—only to dismiss it as "a Type, a Sign, an Emblem, a Shadow, a Symbol" (p. 61)—Swift is able to deliver assaults against a list of victims which identifiably includes, at the least, Dryden, speculative philosophy, (particularly that of Englishmen),[36] judges, lawyers, numerology, the Dissenters in general and the Presbyterians more particularly, John Dunton, and the conventions of the contemporary theater. It is impossible in the limits of this discussion to note the precise way in which each of these thrusts is delivered, but the range of satiric techniques is very great. Thus, for example, the pulpit chiefly suffers through "guilt by association" with the other two mean "Oratorial Machines,"[37] upon first being mentioned, but Swift embroiders upon his conceit so that the physical appearance of a dissenter's pulpit is made to convey, through a fine mixture of metaphor and pun, a variety of epithets applicable to Puritanism itself (p. 58). John Dunton,[38] on the other hand, is merely

[36] *Tale*, p. 56. The reference to "these North-West Regions" points, as the editors remark, to English philosophers as suffering peculiarly from *"Inclemencies of Air."*

[37] "Would any Christian," asks Wotton, "compare a *Mountebank's Stage*, a Pulpit, and a *Ladder* together?" (*Reflections*, p. 530). And in his initial introduction of the "machines" Swift does nothing to qualify the image of the pulpit (although subsequently announcing his preference for those made of *Sylva Caledonia*). Here, as in the categorically debasing device of the three brothers, religion in general seems to suffer in a way which, though hardly the basis for an accusation of deliberate impiety, is difficult to reconcile with the rigorous devoutness Swift is to display within a few years.

[38] As Guthkelch and Nichol Smith point out, the assertion that John Dunton is about to publish a 12-volume edition of gallows-oratory is without foundation.

introduced with heavy sarcasm as a "worthy Citizen and Bookseller" and made the protagonist of a completely fictional and meanly preposterous publishing enterprise (p. 59).

Attacks of this kind, for all their diversity, are quite obvious as the author's argument proceeds. There are, to be sure, fugitive postures in which the wit of Swift appears virtually undisguised; the rejection of the Bar and the Bench as Oratorial Machines (pp. 56–57) is one of these. But here, as elsewhere, the author (by professing that a mystical respect for the number Three has chiefly prompted his choice) quickly slips back into his ingenuous servility toward the practices of "other Philosophers and Great Clerks" (p. 57).

These overt sallies do not, however, exhaust the assaults upon particular satiric victims, since closer scrutiny reveals, I believe, a special dimension of pointed malice in passages which, even without complete explication, serve an apparent satiric purpose. Thus, for example, the quotation from Virgil, in the very first paragraph,

> —Evadere ad auras,
> Hoc opus, hic labor est (p. 55)

is sufficiently amusing as, one assumes, a patently strained effort to introduce a classical tag. Swift's own note, however, cites Dryden's translation of the *Aeneid*,[39] and the warping of these edifying lines for purposes of this sort of foolery is hardly flattering to the translator.

Beyond this, however, the statement that this project is "altogether worthy of such a Hand" is hostile sarcasm which reveals Swift's recently-acquired animosity for the publisher of the *Athenian Mercury*. For an account of Swift's disaffection from the Athenians, see Mabel Phillips (DeVane), *Swift's Relations to Science* (Ph.D. diss., Yale, 1925).

[39] The observation that it is "as hard to get quit of *Number* as of *Hell*" seems very forced, but it provides the occasion for a solemn reference to Virgil and, more important, to the translation of Dryden which, in the epistle to Posterity, has been listed along with the productions of Durfey and Nahum Tate as a leading literary product of the age. The fragment quoted must be seen in its context; in *Aeneid*, vi, the Sybil, speaking to Aeneas of his proposed journey to Hell, warns

> "The gates of hell are open night and day;
> Smooth the descent and easy is the way;
> But, to return, and view the cheerful skies—
> In this the task and mighty labour lies."
>
> (Dryden's *Works*, ed. Scott and Saintsbury, XIV, 405.)

The quotation is hardly vicious satire, but had Dryden lived to see his lines gratuitously introduced in this context, he might well have been resentful.

A more significant question is raised by the style of the opening section, for beyond its mere sententiousness and heavy mock-deference, it is couched in a pseudo-scientific jargon which before now has prompted scholarly conjecture as to its parodic intention.[40] Two paragraphs which are particularly notable for the multiplicity of their satiric accomplishments are worth quoting:

AND I am the readier to favour this Conjecture, from a common Observation; that in the several Assemblies of these Orators, Nature it self hath instructed the Hearers, to stand with their Mouths open, and erected parallel to the Horizon, so as they may be intersected by a perpendicular Line from the Zenith to the Center of the Earth. In which Position, if the Audience be well compact, every one carries home a Share, and little or nothing is lost.

I confess, there is something yet more refined in the Contrivance and Structure of our Modern Theatres. For, First; the Pit is sunk below the Stage with due regard to the Institution above-deduced; that whatever *weighty* Matter shall be delivered thence (whether it be *Lead* or *Gold*) may fall plum into the Jaws of certain *Criticks* (as I think they are called) which stand ready open to devour them. Then, the Boxes are built round, and raised to a Level with the Scene, in deference to the Ladies, because, That large Portion of Wit laid out in raising Pruriences and Protuberances, is observ'd to run much upon a Line, and ever in a Circle. The whining Passions, and little starved Conceits, are gently wafted up by their own extreme Levity, to the middle Region, and there fix and are frozen by the frigid Understandings of the Inhabitants. Bombast and Buffoonery, by Nature lofty and light, soar highest of all, and would be lost in the Roof, if the prudent Architect had not with much foresight contrived for them a fourth Place, called the *Twelve-Peny Gallery,* and there planted a suitable Colony, who greedily intercept them in their Passage (pp. 60–61).

The initial image of the audience is offered in obvious derision of the slack-jawed, uncritical auditors who surround the mountebank, the gallows-orator, and, particularly, the dissenting preacher. And, in the latter paragraph, the delightful invention by which the physical properties of sound are attributed to the substance of the drama to account for the construction of contemporary theaters is an amusing reflection on the quality of the stage.

[40] Guthkelch and Nichol Smith suggest that a reference in Browne's *Vulgar Errors* (in a chapter dealing with the ring-finger!) is a possible influence for the notion of a cosmically oriented posture (*Tale,* pp. 60–61), while for Mrs. Starkman the passage as a whole is part of the general satire against the "new science" (pp. 64 ff.).

To those, however, who are aware of Swift's satiric preoccupation with the new science, the bogus-mechanical exposition of these and surrounding paragraphs has a significant ring. The foundation of these rather elaborate conceits is a deliberately simplistic acceptance of the physical properties of sound. For a model of this kind of discussion, we are prompted to turn (as at least one scholar has done for the explication of comparable passages elsewhere in the *Tale*)[41] to the Royal Society's *Philosophical Transactions*. And the *Philosophical Transactions* for February 20, 1683–84, contains "An Introductory Essay to the Doctrine of Sounds" in which certain parallels are drawn between optics and acoustics and which concludes with three "problems" in which the author's theory is applied. The first two of these are particularly striking and are as follows:

The first [problem] is, *To make the least Sound* (by the help of Instruments) *as loud as the greatest;* a whisper to become as loud as the shot of a Canon. . . .
The second is, *To propagate any* (the least) *Sound to the greatest Distance.*

For the solution of these problems, a diagram is offered, with the accompanying explanation:

You are to conceive that (rude) *Semiplane,* as Parallel to the Horizon. For if it be Perpendicular thereunto, I suppose the upper extremity will be no longer *Circular* but *Hyperbolical,* and the lower part of it suited to a greater circle of the Earth. So that the whole *Phonical* Sphear (if I may so call it) will be a solid *Hyperbola,* standing upon a *Concave Sphaerical* Base. I speak this concerning *Sounds* made (as usually they are) nigh the Earth, and whose Sonorous medium has a free passage every way. For if they are generated high in the Air, or directed one way, the case will be different; which is partly design'd in the equality of that draught.[42]

Swift's quotation from Lucretius, immediately preceding the passage I have quoted, is at most a facetious epigraph for his discussion[43] in

---

[41] See R. C. Olson, "Swift's Use of the *Philosophical Transactions* in Section V of *A Tale of a Tub,*" *Studies in Philology,* XLIX (1952), 459–67.

[42] *Philosophical Transactions of the Royal Society of London,* XIV (1684), 487–88.

[43] I am inclined to feel that the repeated appearance of Lucretius in the *Tale*—like that of Epicurus and quite possibly of Paracelsus and even Descartes—is as a symbol of impiety and outlandish belief rather than as a direct object of satiric attack. A tag from Lucretius is quoted, with transparent facetiousness, along with a gibberish Marcosian heresy from Irenaeus, on the title-page of the *Tale,* and at seven more points within the text. In each instance, the reference appears in a passage in which, by substance, diction, or both, Swift has assumed one or another of the identities he

comparison with the sustained mechanistic treatment of sound in the article from the *Philosophical Transactions*. The account of how sound is "begotten," "beaten," "falls upon bodies," "broken and extinguisht," and even how "in a Church, the nearer the Preacher stands to the wall ... the better he is heard" may well be a thoughtful exposition of acoustical science, but it also provides a splendid object of ridicule for the unscientific Ancient. What is, however, more striking is the complete title of the scientific paper, which gives us the name of its author and the circumstances of its original delivery:

An introductory Essay to the doctrine of *Sounds,* containing some proposals for the improvement of *Acousticks;* as it was presented to the Dublin Society Nov. 12. 1683, by the Right Reverend Father in God *Narcissus* Lord Bishop of Ferns and Leighlin.[44]

The Right Reverend Father, it need hardly be added, is Narcissus Marsh, recently made Bishop of Ferns and Leighlin, but at the time his paper was delivered, still provost and resident of Trinity College, Dublin, in which, at the same moment, Jonathan Swift was in the second year of his undistinguished academic career.[45] And he is, of course, the same Marsh whose caution in 1694 delayed Swift's ordination and prompted his famous "penitential" letter to Temple, who seems to have had some part in Swift's failure to become Dean of Derry and the delay in his securing the prebend of Dunlavin, and who, as Primate of Ireland, together with King, commissioned,

---

clearly seeks to mock or discredit. At two of these points he expressly speaks in the character of a "Modern Author" (pp. 123 and 208) and is obviously carrying on in the same flamboyant fashion at a third (p. 142). His pseudo-scientific style in the present passage is echoed in his account of "great Revolutions" (p. 164). There is a display of mock erudition in the pedantic digression on critics (p. 100) and in the exposition of Aeolist doctrine (p. 150). In every instance, that is, there is a more direct satiric victim than Lucretius, whose name, Swift seems to assume, is regarded with sufficient hostility so as to stigmatize whatever argument it is invoked to support. The point is worth noting, I think, because it makes clear the distinction between the immediate satiric victim and the more remote figure who, however hostile his position may be to Swift's own, does not really bear the brunt of the satiric attack.

44 *Philosophical Transactions,* XIV, 472.

45 For biographical details about Marsh, see *DNB,* XII, 1101–3, and George T. Stokes, *Some Worthies of the Irish Church* (London, 1900), pp. 65–141; the latter contains interesting information concerning the Dublin Philosophical Society. Forster's account of Swift's college career (pp. 27–49) remains one of the most detailed. See also John Barrett, *An Essay on the Earlier Part of the Life of Swift* (London, 1808).

supervised, and apparently vexed Swift on the mission of the First Fruits.[46] He is the Marsh who kindled in Swift a smoldering animosity which burst into furious flame in the devastating "Character of P[rima]te M[ars]h" and may well account for the assault on the conception of man as *animal rationale* in the final book of *Gulliver's Travels*.[47] Swift's open hostility toward Marsh has been variously attributed to political bickering within the ecclesiastical establishment and to the affair of the delayed ordination.[48] The veiled attack in the *Tale,* however, certainly points to an early beginning to this animosity and hence to the latter conjecture—if not to an even earlier origin in the uncongenial association of Marsh and Swift at Trinity College.[49]

[46] *Correspondence,* I, 13; 104-6; Forster, pp. 242-43; *Journal to Stella,* I, 80; II, 675, 676. Louis Landa in *Swift and the Church of Ireland* (Oxford, 1954) suggests (pp. 29-31) that Marsh may have been largely instrumental in Swift's failure to be considered for the vacant deanship of Derry in 1700 as well as for the delay later in the same year of Swift's appointment to the prebend of Dunlavin (pp. 44-45). Professor Landa, pointing out that the prebend was in Marsh's gift, asserts that "there is an obscure circumstance that occasions some doubt of Marsh's attitude—an inexplicable delay in conferring the prebend on Swift" and continues that "it is an inference, but a reasonable one, that for some reason Marsh did not hold Swift in high estimation. . . ." If, as is most likely, the "Introduction" was written in 1697 (see *Tale,* p. xlv), Swift's parody of Marsh points to a hostility between the two which antedates by three years the affairs of the deanery and prebend.

[47] See R. S. Crane, "The Houyhnhnms, the Yahoos, and the History of Ideas" in *Reason and the Imagination: Studies in the History of Ideas, 1600–1800,* ed. J. A. Mazzeo (New York and London, 1962), pp. 231–53. Among other achievements of this excellent article is the compelling argument that the Houyhnhnm-Yahoo myth assails the logical definition of man as *animal rationale* as it appears in, *inter alia,* Marsh's *Institutio logicae,* the text introduced at Trinity College by the then provost during Swift's shaky undergraduate career.

[48] See the "Character of Primate Marsh" in *Prose Works,* ed. Temple Scott, XI, 188.

[49] The hypothesis that the hostility began during Swift's college days is just a bit more than a tempting conjecture. It is hard to discover doctrinal or political differences between the two men (a fact which has led Denis Johnston in his *In Search of Swift,* p. 194, to the mistaken conclusion that Swift "consistently approved" of Marsh). When, in 1694, Swift sought ordination, Marsh's zeal in inquiring into his "Learning and Morals" may, as Professor Landa suggests (p. 6), have been a natural display of habitual austerity, but Marsh "was pleased to say a good deal" to Swift (*Correspondence,* I, 13). The skepticism which this suggests and which could be allayed by evidence of Swift's good conduct while in Temple's service must presumably have been engendered during the period prior to Swift's joining Temple (1689).

Aside from Wotton's account of scientific achievement, many, if not most, of the strictly scientific writings which are attacked in the *Tale* were published, I believe, during Swift's college years. Olson traces Swift's derogatory references to the *Philo-*

Such paragraphs as these invite a sort of stocktaking in which, by noting the rather clear strata on which the satire operates, we can gain some insight into the notable complexity of Swift's art. The stylistic and substantive parody of Marsh's writing is probably the most particular and pointed achievement of the passage, yet an understanding of this aspect of the satire is obviously not indispensable to a satisfactory reading of the section. For, as is so often true, Swift's concurrent satiric achievements have abundant charm and power in their own right, as we can see in the droll image of orators and of the theater. Characteristically, Swift is not content to produce a mere debasement of his victim's manner but allows his own wit to emerge in the construction of fantasies which carry their own impact. This performance, moreover, is undertaken in the course of defending the basic "proposition" that public attention can be gained only by a "superior Position of Place." And this assertion is itself a two-edged weapon; it is a parody on the mechanistic reduction of

---

sophical Transactions and notes that the articles which Swift derides all appeared between the years 1684 and 1686, inclusive. To these objects of satiric attention we may add the present apparent parody on Marsh and possibly a description of the role of a "polypus" in producing epilepsy and associated disorders which suggestively resembles the early part of the "Digression concerning Madness" (see Philosophical Transactions, XIV, 537–48). It may be further suggested that the great majority of scientific "projects" which emerge satirically in the Third Book of Gulliver's Travels (and for which Mohler and Nicolson understandably seek models as close in time as possible to the writing of that work) have close analogues in reports to be found in the Philosophical Transactions for the three early years in question.

It seems reasonable to believe that the unscientific Swift's most thorough exposure to detailed accounts of scientific inquiry took place during his college years, when the zeal of Provost Marsh and of Swift's tutor, St. George Ashe, combined with the influence of the newly formed (1683) Royal Dublin Society to force the attention of Trinity undergraduates to matters scientific. That, even at this time, such worthy efforts were met with skeptical irreverence is suggested by the ridicule directed against the "Fresh Philosophers of Dublin" in which the students of "rude, undisciplined" Trinity College may well have had a leading part (see Stokes, pp. 83, 138–41).

Olson is properly reluctant to assign to this early encounter with the Royal Society and its Dublin offshoot the actual genesis of the Tale. Swift's statement, in chapter v, that "every Branch of Knowledge has received such wonderful Acquirements . . . especially within these last three Years" (p. 129) may, Olson suggests, allude to the three years in which Swift draws so heavily upon the Philosophical Transactions, but may also, as Guthkelch and Nichol Smith assert, refer to the time between the appearance of Wotton's Reflections and the composition of the Tale (1694–97); see Olson, pp. 459–60. The case for the former conjecture is somewhat strengthened, I think, by the fact that the three years in question coincide with the founding and stormy early activities of the controversial Royal Dublin Society.

abstractions (in this case, eloquence) to physical laws, and it reflects, at the same time, on the meretricious orators whose arts can be successfully governed by such grotesque principles. And finally, in the choice of the three "machines" which exploit this bogus law, Swift is able to damn the dissenting pulpit through its association with the stage and gallows-ladder and his facetious explanation of its "mighty Influence on human Ears" (p. 60).

In contrast to the supple flow of Swift's writing, such an inventory seems very ponderous indeed. Yet only an identification of the numerous victims he concurrently assaults can reveal the true nature of the "many-faceted" satire for which he is so famous and make clear the astonishing economy of his apparently playful fantasies.

Although the range of specific targets in the second half of "The Introduction" is greater than that of the earlier pages, Swift's procedure is, on the whole, relatively simple—always provided one distinguishes between primary satiric objects and those which are secondary, incidental, or not true objects at all. The deliberate fashion in which the three machines are equated with fields of literary endeavor suggests that the chief concerns of the chapter will subsequently be literary. These equations begin with the chapter's final glance at religion: the pulpit is refined upon and alleged to represent the "Writings of our *Modern Saints* in *Great Britain*." The equation of the ladder with faction and poetry is accomplished with a hiatus and a few puns. And finally, Grub-street is introduced as the institution analogous to the stage-itinerant, and we are informed that our author has just been "adopted a Member of that illustrious Fraternity" (p. 63).

Having established himself as a temporary spokesman for Grub-street, the author proceeds to what might have been called "a digression on fables." The famous catalogue of Grub-street productions is introduced by the even more famous passage which purports to offer reasons for public neglect of Grub-street performances, a situation which will be remedied only when the great truths underlying the attractive fables of the Society have been properly explained. The introductory passage presents certain problems of importance for Swift's method in the *Tale;* it is, moreover, parodic satire of a particular sort, deserving, for this reason, to be quoted in full:

But the greatest Maim given to the general Reception, which the Writings of our Society have formerly received, (next to the transitory State of all sublunary Things,) hath been a superficiall Vein among many Readers of the present Age, who will by no means be persuaded to inspect beyond the Surface and the Rind of Things; whereas *Wisdom* is a *Fox,* who after long hunting, will at last cost you the Pains to dig out: 'Tis a *Cheese,* which by how much the richer, has the thicker, the homelier, and the courser Coat; and whereof to a judicious Palate, the *Maggots* are the best. 'Tis a *Sack-Posset,* wherein the deeper you go, you will find it the sweeter. *Wisdom* is a *Hen,* whose *Cackling* we must value and consider, because it is attended with an *Egg;* But then, lastly, 'tis a *Nut,* which unless you chuse with Judgment, may cost you a Tooth, and pay you with nothing but a *Worm.* In consequence of these momentous Truths, the *Grubaean* Sages have always chosen to convey their Precepts and their Arts, shut up within the vehicles of Types and Fables, which having been perhaps more careful and curious in adorning, than was altogether necessary, it has fared with these Vehicles after the usual Fate of Coaches overfinely painted in gilt; that the transitory Gazers have so dazzled their Eyes, and fill'd their Imaginations with the outward Lustre, as neither to regard or consider, the Person or the Parts of the Owner within. A Misfortune we undergo with somewhat less Reluctancy, because it has been common to us with *Pythagoras, Aesop, Socrates,* and other of our Predecessors (p. 66).

There has been some tendency on the part of critics to read this paragraph as a witty but essentially earnest comment upon superficiality and depth, appearance and reality, or the nature of true wisdom—as, in effect, a genuine adumbration of the brilliant "fool among knaves" section of the "Digression on Madness."[50] But the ideas expressed here seem clearly to be those of a "Grubaean sage." Although we cannot assume that Swift sustains this role—or any other his *persona* temporarily adopts—in the face of evidence to the contrary, at those points where he *does* so label himself, we must keep his identity in mind. The "wisdom" of which he speaks so solemnly here is the Grubaean concept of wisdom and thus nothing more than the "moral" or hidden "truth" contained in fables, the product of Grub-street. Moreover, there is neither eloquence nor conviction in the string of ludicrous similes which Swift produces. Farfetched, trivial, and (in the mad business of hens, eggs, nuts,

[50] See, for instance, Carl Van Doren, *Swift* (New York, 1930), pp. 41–42, in which a popular biographer finds Swift's sentiments, however brilliantly expressed, to be those of Temple's attacks on the superficiality of modern learning.

and teeth) comically irrelevant, the "argument" can hardly be viewed as anything save the adornment of a platitude with a series of extravagant and unilluminating figures. For if one takes the passage soberly, it is assuredly a pompously didactic exposition of a thoroughly unoriginal proposition.

Swift, we know, was inordinately sensitive to banality, both in the style and substance of contemporary writing. Elsewhere he speaks of being "offended with many Writers of Essays and moral Discourses, for running into stale Topicks and thread-bare Quotations, and not handling their Subject fully and closely."[51] The "old beaten story," frozen into the formulae of dedications, prefaces, digressions, and apologies, is certainly familiar enough to readers of the *Tale* to put them on their guard against the sententious platitudes of the passage before us. Thus warned, the reader cannot, in my opinion, discover here a "meaning" more profound than that embodied in a series of figures or fables in miniature, striking chiefly because of their incongruously mundane character and described as "momentous truths" in a spirit of patent facetiousness.

This combination of the insipid and the grotesque, therefore, points rather clearly to a parodic intention; if the passage is not the straightforward statement of an authentic conviction, it suggests that Swift has assumed a satiric posture. One might be content with an interpretation of Swift's words as a parody of Grub-street style and substance in general—as a mock-defense of fables in the mean manner of a typical but anonymous literary hack. But the defense of fables is a special kind of argument, and the dogged enumeration of ludicrous similes has a ring of particularity; they suggest that, at the least, we search for a single object of parody. And, once again, we find ourselves examining the work of L'Estrange. We know that, with reference to a passage separated from the present one by only a few pages,[52] Swift was prompted by certain critical strictures to admit, in a note and in his "Apology" to the fifth edition of the *Tale,* that he sought to "personate L'Estrange, Dryden, and some others." We have already referred to the "Preface" to L'Estrange's *Aesop* as a possible source for the title of Swift's book. It is this same

---

[51] In the dedication to "A Tritical Essay upon the Faculties of the Mind," *Prose Works,* I, 246.

[52] *Tale,* pp. 69–70.

preface which provides some unusually suggestive features if read in connection with the present "digression on fables."

L'Estrange's "Preface" is chiefly an advocacy of fables as instruments of unmatched effectiveness for moral instruction. The most important aspect of his argument can be indicated by quoting a passage which should also suggest features of style which dominate the entire preface:

'Tis in the very *Nature* of us, first, to be Inquisitive, and Hankering after New and New [*sic*] *Sights* and *Stories*: and 2dly, No less Sollicitous to Learn and Understand the *Truth* and *Meaning* of what we See and Hear: So that betwixt the Indulging and Cultivating of this *Disposition* or *Inclination,* on the *One* hand, and the Applying of a Profitable *Moral* to the *Figure* or the *Fable,* on the *Other,* here's the Sum of All that can be done upon the Point of a *Timely Discipline* and *Institution,* toward the Forming of an Honourable and a Vertuous Life. . . . To Speak All, in a Few Words, *Children* are but *Blank Paper,* ready Indifferently for an Impression, Good or Bad (for they take All upon Credit) and it is much in the Power of the first Comer, to Write Saint, or Devil upon't, which of the Two he pleases.[53]

Nor are these rules applicable only to children, for L'Estrange argues,

. . . there's Nothing makes a deeper Impression upon the Minds of Men, or comes more Lively to their Understanding, than Those Instructive Notices that are Convey'd to them by Glances, Insinuations, and Surprize; and under the cover of some *Allegory* or *Riddle*. But, What can be said more to the Honour of this *Symbolical* Way of Moralizing upon *Tales* and *Fables,* than that the Wisdom of the Ancients has been still Wrapt up in Veils and Figures; and their Precepts, Councels, and Salutary Monitions for the Ordering of our Lives and Manners, Handed down to us from all Antiquity under Innuendo's and Allusions?[54]

In defending his own treatment of the *Fables,* L'Estrange deals with some editorial problems and then concludes with the passage to which we have already referred in discussing the title of *A Tale of a Tub:*

[53] *Fables of Aesop and Other Eminent Mythologists with Morals and Reflections,* Sig. A1ᵛ.

[54] Sig. A2ᵛ. It is worth noting that Swift twice employs the term *Innuendo* in the same sense as does L'Estrange, a usage at least rare enough to warrant a note by Swift's modern editors (*Tale,* p. 114).

This *Rhapsody* of *Fables* is a Book Universally Read, and Taught in All our Schools; but almost at such a Rate as we Teach *Pyes* and Parrots, that Pronounce the Words without so much as Guessing at the *Meaning* of them: Or to take it Another way, the Boys break their Teeth upon the Shells, without ever coming near the Kernel. They learn the *Fables* by *Lessons,* and the Moral is the least part of our Care in a Child's Institution so that take Both together, and the One is stark Nonsense, without the Application of the Other; besides that the Doctrine itself, as we have it, even at the Best, falls Infinitely short of the Vigour and Spirit of the Fable. To supply this Defect now, we have had several English *Paraphrases* and *Essays* upon *Aesop,* and Divers of his Followers, both in *Prose* and *Verse:* the Latter have perchance Ventur'd a little too far from the Precise Scope of the Author upon the Privilege of a Poetical License: and for the Other of Ancient Date, the *Morals* are so *Insipid* and *Flat,* and the *Style* and *Diction* of the *Fables,* so *Coarse* and *Uncouth,* that they are rather Dangerous, than Profitable, as to the Purpose they were Principally Intended for; and likely to do Forty times more Mischief by the One than Good by the Other. An *Emblem* without a *Key* to't, is no more than a *Tale of a Tub;* and that Tale sillily told too, is but one Folly Grafted upon Another.[55]

L'Estrange's sententious exposition of simple-minded propositions, his pompous reliance on rude similes (among them the "nut" figure which, with an amusing twist, appears in the *Tale*), and his solemn assumption that profound wisdom lies wrapped in the "veils and figures" of popular fables all have their counterparts in Swift's playful argument. Beyond this, there is L'Estrange's assertion that his work will at last truly "supply" a "defect" which has hitherto marked translations of the fables, a manifestation of self-esteem echoed in Swift's claim, immediately following the passage quoted in the *Tale,* that his own great labors will provide that "neither the World nor our selves may any longer suffer by such misunderstandings."

The vulgar style, the egotism (ill-concealed by various humble professions), the shoddy reasoning and rhetoric of L'Estrange's preface may well—like his habit of addressing posterity—have appealed to Swift as features richly deserving the scorn of the parodist. Over and above these literary infirmities, however, L'Estrange's preface contains a doctrine which, in the light of the first chapter of *A Tale of a Tub,* is almost the direct antithesis of Swift's own beliefs. For L'Estrange advocates, as necessary and desirable, the

[55] Sig. A4ᵛ.

notion that instruction and reform are best accomplished by flamboyant and pleasurable devices, painless methods of reproof and correction which beguile men into the path of virtue and wisdom. Aesop's great achievement, for L'Estrange, was an "Art of Schooling Mankind into Better Manners; by Minding Men of the Errors without Twitting them for what's Amiss, and by that Means Flashing the Light of their Own Consciences in their Own Faces."[56]

Here assuredly is a formula to set Swift's teeth on edge! Secure sympathy and attention by any means at your disposal; follow this with gentle admonition, universally applicable to sinners eager to profit by instruction! To the speeches of jugglers, jailbirds, and fanatics, let fables be added! And then let wise men unlock with "keys" the "emblems" which embody universal truth! One is tempted to reconstruct for Swift a fierce conviction that if *this* be instruction and reform, then let his own "keyless" and merciless assault on folly be damned as "no more than a tale of a tub."

The catalogue of Grub-street productions, to which the passage we have been discussing purports to serve as a preamble, lists seven works. The titles listed have attracted scholars chiefly because they provide evidence that Swift was familiar with hermetic and alchemical writings, Pythagorean theories of the soul, and Talmudic scholarship.[57] It is true that these paragraphs can be said to deride mystics, cabalists, alchemists, and the like to the extent that the special language of such worthies is plainly employed in a ridiculous task. Yet the appearance here—as elsewhere in the *Tale*—of these generally discredited kinds of occult inquirers is not, in my opinion, as the chief object of Swift's satire. It is plain that, of the seven works listed, five are vulgar pieces of folk-literature or familiar myth.[58] The addition of *The Hind and the Panther* to this list has an effect so obvious

[56] Sig. A3.

[57] Guthkelch and Nichol Smith use this passage in commenting on Swift's reading (*Tale*, p. liii) and explicate it in their "Notes on Dark Authors" (pp. 353–60). Mrs. Starkman offers further illumination of the preoccupations reflected in the list (pp. 44–56, *passim*).

[58] See Guthkelch and Nichol Smith notes at *Tale*, pp. 67–68. Of the folk tales, only *Faustus* appears to have any significance beyond its wide popular currency. The extravagant and widely differing forms of the Faust legend in the seventeenth century all apparently stemmed from the apocryphal achievements of the fifteenth-century necromancer, thus making the tale a good one for alchemical analysis; see Philip M. Palmer and Robert P. More, *The Sources of the Faust Tradition* (New York, 1936), pp. 81–126.

that discussion is unnecessary. And *The Wise Men of Gotham,* we can see even without the fifth-edition note, is a reference to William Wotton's *Reflections upon Ancient and Modern Learning.*

The entire list, however, achieves greater satiric point than is involved in the inclusion, amid a collection of common folk tales, of the works of two of Swift's chief literary antagonists. Swift is, after all, asserting that these ancient and familiar stories are modern productions and, in doing so, is mocking Richard Bentley's demonstration that no surviving fables can be attributed either to Aesop or Phalaris. Bentley's proof was, as a matter of fact, decisive, and he properly assumed that it would furnish his ally, Wotton, with "a considerable point in the controversy" between the Ancients and the Moderns.[59] Thus, like virtually every other contribution which *A Tale of a Tub* makes to the Ancient cause in this quarrel, the satire on Bentley's treatment of ancient fables fails to provide any substantive refutation whatever of Bentley's demonstration. Instead, it distorts the nature of his claims to an absurd degree (Bentley of course never professed to believe that the fables were of recent date!) and further mocks his scholarly researches by suggesting that the explication of the fables is a work comparable only to the naïve speculations of alchemists, hermetics, and cabalists. Here, assuredly, is the chief function of the "dark authors" in this passage. For the benefit of a sophisticated reader, prepared to dismiss mystical writings as nonsense, the erudition and careful scholarship of Bentley are derisively lumped together with such discreditable researches. Thus the satire on Bentley is twofold. His goals are implicitly distorted so as to constitute the demonstration of the "modernity" of what is irrefutably old and commonplace. His methods are equated with those of idle and irresponsible mystics. And, indeed, the satire becomes threefold as we find the second edition of Wotton's *Reflections,* which includes Bentley's own first *Dissertation* (June, 1697), added to the list of idle folklore.

From this catalogue, the text moves, with all the appearance of flagrant digression, to the famous recital of its author's past sacrifices, sufferings, and thankless contributions to a variety of causes. Despite the fact that Swift's own note calls attention both to Dryden *and* L'Estrange as objects of parody (p. 70), the correspondence between the passage and certain lines of Dryden has received by far the

[59] *The Works of Richard Bentley,* ed. Alexander Dyce (London, 1836–38), I, 78–79.

greater share of critical attention. There are, to be sure, striking instances of a tendency to engage in bathetic recitals of past sufferings scattered throughout the prose of Dryden. But a more precise parallel, I believe, is furnished by L'Estrange, in part by his "Preface" to the first volume of collected *Observators:*

I have been *Baited* with *Thousands* upon *Thousands* of *Libells*. I have created Enemies that do me the *Honour* to *Hate* me, perhaps, next to the *King Himself* (God Bless him) and the *Royal Family.* Their *Scandals* are *Blown Over:* Their *Malice, Defeated,* and whenever my *Hour* comes, I am ready to deliver up my *Soul,* with the Conscience of an *Honest Man,* as to what I have done, in *This Particular:* And I do here Declare, in the presence of an *All-Seeing,* and an *All-Knowing God,* That as I have never yet receiv'd any *Answer,* more than *Cavil,* and *Shuffling,* to the *Doctrine* and *Reasoning* of *These Papers:* So I never *made use* of Any *Sophism* or *Double Meaning,* in Defense of the *Cause* that I have here taken upon me to *Assert:* But have dealt *Plainly* and *Above-Board,* without either *Fallacy* or *Collusion.*[60]

The case for naming the preceding passage as the chief model for Swift's parody is weakened only by the existence of another lamentation by L'Estrange which bears an equal, if not a greater correspondence to the complaints of Swift's persecuted scribbler. It is to be found in one of the prefatory addresses to Posterity which, as we have already said, dot *A Brief History of the Times:*

But *Men,* I perceive, do not allways know their *Own Minds;* for after I had stood the *Uttermost Malice* of the *Common Enemies* of the *Church,* and *State,* for *allmost Four Years together,* during the course of *These Papers;* and without the least *Change* of *Mind, Resolution, Countenance,* or so much as of *Pretence:* After I had, I say, born all manner of *Indignities* for the sake of *Both;* (divers *Practices* of *Perjury* and *Subornation* against me, over and above) and all This, purely for the Love of *Common Justice,* and out of a Sense of what I owe to my *Prince,* and Country; I found my self in February Last was Two Year, to my *Great Admiration,* Deliver'd over to *New Tormentors;* and I have been Treated at such a Rate, by *Another Sort of People,* that the *Venom* and the *Scurrility,* the *Rage,* and the *Slander* of my *Profess'd Adversaries* was but a *Flea-biting* to the *Wounds* and *Reproaches* that I have suffer'd ever since, from several of my *Pretending Friends.*[61]

[60] Roger L'Estrange, "Preface" to *The Observator in Dialogue,* Vol. I (London, 1684).

[61] *A Brief History of the Times in a Preface to the Third Volume of the Observators* (London, 1687), pp. 1–2. This edition prints the "History" separately in 8vo;

If the resemblance between the style and substance of L'Estrange and those of Swift's woebegone hack does not make it certain that L'Estrange is the chief victim of Swift's mock lamentation, the likelihood of this identification is further strengthened by Swift's reference to "Popish Plots and Meal-Tubs." L'Estrange clearly regarded himself as the official recorder of the Plot, and in the canon of his works, controversial literature occupies the dominant place.[62]

The passage, as we have noted, deliberately appears as a digression, and Swift moves on to his concluding paragraphs with the phrase, "but to return . . ." (p. 71). Yet in terms of the general satiric direction of the chapter, the passage has a relevance which makes it both appropriate and effective. In his attack upon specific literary enemies, Swift has taken upon himself the Grub-street stigma, professed his faith in numbers, alchemy, and mystic lore, and announced his dedication to a bizarre and menial literary project. If, while assuming one of these readily changeable but uniformly contemptible roles, he speaks with the voice of Dryden or L'Estrange or declares his admiration for Wotton or Bentley, the satiric result is perfectly clear.

In the final two paragraphs of the chapter, the framework of an "Introduction," upon which all of the preceding satire is suspended, again emerges very plainly. For here the author is defending the "principal" title of his book as one modeled after the Grub-street fashion and his multiplicity of "lost" subtitles as an improvement upon Dryden's laudable practice of appointing many "God-fathers." Once more the *Tale* purports to embody the best Grub-street tradition, but the point of the satire is achieved only when Dryden is permitted to share with Grub-street the dubious honor of serving as a model. And from this thrust, the author speedily moves to a bit of nonsense which is purely comic: his project for a multiple dedication has failed, for the forty Lords whom he asked to serve as godfather, "all made it a Matter of conscience and sent . . . their Excuses." It is conceivable that this prudent aversion, on the part of the nobility, to extend patronage to an importunate scribbler has some specific historical antecedent. If so, it has been lost to us, and with it whatever claim the passage may make as genuine satire. The posture is a

---

the "History" actually appeared earlier in the same year as a preface to the folio third volume of collected *Observators*.

[62] Kitchin, *Sir Roger L'Estrange*, esp. pp. 222–59.

good traditional comic one, however; it is simply the momentary revelation, by the performer, of his own ineptitude, his egregious failure to achieve the kind of goal on which he patently sets the greatest store. As such, it is an amusing note, entirely consistent with the low opinion of himself and his undertaking which the author has constantly managed to convey, and it is with amusement, above all else, that we conclude at last the introductory materials and await the unfolding of the narrative.

We are now in a position to assert that the apparent disorder of the chapter acquires perceptible arrangement not only by the way in which it carries out its superficial introductory mission but by the strategic disposition of satiric elements. Enough has already been said about the "three machines" to suggest that the particulars of satire are only incidental to their introduction and that it is in the second or "Grub-street" section that these particulars become, for the most part, the central object of the writer's attack. The "mystery" of the machines is dramatically unveiled, and, by the author's identification with the Grub-street brotherhood, it is on this Society alone that our attention is ultimately concentrated. This is not to say that Grub-street is the principal satiric victim. Swift uses this pejorative term as a weapon to degrade his specific enemies. The machines have been discussed, in a manner appropriate to a discursive introduction, as a means of claiming popular attention; they have been explicated, in a manner as comic as it is satiric, and in the explication Grub-street has emerged as a central notion. Once Grub-street is before us, the assault can proceed. And as always in these crucially located, purely satiric sections, the objects of the assault emerge specifically and plainly—Dryden, L'Estrange, Wotton, and Bentley.

Here it seems proper to revert to an earlier question. Does our emphasis upon particular satiric victims impede analysis? Does it imply a diffuseness which destroys the principles of order to be found in "thematic" interpretations or attempts to establish comprehensive satiric objectives? The answer would seem to be that such attacks are unsystematic and unrelated to their context only to the extent to which Swift deliberately allows them to be. Thus the covert parody of Narcissus Marsh may appear gratuitous and quite unrelated to Swift's central assaults upon his literary victims. But, at the same time, the spurious acoustical theory by which the parody is achieved is a well-integrated element in the account of the three machines—an amusing and relevant "explanation" of the phenome-non to which he has addressed his attention. Thus we have a passage which can be satisfactorily read for its essential comic qualities, as a plausible portion of a prose structure which leads ultimately to very pointed satire, or as, in itself, a gross parodic debasement of the writings of a particular individual. For, as we have pointed out, satiric and non-satiric achievements are by no means mutually exclusive; to distinguish between them, however, allows us to discover in such a reasonable and amusing passage as the one on "sounds" an additional, entirely satiric dimension of a kind which can only increase our admiration for Swift's multiple accomplishment.

In the later attacks upon Bentley, Wotton, L'Estrange, and Dryden, however, we encounter the unequivocally satiric procedure to which the section as a whole is directed. The incidental satiric thrusts and comic posturings reach a focus in the Grub-street section; the identity of Swift's *persona* as a Grub-street hack has been unobtrusively and engagingly established so that the positions he adopts and the objects of his admiration will be automatically stigmatized by his own conceit, obtuseness, and vulgarity. This is simply satiric strategy. We may remember the three machines and the Grub-street catalogue as the most striking devices of the chapter, but to the extent that true attack is undertaken in these pages, Wotton, Bentley, L'Estrange, and Dryden are crucially its victims.

Finally, however, one may ask whether, beyond the strategically planned assaults against men who, for various historical reasons happen to be his enemies, Swift proceeds from any broader principle. The question is proper not only because one naturally seeks the grounds which account for the aversions of a thoughtful man but also because in such principles are to be found the likeliest source for whatever significant development *A Tale of a Tub* displays in its entirety. And there is a general direction taken by Swift's strictures in this chapter which suggests an awareness of particular artistic vices which call for correction.

I have already suggested that, in the notable passage on "wisdom," there is mockery, achieved in several ways, of the easy and simplistic defense of fables, offered by such writers as L'Estrange, as palatable purveyors of salutary truths. I have suggested, too, that there is some connection between Swift's skeptical view of fables and the "oratorial machines," those ridiculous devices whereby unworthy men attain a spurious ascendancy over their uncritical fellows. More than this, the image of the "machines" allows Swift to ape the ways of those who "explicate" fables, for the author asserts that his scheme "contains a great mystery, being a Type, a Sign, an Emblem, a Shadow, a Symbol, bearing Analogy to the spacious Commonwealth of Writers" (p. 61). Here, quite as much as in the catalogue of Grub-street productions, the solemn explanation of the obvious is mocked. But the principal target is not Bentley, but rather those who, like L'Estrange, soberly attach inordinate wisdom to the tales of Aesop and other fableists of antiquity.

The full extent to which the notion of splendid truths, agreeably conveyed through symbols and allegories, does violence to Swift's basic convictions is not made clear in the *Tale* until one reaches the "Digression concerning Madness," about which I shall have more to say in my final chapter. From the "Introduction," nonetheless, it is clear that the majority of Swift's assaults upon particular victims proceed from a deep aversion to certain kinds of false claims to knowledge and the fraudulent modes of discourse by which they are advanced. The pat, "universal" precepts, sugar-coated to the taste of an ignorant multitude, plainly violate the beliefs which, among other things, Swift advances about satire itself. The "oratorial machines," instruments though they are for the attack on the Puritan pulpit, are more fundamentally a debasing metaphor for all attempts to communicate alleged truth by spurious and flamboyant means, and Swift's sarcastic solemnity in explicating his own "symbols" is a further derisive exemplification of this practice. Where the fatuous belief that men are painlessly educable appears in particular form, whether in the pontifications of L'Estrange or Dryden, such statements are fair game for Swift. And it is on the same score that he is, in this section, contemptuous of the claims for certain and systematic knowledge which Bentley and Wotton have presumably advanced.

The conception of truth as readily mastered, neatly formulated, and delightfully communicated is the error with which this section, for all its diversity, recurrently taxes its satiric victims. In the immediate play of the satire against its targets, however, the sinner rather than the sin remains paramount. We, in our own day, may view such phenomena as *Life* or the *Reader's Digest,* the novels of Ayn Rand, or the palliative pieties of Norman Vincent Peale as manifestations of disturbing public tendencies. A courageous satirist, however, will leave the tendencies to the social scientists and attack the writings themselves. So, I think, it is with Swift. His aversion to easy wisdom, fraudulently begotten and propagated, lends to his specific strictures a sense of consistency and responsibility and appeals to our common capacity for outrage at what is stupid and arrogant. The effect of these consistent principles, however, is not to give unity or general significance to his satiric enterprise but rather to add the power of authentic conviction to the wit and aptness of his individual assaults.

V

Our discussion of the satiric victim has thus far involved works in which the establishment of a particular historic object of the satirist's attack has been possible and in which the consequences of such an identification can quite readily be grasped. Thus we have seen that for both the *Argument against Abolishing Christianity* and *A Modest Proposal,* the recognition of a primary satiric target makes clear the nature and purpose of the fictional position assumed by the putative author and assists in accounting for the function of each element in the "argument" which is advanced by this *persona.* In the much longer, heterogenous construction of *A Tale of a Tub* it is, of course, impossible to detect a sole object of satiric attack (unless, as I have suggested, one produces a term of such breadth and comprehensiveness as to be of little value in accounting for all of the diversified satiric procedures incorporated within the work). Our quest for particularity, however, has permitted us to discover new point in certain specimen selections from the *Tale* and has provided some evidence that elements in that work which share its generally playful or critical character serve, at the same time, as the vehicle for assaults upon very specific targets.

There remains to consider, however, the most controversial implication of our view that the object of satiric attack rests in the historic particular. I have already asserted that in the absence of a discernible satiric target, as I have defined it, we are confronted with writing which cannot be regarded as essentially satiric. We must, accordingly, be prepared to deal with the negative as well as the affirmative consequences of our search for particularity. We must be ready to assert that in many works which are traditionally regarded as satire there are important non-satiric elements and, having identified such elements, must be able to provide some account of their character and function.

The perenially challenging pages of *Gulliver's Travels* receive, I believe, considerable illumination from a distinction between the satiric and non-satiric. Many of the studies which have dwelt upon the "background" of this most famous of Swift's works have, whether deliberately or not, expanded the satiric dimension of the book. The result of many researches has been to supply precisely the historic particulars which are under attack by Swift, to transform, in increasing amounts, parts of the fantasy which the work appears to be at its most superficial level into hostile comment upon specific phenomena in Swift's world.[63]

Such discoveries tend to reinforce the most familiar of all clichés about *Gulliver's Travels*—the proposition that an apparently charming story, while undeniably appealing as such to the youthful or unsophisticated reader, is actually a bitter satiric attack upon authentic follies and abuses. This generalization implies that a "proper" reading of the text, a reading conducted in complete awareness of its most important qualities, must proceed on the assumption that *Gulliver's Travels* is, in its totality, a satiric construction and that the attractive fiction which supports the entire work is merely the mask or vehicle for a sustained satiric assault.

There are, however, great difficulties inherent in such a view. The initial problem—that the objects of Swift's satire are a widely diffuse assortment, sporadically and fragmentarily treated—is not insupera-

---

[63] Certain classical studies of the *Travels* have illuminated its satiric aspect so fundamentally that even ordinary classroom readings of the text today proceed in tacit awareness of the meanings that have been thus supplied. Notable among these studies are Sir Charles Firth, "The Political Significance of *Gulliver's Travels*" in *Proceedings of the British Academy*, IX (1919–20), 237–59; Marjorie Nicolson and Nora M. Mohler, "The Scientific Background of Swift's Voyage to Laputa," *Annals of Science*, II (1937), 299-344; Miss Nicolson's earlier "The Microscope and English Imagination" in *Smith College Studies in Modern Languages*, XVI, No. 4 (1935); and Arthur E. Case, *Four Essays on Gulliver's Travels* (Princeton, 1945). To this distinguished list must now be gratefully added Irvin Ehrenpreis's chapter on "Gulliver" in his *The Personality of Jonathan Swift* (London, 1958), pp. 83–116. In his search for the particular and personal in the *Travels,* Ehrenpreis applies—not, to be sure, with uniform success—a principle which I have regularly urged in these essays. One may differ with him—as I have done elsewhere—in specific readings of the text, yet the ambiguities he resolves and the mistakes he corrects have substantially advanced our understanding of the *Travels* and restored to it the vital immediacy by which it can be distinguished from conventional "imitative" genres.

ble; *A Tale of a Tub* presents similar obstacles to any search for "satiric unity," yet it is an essentially satiric work, sufficiently well organized to be intelligible and effective as such. A far more serious impediment to the consideration of *Gulliver's Travels* as primarily satiric is the magnitude, both in terms of sheer quantity within the text and of our response to the total work, of elements which do not conform to the concept of satire we have been employing. Unless, as seems unlikely, the discovery of specific targets proceeds in the future with vastly multiplied results, many pages of *Gulliver's Travels* will continue to appeal to us for reasons which have little to do with satiric significance.

Within recent years, indeed, there has been some tendency for scholars to ignore the satiric character of *Gulliver's Travels* and, in particular, to impose upon it some of the modes of analysis traditionally applied to purely comic literature. Approaches of this kind are laudable to the extent that they are invited by genuine comic qualities in the book, but one notes in such studies a failure, analogous to that found in purely "satiric" descriptions, to take into account those elements which have no demonstrable relevance to the attainment of comic ends. Thus to regard the work as exclusively either a "satire" or a "comedy" produces interpretations which are inevitably fragmentary. The *Travels* provides, moreover, an excellent illustration of the inadequacy of such hybrid species as "comic satire" or "satiric comedy," if only because it contains so many elements which are grimly non-comic and so many others to which it seems impossible to apply the word "satire" in any productive sense. Above all, to thrust *Gulliver's Travels* into the monolithic mold of a single literary species is an act of violence precisely because the ever surprising *different* literary experiences it provides constitute one of its chief claims upon our enthusiastic attention.

It is, I think, possible to discuss *Gulliver's Travels* adequately only if we are prepared to distinguish between the effects of comedy and of satire, to recognize that these different effects may be sought in closely related passages or even concurrently in a single work, and to suspend our concern for the book's unity in order to discover what Swift is actually doing in every considerable portion of the book.

Thus, for example, I believe we must recognize that the charm and humor of the first book have far greater effect than do any of its satiric procedures—even when we take quite literally all the suggestions which have been made about the correspondence between the Lilliputian world and that of eighteenth-century Europe. The problem of Swift's dominant motive remains insoluble. We cannot reconstruct his intentions and decide whether Lilliput was to him, above all, the satiric arena in which the follies and injustices which burned within his memory would be properly exposed,[64] or whether, on the other hand, the resemblances between his minuscule kingdom and the court of England were satiric touches, added to an original conception of droll fantasy. Whatever his actual motives, however, the fiction, with its intrinsic comic appeal, towers above all satiric design. There is abundant historic reference, but it emerges piecemeal. Our amusement is sporadically elicited at the expense of Walpole or George I or Queen Anne or the conduct of British foreign and domestic affairs; we are aware that the book succeeds in exposing the British court, reduced in stature and with its infirmities accordingly magnified, isolated, and held up to ridicule.

But the reduction and exposure of the particular remain the secondary accomplishments of the Voyage to Lilliput. Its stature in the history of literature is essentially the result of pure imaginative creation, the creation of a world of impossible yet credible homunculi, rendered comic by their physical and moral resemblances to mankind *in general*. To the extent that Gulliver himself and the plight into which he is thrust constitute a true satiric device, he must be equated with a historic counterpart, and obviously we may speak of him, at different points, as the spokesman for a disgruntled Swift or the alter ego of a martyred Harley or Bolingbroke. Far more than these, however, his is the role of ordinary, unspecified man, discomfited by a marvelous imaginative situation from which he is able at last happily to extricate himself in keeping with traditional comic formula.

Gulliver's ineptness among the Lilliputians—like his insignif-

---

[64] In *The Personality of Jonathan Swift* Ehrenpreis convincingly argues that to the extent the First Book reflects affairs in the last years of Queen Anne's reign, it does not represent the abrupt re-emergence of old issues. Swift, says Ehrenpreis, "went over the material in one form or another, from personal letters, through unpublishable essays, into the entertainment of an allegory" (p. 91). As Ehrenpreis goes on to say, however, "One must not confound origins with value. *Lilliput* does not signify a container for private jokes or half-conscious allusions." Here, as elsewhere, in discussing his own scholarship, Ehrenpreis seems tacitly to employ the distinction I have been urging; in my own terms, that is, his recovery of satiric qualities in the *Travels* does not vitiate the broader comic or philosophic impact of the work.

icance among the Brobdingnagians—is not a weakness which can
be attributed to any identifiable group or person; it is the result of
his normal, his universal human qualities, in large part simply of his
ordinary human size. The moral frailties he displays—inflexibility
and vanity, for example—are generic human weaknesses of precisely
the sort we find exploited in comic characterization and action. It is
true, of course, that Gulliver is not regularly an object of ridicule,
whether comic or satiric, for he appears more frequently in the role
of intelligent observer as well as in that of a "hero," whose plight
lays claim, to some extent at least, upon our sympathetic indignation. But to the extent—and it is not a very great extent—that Gulliver is a just victim of his own frailties, he is a comic rather than
satiric victim, and it is accordingly to the qualities of the Lilliputians
themselves that we must look for Swift's satiric target.

It is true that, with the exception of the "Utopian" sixth chapter,[65]
the (Lilliputians appear rather contemptible)than otherwise. Where
our contempt is leavened with laughter, where the Lilliputians are
authentically comic, it is almost always in a situation arising out of
the basic fiction of Book I, in a dilemma or embarrassment attributable to their stature. (On occasion, the stature itself is the chief source
of their discomfiture; this is true of many of their laughable attempts to deal properly with their giant visitor. At other times, however, their stature is employed to augment the ludicrous effect of
their complacency, arrogance, and shortsightedness, all of which are
displayed as generic human failings.) The great image—whether
comic, poetic, or philosophic—whereby man in his pride is reduced
to the stature and power of one of the lesser animals yet retains his
vision of himself as the potent center of the universe is, understandably enough, an inexhaustible source of critical discussion. It is, indeed, the dominant fiction of Book I, if not of the entire *Travels,*
both because of its originality and because of the very universality
with which it exposes man in his myopic self-esteem.

But the particularized strictures of satire, within the Voyage to
Lilliput, proceed in an essentially autonomous fashion. Against the
basically comic episodes attending on the capture and custody of
Gulliver, against even such an incident as the saving of the royal
palace (which, whether or not it is the satiric representation of

---

[65] Where it seems useful, I refer to the text of *Gulliver's Travels* as it appears in
Davis's *Prose Works,* XI. The sixth chapter is found at pp. 41–50.

Queen Anne's distress over *A Tale of a Tub* or the Treaty of Utrecht is certainly most effective as a magnificent bit of wholly imaginative ribaldry),[66] there proceed the attacks upon specific persons and policies which have little or nothing to do with the central giant-among-pigmies device. The attacks upon Walpole and Nottingham,[67] the exposure by reduction to absurdity of political patronage and preferment and of religious factionalism, the ultimate excoriation of Whig policy during and after the War of the Spanish Succession are carried out on grounds which are very indirectly connected with the Lilliputians' size or its contrast with Gulliver's stature. There are, of course, moments of amusement, when one transiently recalls that the moral depravity and vanity under attack are the qualities of creatures only six inches high. These are, however, mere comic by-products, as in this case they must be, if the satire is to have its full effect. For the intrigue and ingratitude of the Whig ministry must be seen as a real violation of the rules of decent human behavior rather than the imagined transgressions of the tiny inhabitants of a mythical kingdom.

The explication of the First Book of *Gulliver's Travels* as satire, therefore, provides a very partial, although important, account both of its structure and its total effect. In the first five chapters, little is to be gained by establishing specific objects of satiric attack; the fictional situation is compelling and the imaginary dilemma of Gulliver is the central source of amusement. The "intruding" sixth chapter, with its characterization of Lilliputian institutions (so in-

---

[66] Sir Charles Firth and Professor Case differ in their interpretations of the episode, and Ehrenpreis, while agreeing with Case that the "extinguishing" represents the Treaty of Utrecht, asserts that the resentment it engenders must be seen as that of the Whigs who impeached the ministers responsible for the Treaty and that the principal victim of their rage is Bolingbroke, rather than Oxford (pp. 87–88). If, as I am inclined to, one agrees with this view, then no satiric purpose explains Swift's introduction of the queen and her palace as the object of Gulliver's unorthodox rescue mission. The *comic* effect of the passage, on the other hand, is considerably heightened by the choice of a royal lady and her residence as "victims" of this indelicate attention.

[67] Nottingham seems today to be the generally accepted historical counterpart for the "morose and sour" Skyresh Bolgolam (*Travels,* p. 26). Swift's disinterment of an ancient and long-retired enemy for satiric purposes is rendered plausible enough by Ehrenpreis' thesis about Swift's continuing preoccupation with the affairs of the queen's time. Nottingham's role in Gulliver's adventures, however, is anachronistic and provides a good instance of the fragmentary and fugitive appearance of satiric assaults within the larger, systematic framework of the fiction.

consistent with the context provided by the rest of the book that Gulliver must explain and justify it)[68] is largely satiric and, to the extent that it is satiric, quite superfluous within the fictional construction. As the book progresses, it is precisely at those points at which the giant-among-pygmies situation ceases to provide interest and amusement that the search for the particularized objects of genuine satire becomes necessary. From the tiny kingdom come manifestations of treachery and ingratitude for which we are unprepared; a grotesque bill of impeachment, largely without Lilliputian stamp, is reproduced in full (pp. 52–53); Gulliver's position becomes untenable for reasons which have nothing directly to do with his size but with the special reaction of his hosts to a special series of occurrences. What, as pure fictional comedy of the sort with which the book begins, would be humorless and rather artless acquires meaning and relevance only because Swift's assault—and our attention— are now directed not to a mythical kingdom but to the vexed particulars of English history following the Peace of Utrecht. In effect, the comic fiction which has been developed by the earlier chapters yields, toward the conclusion of the book, to a series of satiric incidents in which the attack depends only tenuously upon the central conceit of the microcosmic kingdom.

I have already said a good deal to suggest that I find this comic conceit, with its originality, its delightful elaboration, and its mocking assault upon the complacency of mankind in general, to be the chief source of satisfaction in the voyage to Lilliput. There are, no doubt, those who would assert that the satire of the later chapters, if only because of its location, constitutes the point to which the entire book is directed, that the beguiling fiction is merely an initial device which leads us to the bitter attack on Whig policy which is the true "climax" of the voyage. Granted it is possible—although by no means necessary—to assert the primacy either of the satiric or the comic in the first book, I should argue only that two very different kinds of thing are achieved within its pages. And I should suggest, moreover, that the awareness that particular men, institutions, episodes, and beliefs are under attack is the distinctive mark of our response to whatever is truly satiric in this engaging fable.

[68] "In relating these and the following Laws, I would only be understood to mean the original Institutions, and not the most scandalous Corruptions into which these People are fallen by the degenerate Nature of Man" (p. 44).

Many of the things we have said about the voyage to Lilliput apply equally to Gulliver's sojourn among the Brobdingnagians. Both the comic power and philosophic suggestiveness of his encounter with these huge creatures are, of course, strongly enhanced by the contrast between the basic dilemmas, with respect to human size, of the first two books. As in the voyage to Lilliput, Gulliver's principal difficulties are the result of his size, coupled, to be sure, with varying manifestations of vanity, ineffectual valor, and timidity. And again, Swift is willing to exploit whatever aspect of the discrepancy between the size of Gulliver and his hosts seems convenient for comic purposes. Gulliver is at times the frustrated, squeaking victim of his vastly powerful captors; in other passages, notably those in which his stature provides him with "microscopic" vision of the giants, the Brobdingnagians themselves are held up to comic exposure. There are, again, transient satiric thrusts, achieved through a variety of techniques which range from parody[69] to the malicious fantasy which attacks the Maids of Honor. With the dialogues between Gulliver and the Brobdingnagian king, however, the comic quality becomes secondary in the presence of the most sustained satire we have yet encountered in the *Travels*. The dialogue, to be sure, remains closely related to the central fictional conceit, unlike the events which conclude the voyage to Lilliput, for Gulliver's tiny stature and comparative impotence lend a particular irony to his grandiose account of western civilization. It is, of course, the ludicrous size of his tiny visitor which, at the most obvious level, prompts the king's famous characterization of Gulliver's countrymen as "little odious vermin." On the other hand, the essence of the satiric procedure, whereby the legal, political, and ecclesiastical institutions of England are exposed in a manner to justify the king's reaction, does not depend upon the contrast in stature between the two parties to the dialogue. Swift's technique here is largely that of heavy sarcasm in which the naïvely boastful Gulliver parades before the king a highly

---

[69] Stylistic parody is relatively rare in the *Travels,* and where it appears is, in one way or another, made compatible with the broad outlines of Gulliver's character. The nautical jargon (p. 68) with which Swift apes such models as those found in Samuel Sturmy's *Mariner's Magazine* is entirely appropriate for a sailor, while the scientific explanation of the Flying Island is plainly offered as a "Philosophical Account" (pp. 151–54). In his almost exclusive reliance upon narrative events, Swift thus severely limits the use which he can make of a satiric device he elsewhere employs with major effects.

selective account of the English state, while the king responds with
the devastating penetration of the *faux ingénu*.[70]

It is interesting that the third book of *Gulliver's Travels,* generally
considered the least successful,[71] is the most thoroughly and genuinely satiric of the four. Within the repellant nations which Gulliver
visits on his third voyage, Swift has isolated and wildly distorted
many important and readily identified aspects of contemporary science, learning, and politics. To his slender fictional thread he has
tied, as well, scathing and unmistakable comments on Anglo-Irish
affairs, a myth which may well be satirically directed against common habits of thought concerning immortality, and a final savage
attack upon the Dutch nation.[72]

The explication of Book III in terms of particular satiric targets
yields very different results from similar inquiries into the other
books of the *Travels*. For when the historical victims have been iden-

[70] Ehrenpreis has shown the resemblance of the Brobdingnagian king's views to
those of Sir William Temple and has suggested that Moor Park memories of Stella
and Dorothy Osborne Temple have also colored the portraits of Glumdalclitch and
the giant queen (pp. 92–99). Such "identifications," tenable as they seem to me, obviously do not affect my interpretation of the satiric quality of the Second Voyage,
since of course none of these three figures is the victim of satiric assault. Whatever
the source of its principles, the king's shrewd and unaffected attack is unmistakable
in both its substance and direction.

[71] The comparative inferiority of the Third Voyage was marked, as Quintana reminds us, "by the first readers of the satire" and the judgment "has never been re-
versed" (*The Mind and Art of Jonathan Swift,* p. 315). (Quintana himself continues
to concur in this verdict; see *Swift: An Introduction* [Oxford, 1955], p. 51.) The well-
established fact that the Third Voyage was the fourth and last in order of composition cannot, I think, have the slightest bearing on the analysis of the *Travels,* since
the sequence of voyages in published form reflects Swift's deliberate intention. Of the
efforts to affirm the excellence of the Third Voyage, an excellent specimen is John H.
Sutherland, "A Reconsideration of Gulliver's Third Voyage," *Studies in Philology,*
LIV (1957), 45–51; arguing from the standpoint of the *Travels'* total plot, Sutherland
asserts that "Swift must have seen that he would have to expose Gulliver to more
disillusioning experiences and that he would have to show him reacting to such
experiences with some understanding, before he could present him as an easy and
immediate convert to the Houyhnhnms" (p. 51). However effective such defenses
of the Voyage's literary excellence may be, they ignore, at the very least, the matters
of narrative structure and sustained fiction which so clearly set the Voyage apart from
the other three.

[72] That the assault upon the Dutch—an "actual" nation—can be unobtrusively incorporated into the impossible adventures of the Third Voyage suggests how un-
important it is that, in this book, Swift adhere to a single level of fantasy. A similar
direct encounter with the alleged realities of international affairs would patently be
out of place in the two earlier voyages.

tified and the satiric character of the book established, there is very little in the way of comic plot, situation, or characterization which can be said to function independently. It is precisely this fact which accounts, in my opinion, for general dissatisfaction with the third book. The engaging narrative and the comic imagination of the two earlier books supply their fiction with a life of its own, with the appeal which entirely justifies the reputation of the *Travels* as a "children's story." Without this lively independent power, the fiction of the third book is a thin and subordinate apparatus. What pleasure we derive from this portion of Gulliver's voyaging is the pleasure afforded by punitive satire.[73] The inhabitants of Laputa, Lagado, and the rest have little comic appeal in their own right. Gulliver's sojourn in these realms provides only the thinnest of plots, and the occasional comic situations in which we find him are, at most, embodied in isolated episodes which lack central relationship to any sustained narrative structure.

The effect of Book III is thus almost entirely dependent on our recognition of the historic particulars—men, institutions, practices, and doctrines—with which Swift has peopled his mad kingdoms, savagely distorting them in the process. If the book could be viewed as a single, independent work, it might well be regarded as a brilliantly successful specimen of punitive satire, for, with even a minimal acceptance of Swift's prejudices, the reader can doubtless find considerable grim amusement in this bizarre debasement of important men and affairs. Our dissatisfaction with the book arises, I believe, chiefly from its appearance as an almost entirely satiric undertaking within a larger context from which we have come to expect many of the satisfactions afforded by comic, poetic, and other kinds of non-satiric art. In short, Book III suffers precisely because it is pre-

---

[73] An exception to this generalization is the episode with the Struldbruggs (see below) and possibly Gulliver's sojourn in Glubbdubdribb. In the latter instance, as in the former, Gulliver is clearly compelled to change his opinions, perhaps in a rather fundamental way; a detailed discussion of his "discoveries" in this section is offered by Edmund Reiss, "The Importance of Swift's Glubbdubdribb Episode," *Journal of English and Germanic Philology*, LIX (1960), 223–28. When a satiric figure moves to this kind of new awareness—however distorted may be the "truth" he apprehends—the effect tends to be persuasive since, to some extent, we are invited to share in his newly acquired views. Thus it might be argued that the sorcerers of Glubbdubdribb provide a novel formulation of the disparity between fact and the attractive falsehoods in which it is cloaked by history.

dominantly and forthrightly satiric but is a portion of a larger work of which this is by no means true.

In discussing the non-satiric qualities of the first three books of *Gulliver's Travels,* I have chiefly stressed those parts in which the fiction, transcending the satiric attack upon particulars, assumes an essentially comic quality. The "victims" of Swift's derision, that is, have, in such portions, lacked either the authenticity or the particularity of the satiric target, and we have laughed at the expense of all mankind or at the humor in situations which have no clear counterpart in the world of historic experience. But at certain points in these books there are also specimens of that kind of writing which, while it relies upon fictional devices and can even, in a broad sense, be considered polemic, is primarily neither comic nor satiric but substantially philosophic. One discovers in such sections a gravity and a magnitude of theme which discourage all search for comic qualities; at the same time, the very universality of the subjects to which they are addressed prevents the establishment of the particular victim who is the true satiric quarry.

To the extent that Gulliver's address to the Brobdingnagian king exposes the vice and folly which make of all humanity, rather than of eighteenth-century Englishmen alone, a "pernicious Race of little odious Vermin," we are confronted with an account of generic problems of human conduct. It is still, to be sure, western and more particularly English civilization which seems to arouse the king's contempt, since he is willing to distinguish between Gulliver and "the Bulk of your Natives," yet here, and especially in the ensuing chapter with its account of the king's "incredible" aversion to the idea of gunpowder, there is a pervasive exposure of accepted human values which is addressed as much to the broadest questions of morality as it is to the folly of specific, temporally limited customs.

In Gulliver's encounter with the Struldbruggs, in Book III, there is yet again a fictional incorporation of the problems arising from some of the deepest of man's hopes, his fatuousness, and his lot on earth. Recent studies suggest that the Struldbrugg myth can be seen as satirically directed against a form of heretical thinking which, as an accompaniment to new views of science and of human progress, has a clear historical identity.[74] It is also possible that the place of the

[74] See, in particular, J. Leeds Barroll III, "Gulliver and the Struldbruggs," *PMLA,* LXXIII (1958), 43–50.

aged in society had in Swift's day—as it has so clearly acquired in
ours—particular aspects inviting critical attention of the sort which
can supply specific satiric meaning to the Struldbruggs. Yet the vision of a world in which life itself is not to be cherished, in which
experience is seen as the accumulation of sorrow and infirmity, in
which ripeness is nothing and rottenness all, is, in all its horror,
philosophic.

Now while the fourth book of the *Travels* is rich in satiric materials—in assaults, that is, upon particularized kinds of men and institutions and habits—the final, comprehensive "meaning" of Swift's
disturbing fable cannot, I think, be regarded as essentially satiric. As
we have indicated, the most useful scholarly attempts to explicate
the earlier books have provided historic particulars to which the contents of Swift's fiction correspond or which, in some way, become
the object of attack by Swift. Such attempts in connection with
Book IV are rare, although on occasion they have provided most useful suggestions as to the reasons why Swift produced certain of his
inventions.[75] On the whole, however, Book IV does not invite us to
seek illumination in sources beyond the text itself. Instead, Gulliver's
adventures with the Houyhnhnms have been continually drawn
upon by those concerned with establishing Swift's basic beliefs and
attitudes—with setting forth the doctrines which, presumably, informed not only this book of *Gulliver's Travels* but much else which
Swift wrote. In a later chapter I shall be interested in discussing
these doctrines. For the present, the point is that without some notion, however controversial, of a fundamental view of man's nature
and achievements which, far more than specific assaults or engagement in ephemeral issues, provides the "meaning" of Swift's tale, we
have, at best, a fragmentary understanding of the book. Whatever is
didactic about "A Voyage to the Houyhnhnms" is, to be sure, re-

75 Much recent discussion has, of course, been devoted to the Houyhnhnms themselves and to Gulliver's extravagant response to their qualities. These studies can
often be viewed as efforts—of precisely the sort I have been urging—to establish an
authentic satiric victim by equating Houyhnhnm values (and Gulliver's participation
in them) with such specific beliefs as those of the deists. In my text, I shall subsequently have more to say about these undertakings. For the present, it is sufficient
to note my belief that in only one recent study—Professor Crane's "The Houyhnhnms,
the Yahoos, and the History of Ideas"—is a hitherto-unsuspected object of satire (the
logical doctrine of man as *animal rationale*) convincingly established. Whether this
doctrine, or the text in which it appears, constitutes the ultimate object of Swift's
assault is a question which is considered in my final chapter.

lated in some way to the strictly satiric elements within that book
and within the *Travels* as a whole. When principles are properly
established, the satirist's strictures against his enemies obviously acquire new authority and force. But the principles themselves, however unorthodox their substance or fantastic their mode of appearance before us, are not, in themselves, satiric. In the final analysis,
the tale of Gulliver's experience among the Yahoos and their masters
is neither a concentrated attack nor a comic fabrication. It is, instead,
a mythical statement of a profound and terrible belief about the
human condition.

We have spoken earlier of that species of philosophic myth which,
because it is cheerless and even destructive with respect to the state
of man, has a good deal in common with the characteristic attack of
satire. Such myths, however, are not ultimately to be regarded as
polemical assaults but as statements of belief concerning those questions which are fundamental for all thinking men at all times. If
they achieve incidental thrusts against specific targets (as do some of
Plato's dialogues and as does Book IV of *Gulliver's Travels*), these
should certainly be recognized wherever possible, yet they must not
be confused with the ultimate significance of the fictional invention.
Thus to regard the "Voyage to the Houyhnhnms" as satiric is to deal
with but a fraction of it. It must be seen, and I shall presently turn
to it, as the expression of answers to the kind of universal question
which are the province not of the satiric but of the philosophic mind.

I have, then, been arguing that there are very important elements
in *Gulliver's Travels* which, since they do not constitute attacks upon
historic particulars, lie beyond the satiric spectrum and represent, instead, several other kinds of literary art. The fiction in *Gulliver's
Travels* is, of course, continually present. It is, in fact, precisely at the
many points where the fiction arises above all correspondence with
historical reality and becomes a patent and complete artifice that the
comic, as opposed to the satiric, power of the work can be most
clearly felt. Where the fiction lacks the relationship to historical reality and thus loses satiric impact, the result is often entirely comic,
since Gulliver or various of his hosts frequently suffer the exposure
or embarrassment characteristic of comic "suffering." In addition,
however, we have noted a further kind of non-satiric writing in passages which, although incorporated within the governing fiction of
the entire work, cannot be truly said to attack—or, if they do attack,

have as their objects aspects of man and his world so broad and basic as to require that their consideration be essentially didactic and philosophic.

The reader will recall my distinction between "persuasive" and "punitive" satire. In a work like *Gulliver's Travels,* fiction is ever present and often, as fiction (rather than as symbol or surrogate for historical reality), dominates our attention; the satiric frequently yields to the non-satiric through the absence of specific objects of attack and even through the absence of attack of any sort. In such a work, we may expect the actual satiric elements to be of the sort we have called "punitive." For in the punitive portion of the satiric spectrum we have located the satire which lies closest to comedy, since it frequently treats the historically authentic victim in precisely the manner in which comedy treats an imaginary dupe. This species of satire can, I think, be seen to dominate the satiric elements in the first three books of the *Travels.* There is little real "exposure" here. In representing historically recognizable men, classes, and activities in a degrading and ludicrous light, Swift appears to rely upon our acceptance of them as stock material for such treatment.

To declare that much of *Gulliver's Travels* is not truly satiric, to assert that the satire it contains provides the quasi-comic satisfactions of the punitive type rather than the novel insights and altered opinions of the persuasive, is not to asperse the extraordinary attainments of Swift's great book. On the contrary, such distinctions tend to direct attention anew to the unique diversity of Swift's accomplishments. Precisely because these accomplishments are so varied, an analysis which seeks to describe the entire *Travels* as satiric is almost as inadequate as a formula which forces this singular document into the shape of the "comic novel" or some similarly rigid literary type. In the absence of a label which can successfully account for hugely diverting imaginative fiction, savagely pointed punitive satire, and a profound and challenging myth which embodies fundamental assertions about the state of man, it becomes all the more important to recognize that no one of these elements subsumes or "accounts for" the others. In the last analysis, it is the very diversity of these elements, together with the brilliant independence with which each asserts itself, that constitutes the triumphant uniqueness of *Gulliver's Travels.*

VI

Quite apart from what it may help us to see in any particular work the definition of the satiric victim which we have been employing raises some broad questions about satire in general. The particulars of history are, after all, transient and elusive. Can a satire which continues to engage many readers, centuries after it was composed, be truly "understood" only by the discovery of particular facts which have long been forgotten? Equally important, assuming that the facts do not disappear, that they are widely known or can be readily recovered, can we be expected to share the convictions, predilections, and passions with which they were originally viewed? If punitive satire proceeds from our willingness to accept the culpability of its victims and to rejoice uncritically in the discomfiture which they undergo, can we entertain such attitudes toward men and institutions long dead and forgotten—or often, to our own eyes, far more sympathetic figures than the satirist would have us believe? If true persuasive satire seeks to alter our opinions, what sentiments or knowledge can we bring to bear on issues which are irrelevant to our own concerns?

In previously mentioning this problem I have suggested that, in pursuit of the satiric victim, we have to suspend our own twentieth-century preoccupations and reconstruct the character of the satirist's original audience. To join this audience is a procedure appropriate to the scholar or critic, but for the common reader, however alert and sensitive, it may well seem formidable. In short, the text which, in Dr. Johnson's phrase, is able to "please many and please long" is not one whose comprehension depends upon abundant footnotes. If then, true satiric writing is addressed to precisely the kind of object which tends to be ephemeral and limited, how can a satire persist, in lively and intelligible form, from one generation to the next?

The first fact which must be faced is that, to be sure, much satire is as short-lived as the issues to which it is addressed. Like any form of pamphleteering, satire tends to claim the attention of the reading public only so long as that public is capable of a concern, approximating that of the satirist himself, for the questions under discussion. It is not surprising that there have been periods of literary history—of which late eighteenth- and early nineteenth-century England provides a good example—in which huge quantities of satiric literature have been produced and read, only to disappear, within a few years, from the awareness of all but a few specialists. Like the great majority of tracts of every kind, the outpourings of satirists tend to enjoy the transient currency of "popular" literature. Most satire does not, indeed, "please many and please long."

As a corollary to this, we should be prepared to note that many so-called satiric works which have become immortal are either not satiric to any appreciable extent, or claim continuing interest on grounds other than their satiric achievement. The *Satires and Epistles* of Horace, for example, are not, within the definitions we have advanced, exclusively satiric works. They are, quite properly, *sermones,* far more closely related to their ancestral *lanx satura* than, for example, to the satiric allegory of *Absalom and Achitophel* or the bogus proposals and arguments of a Swiftian *persona*. The same general thing can be said of most of Donne's *Satires* and of such an exercise in moralizing as Johnson's *The Vanity of Human Wishes*. There are, moreover, works which, as our discussion of *Gulliver's Travels* strongly suggests, survive chiefly, if not exclusively, for reasons other than their satiric qualities. Pure comedy or wit, philosophic insight, stylistic virtuosity in prose and verse—these can, in satire as in other literary forms, sustain the interest and admiration of readers who are quite indifferent to the substance to which, originally, these other qualities were mere embellishments.

Yet, although we grant that most satiric works are speedily forgotten and that others survive for reasons other than their satiric excellence, there remains such satire as Swift's, which—even in the case of many elements in *Gulliver's Travels*—claims our lasting admiration for no other reason than its success as satire. How, in the light of our insistence upon the temporal and particular nature of the satiric object, can the survival and stature of such writing be explained?

It is obvious, first of all, that the historic particular is not necessarily or totally unique and that the controversies of one age clearly have their echoes in another. Among the literary sins, for example, to which Swift addresses himself, there are those which have survived, almost unaltered, to weaken and vulgarize the writing of our own time. Inordinate partisan zeal, religious bigotry, political corruption, and barren pedantry—all of them among the vices with which Swift taxes his foes—remain with us as phenomena so real

that we are understandably interested in their appearance, however
differently manifested, within another age and nation. It is, to be
sure, Dryden and L'Estrange, Wotton and Bentley, who are Swift's
true victims, and vulgarity, arrogance, and ill-mannered pedantry
are but the crimes with which these individuals are taxed. Yet vice
and folly, like the roots of most kinds of controversy and excitement,
tend always to interest us, and their manifestations and the activities
they produce can compel our attention, even in circumstances quite
remote from our own. It is dangerous, of course, to "modernize" the
facts and personalities of a past age. Walpole cannot be converted
into a present-day political boss; history produces no synonym for a
Jacobite; Swift's "proposal" is, in truth, understandable only when
we know that it is calculated for the "one individual Kingdom of
Ireland, and for no other that ever was, is, or . . . can be upon Earth."
At the same time, the singularity of historical phenomena is no bar to
our understanding them, and with the understanding of human motives, difficulties, and decisions can come engagement in the convictions which drive the satirist to the practice of his art. With such
an engagement we become, as it were, vicarious spectators of the attack, able, like the avid reader of history, to follow with excitement
the course of an encounter whose issue has long since been resolved,
and often forgotten. If, in the motives of our spectatorship, there is
something of malice, some hint of a fierce satisfaction at the outrage
or embarrassment which, in a bygone day, was a painful actuality
for the satirist's victim—well, satire is not traditionally a benign art
nor are its devotees notable for softness of heart.

Yet, to identify the persistent appeal of great satire, we have, I believe, to look beyond the timeless questions which satire tends to reflect or the satisfactions we derive from attack, whatever its grounds.
For the immediate effectiveness and the permanent attractiveness of
satire depend most crucially not upon the fierceness or justice of the
attack itself, but upon the artifice by which satire lays claim to be
regarded as a literary form. Put most simply, it is not the plight of
the Irish, the wisdom or rectitude of Swift's views, the reflection, in
Irish suffering, of timeless problems of human need which make of
A Modest Proposal one of the monuments of satiric literature. It is
the invention, the shocking, totally original conceit of the cannibal-
istic proposal itself, which is the unique product of Swift's satiric
genius. Between a Swift or a Voltaire and the most contemptible

specimen of cheap, sarcastic pamphleteer there may be no difference whatever in satiric purpose or victim. The difference is to be found in the creative imagination, in the literary inventiveness, in short, in the *fictional* element which is as indispensable to the satirist's art as is the attack itself. It is with this element and its power, in the hands of an artist such as Swift, to make of the attack upon the historically particular a source of permanent literary satisfaction that the following chapter will be concerned.

CHAPTER III

The Satiric Fiction

*I*N ORDER TO SAY much about the function of the satiric fiction in writings as varied as Swift's, we shall have to recur to our distinction between punitive and persuasive satire. For there is every reason to expect that the satirist's artifice when he is seeking to satisfy us with the apt castigation of his victim will assume a different form from that by which he seeks to alter or intensify our opinions. The ends of punitive satire, so closely related to those of comic writing, are attainable largely through the ingenuity by which the satiric invention represents the discomfiture of a culpable victim. In persuasive satire, on the other hand, the effectiveness of the fiction is fundamentally judged not by the satisfaction which it affords but by its success in inducing the audience to discover premises, draw inferences, detect resemblances, and ultimately formulate conclusions by affirmative acts of understanding. As we have pointed out, the fiction which is basic to *A Modest Proposal* is brilliantly successful because it is arresting, because it formulates an appalling problem to permit one uncomfortable but crucial inference and, ultimately, to urge a course of political action.

The more manifestly punitive is the function of any satiric undertaking, the more directly do the vitality and aptness of the fiction determine the satirist's success. Thus, for example, cursing and conventional invective, for all their simplicity, fall within the limits of the satiric spectrum, as we have defined it, and tend (if, as is usually true, they involve only malicious epithets and hostile wishes) to be entirely punitive. Such forms of vituperation are ordinarily dreary and vulgar chiefly because they are uninventive and lack any appreciable artistic magnitude. The man who coins a new epithet or who employs authentic imagination in his malignant wishes for his enemies is, within obviously modest limits, a legitimate satirist. Whether or not invective is an essentially mean art, it is an ancient and persistent one in many societies and is unabashedly employed by some of the most illustrious writers of English.[1]

Swift's gifts for this species of satiric performance are abundantly displayed at many points in his works. His verses in particular are rich in sheer degrading epithet, and among them are poems which can be regarded as little more than systematic assortments of scurrilous labels, gaining attention largely because of the aptness of their opprobrium and for their prosodic and linguistic facility.[2] Swift's

[1] See Robert C. Elliott, *The Power of Satire* (Princeton, 1960), especially pages 3–48 and 285–92. Both the outright curse and the mere multiplication of degrading epithets are rather more common in purely imaginative literature than in genuine satire. Many hostile "characters" in the tradition of Samuel Butler, however, involve little more than the direct, if exaggerated or false, attribution of distasteful qualities to a particular victim. And such a famous passage as the "Sporus" portrait in Pope's *Epistle to Dr. Arbuthnot* is chiefly a catalogue of repellent qualities ruthlessly assigned to Lord Hervey.

[2] There is considerable reliance upon pure invective in such poems as "The Description of a Salamander" (*Poems*, I, 82), "The Author upon Himself" (I, 193),

willingness to engage in this mode of abuse is seen, moreover, in numerous passages of his prose, notably in his violent personal assaults on such men as Wharton, Steele, Marsh, Marlborough,[3] and many others, but also in the blunt, presumably spontaneous marginalia with which he graced the published editions of writers like Tindal, Clarendon, and Burnet.[4]

In its brevity and simplicity, invective is not a form which invites much literary analysis, however fascinating it may be to the anthropologist or historian of popular culture. But beyond the frequency with which even so artful a writer as Swift is prepared to employ it, invective should interest us because it embodies, in uncomplicated and unadulterated form, precisely those elements which are most essential to the more elaborate forms of satire. A curse or an epithet is manifestly a fiction—a degrading label or an imagined painful or humiliating experience suffered by the satiric victim. And the effectiveness of this fanciful artifice rests chiefly upon the appropriateness, if not the absolute justice, of the abuse which its object undergoes.

If the malicious, punitive fiction which marks invective is extended, however, we are confronted with a form of satiric art which claims greater attention. For, as I have earlier indicated, one form of substantial satiric construction is the abusive or derisive fable whose total fabric is imaginary and in which the historical victim of satire is exposed to a fictional discomfiture which bears little or no analogy to actual fact. Of such a kind, as has been said, are works like *The Dunciad* and *Mac Flecknoe* which (save for the initial conceit which implies that if there were a kingdom of Dulness, it would be ruled

---

"Wood, an Insect" (I, 350), "A Libel on Doctor Delaney" (II, 479), and, in fact, many if not most of Swift's verse assaults on specific individuals. Specimens of verse which I should regard as almost exclusively invective are "The Character of Sir Robert Walpole" (II, 539) and "Clad All in Brown" (III, 786), the latter a revolting imitation of Cowley in one of Swift's unrestrained attacks upon Richard Tighe.

[3] See *A Short Character of His Excellency Thomas Earl of Wharton* (*Prose Works*, III, 177–84); *A Character of Primate Marsh* (*Prose Works*, ed. Temple Scott, XI, 189–90); the characterizations of Steele in *The Importance of the Guardian Considered* (*Prose Works*, VIII, 4–25) and *The Public Spirit of the Whigs* (*Prose Works*, VIII, 31–68); and the sketches of Marlborough and other opponents of the Harley administration in *The History of the Four Last Years of the Queen* (*Prose Works*, VII, 7–11).

[4] See notes on Tindal in *Prose Works*, II, 84–107. Swift's remarks on the histories of Clarendon and Burnet are printed in *Prose Works*, ed. Temple Scott, X, 291–368.

by the protagonist-victim) rarely ask us to discover by analogue or inference any authentic fact or issue which the fiction disguises. We derive our satisfaction instead from a sustained "quasi-libel," differing from genuine libel only because it does not ask us for a moment to believe in its preposterous substance but instead seeks to divert us with a patent but sympathetic falsehood.

When practiced unimaginatively, such kinds of punitive satire can obviously be puerile and often revolting, bearing a strong family resemblance to the more derogatory forms of grammar-school *graffiti*. The power of the quasi-libel to command admiration depends largely upon the art—art much like that of the comic writer—by which the elements of imaginative fiction are exploited. Its satiric effectiveness requires as well that the imagined abuse of the victim appear sympathetic to us; the grounds for such a response are not, as a rule, provided within the developing fiction of the punitive satirist, but tend to exploit common opinion in assailing a victim who is, as it were, "ready-made" for slaughter.

Specimens of this form of pure punitive assault are not uncommon in Swift's writings. They appear in their simplest forms among his poems, some of which—including, for instance, the thoroughly indelicate verse called "The Problem" and the more artful if equally earthy ballad on "The true English Dean to be hang'd for a Rape"[5] —are barely redeemed by nimble versifying from the class of idle and malicious obscenity. And such a trifling prose piece as *A Hue and Cry after Dismal*—though the historic occasion provides a somewhat more respectable motive—is a totally imaginary product of malicious exultation.[6] There are, however, far more substantial portions of Swift's prose in which the fiction, although serving the ends of punitive satire, lays an autonomous claim on our attention and, by the power of the author's imagination, provides a literary experience very close to that of superior comedy.

Nowhere does this kind of satiric art appear to better advantage than in *The Battle of the Books*. With her usual acuteness, Miss Kathleen Williams has noted a number of ways in which this work of Swift's differs strikingly from other productions of his which are

---

[5] See *Poems*, I, 64; II, 516. Although poetic fictions of a far more ambitious sort serve Swift for purposes of both satire and panegyric, the short verses I mention display the quasi-libel in its most transparent form.

[6] *Prose Works*, VI, 139–41.

of comparable magnitude and importance. She has asserted, among other things, that in the *Battle,* "the intention of the satire is limited, and not of a kind to inspire Swift's most characteristic effects, and the method is, consequently, comparatively uncomplicated."[7]

The satiric intention is, indeed, limited, particularly so if we anticipate from the *Battle* the shifting diversity of purpose, the profundity, the complexity of satiric procedures, and the powerful flashes of polemic assault which are to be found in *A Tale of a Tub* or *Gulliver's Travels.* As a repository of the common charges and hostile stereotypes, the issues and the self-assigned roles which marked the Ancients-Moderns controversy, the *Battle* is of legitimate interest to the historian of ideas. It is true, too, that the work embodies throughout—and in no place more illuminatingly than in the fable of the spider and the bee—pervasive issues of morality, theology, and metaphysics to which Cartesian rationalism and the self-assurance engendered by the new science may have given an immediacy peculiar to the age.[8] Yet what is thus reflected in the *Battle* is reflected in the entire warfare between the Ancients and the Moderns, of which the English version was but a peripheral manifestation and the encounter between Sir William Temple and his learned foes at most a belated skirmish.[9] It is extremely difficult to demon-

---

[7] Kathleen Williams, *Jonathan Swift and the Age of Compromise* (Lawrence, Kansas, 1958), p. 124.

[8] It is doubtless true that, as Miss Williams says, Descartes "was progenitor of the race of modern system-makers, who was representative of all that was presumptuous and dangerous in rationalizing modernism" (p. 125). The "progenitors" of modern folly could also include, as Swift himself implies (*Tale,* p. 166), Epicurus, Diogenes, Lucretius, Paracelsus, "and others." Such men may be seen as "representatives" of the *kind* of error which is attacked in both the *Tale* and the *Battle,* but the currents of thought which can be traced to them cannot tempt us to ignore the specific contemporary antagonists who serve as the primary victims of Swift's satire.

[9] Quintana reminds us that Swift's role in the Ancients-Moderns controversy is comparatively remote from the central substantive issues and that his attack centers chiefly upon the pedantry and bad manners of the Bentley-Wotton faction; see both *The Mind and Art of Jonathan Swift,* pp. 76-77, and *Swift: An Introduction* (London, 1955), pp. 44, 55-56. R. F. Jones, in his history of the Ancients-Moderns controversy, is at pains to point out that even Temple, in his *Essay upon the Ancient and Modern Learning* (1690), provides "only a revival of those attacks on the new science and the Royal Society that characterized the Restoration"; see *Ancients and Moderns: A Study of the Rise of the Scientific Movement in Seventeenth Century England* (2d ed.; St. Louis, 1961), p. 267.

strate that, in any significant fashion, the cause of the Ancients in general or of Temple in particular was advanced by the *Battle*.[10]

Like various portions of *A Tale of a Tub* which tempt one to view them as blows struck by Swift, the satirist, against Bentley, the scholar, the *Battle,* if viewed as persuasive satire, accomplishes very little in exposing or even underscoring Bentley's infirmities or errors. In a careful study of Swift and contemporary science, Mabel Phillips (De Vane) has summarized the strategy of Bentley's enemies, Swift among them, as follows:

> If Bentley was an easy victor, as all later scholars have admitted, his opponents had a very great advantage. Few of them apparently knew that they were beaten; and the public at large certainly did not know it. Bentley was so far ahead of his contemporaries that they had no comprehension of what he had done. They considered his works in the light of their own abilities. If one of them had written the *Dissertation* in that form, he would have had to guess at most of it. They had no conception that it represented accurate knowledge painstakingly acquired. It seemed to them that Bentley was talking about things of which no man could really have positive knowledge. They could not meet him on his own ground, although there was some slight attempt to do so. The consequence was that the answers to Bentley rather avoided the main issue.[11]

It does not seem too much to say that the "main issue," at least as it lay between Bentley and his responsible critics, fails to appear in either *The Battle of the Books* or in *A Tale of a Tub*. What we are confronted with, instead, is in the latter, at least, a fictional construction in which the self-assurance, ill-nature, and pedantry of Bentley and his associates are taken for granted and an elaborate campaign of mirthful abuse is conducted at their expense. Implicit in Mrs. De Vane's account of the matter is a distinction between persuasive satire, directed "to the point" and inviting reflection with respect to a common matter of controversy, and a mode of ridicule exploiting the preconceptions (or indeed ignorance, in this instance)

[10] Swift's lack of engagement in the substantive issues of the controversy has led one student to the extreme view that he was indifferent—and indeed somewhat unsympathetic—to Temple's position; see Philip Pinkus, "Swift and the Ancients-Moderns Controversy," *University of Toronto Quarterly,* XXIX (1959), 46–58.

[11] Mabel Phillips (De Vane), *Swift's Relations to Science* (Ph.D. diss., Yale University, 1925), p. 92.

of an audience seeking only new and entertaining ways of sharing in the mockery of the common enemy.

If, in fact, we explore the persuasive aspects of the *Battle,* the entire Ancients-Moderns controversy is the historical phenomenon which tends, if anything does, to appear in a new light. For in adopting as his comprehensive structure the mock-epic formula, Swift has courted the danger of reducing the whole struggle, including both sets of antagonists, to the status of an inconsequential encounter upon trivial grounds. This is indeed a traditional and often inevitable result of the pseudo-elevation implicit in the mock-heroic technique. In the *Battle,* even the Ancient writers and their adherents, Boyle and Temple, may appear—like Belinda in *The Rape of the Lock* or Parson Adams in his encounter with the dogs— somewhat ludicrous, precisely because their "heroic" roles are actually mock-heroic, and, in attributing virtues to them, the author cannot drop the sarcastic mode to which his inclusive satiric device has committed him. Thus it might be argued that, if anything is actually demonstrated or strikes us with the force of a new insight in the *Battle,* it is that the passion and self-importance with which the entire controversy has been conducted are quite disproportionate to the issues at stake.

To offset this tendency of the work and establish its most memorable effects, we must depend largely upon the novel imaginative qualities of Swift's performance. His sheer linguistic virtuosity, with its brilliant manipulations of tempo, its hilarious juxtapositions of the heroic with the most pungent vulgarity, its ingenious pursuit of epic devices and parallels—remains a principal source of our satisfaction in his achievement. The characterization and actions of the Modern writers and their apologists are grotesque beyond the point of caricature, bearing little relevance to historical facts. The grounds for this savage debasement are shaky; a true portrait of Bentley and Wotton shows little of the eclecticism, abusiveness, and arrogance with which Swift has endowed them. Even as members of Swift's original audience, we would have found it difficult to derive from this extravagant fabrication the slightest reasons for alarm, anger, or indeed any new dimension of contempt for the actual figures who are represented in this wild fantasy.

Miss Williams asserts that the *Battle* "is perhaps the least interesting, as well as the least characteristic, of Swift's longer satires."[12] It assuredly loses interest, as well as excellence, if we demand from it the same qualities and the same effects which are provided not only by such longer works as the *Tale* and the *Travels* but by such power-fully persuasive satires as *A Modest Proposal*. It will not do to assess the *Battle* with the sobriety to which even the apparently playful disorder of the *Tale* invites us. There is no "argument," however oblique, to be disinterred from its pages, for the apparent analogy with the historical development of the controversy, implicit in the opening account of the two summits, speedily evaporates in the mélange of dialogue and fanciful incident which follows. In its de-liberately episodic structure and its pseudo-artlessness, there is little sense of satiric strategy or climax.

It is true that, in the discourse between the bee and the spider, there is a superb figurative concentration of the vices of one side and the virtues of the other. In the same passage, moreover, there is a fine Swiftian multiplicity of satiric means and ends: the analogical and parodic fiction; the vulnerable satiric objects which include not only a number of general Modern habits but such individuals as Bentley, Wotton, and Burnet; the charges which incorporate, at the least, vanity, pedantry, malice, and parasitism. Even here, however, the section appears to me most notable when viewed as, in a sense, an extended and rigorously controlled epithet. The apt choice of the spider as the symbol of varied Modern vices is thus enriched by the creature's language and actions, in addition, of course, to the elabo-rate particulars of the analogy which are supplied by the bee. The bee's closing words are, after all, the most eloquent summary of the entire controversy which Swift ventures to supply:

So that, in short, the Question comes all to this; Whether is the nobler Being of the two, That which by a lazy Contemplation of four inches round; by an over-weening Pride, which feeding and engendering on it self, turns all into Excrement and Venom; producing nothing at all, but Fly-bane and a Cobweb; Or that, which, by an universal Range, with long Search, much Study, true Judgment, and Distinction of Things, brings home Honey and Wax.[13]

This is a superlatively concise and colorful statement of the case. But

[12] *Jonathan Swift and the Age of Compromise*, p. 122.

[13] *Tale*, p. 232.

the "case," of course, rests neither on logic nor discernible fact but on a hyperbolic distortion of the alleged habits of the Moderns. What we can chiefly admire here is magnificently talented name-calling.

In its joyous pummeling of particular men, books, habits, and ideas, the *Battle* is almost exclusively satiric. But we shall, in truth, find it a "disappointing document" if we look to it for a satiric effect which it does not claim. It makes no appeal to our sense of responsible conviction; it provides us with no acceptable grounds for its particular strictures, still less with the kind of thoughtful principles which lie, however concealed, in those of Swift's works which seek seriously to alter or strengthen our opinions. The satisfactions of the *Battle* are largely literary satisfactions. They are the results of imaginative, uninhibited, though highly controlled literary artifice. For here Swift has made dupes of his enemies—the dupes of true comic literature in every sense save for their historic actuality—and the proper measure of his success lies not in the conviction of his audience but in its laughter.

II

What we have been saying about *The Battle of the Books* applies, I believe, with considerable force to the narrative portions of *A Tale of a Tub*—to the allegorical account of Christianity which is embodied in the tale of the three brothers. It is interesting that of this narrative, too, Miss Williams asserts that it "has less, in itself, than Swift's usual power, and perhaps the lowering of intensity has the same cause here as in *The Battle of the Books,* that all is too plain; the work has been done for us."[14] From our point of view, it is perfectly true that "all is too plain" for persuasive satire, that species of assault which provokes us through its demands upon our powers of inference, comparison, and common sense to arrive at novel conclusions. Such "work" has, indeed, "been done for us," and we are prepared, at the outset, to share in the aversions and affinities upon which the structure of punitive satire is erected. Swift's "power" is assuredly of more than one kind, and the power to delight is not necessarily the same as the power to convince.

When reduced to its simplest terms, the narrative of the three brothers has a kind of transparency and patness which is somewhat

[14] *Jonathan Swift and the Age of Compromise,* pp. 134-35.

alien to Swift's greatest satiric fabrications, whatever the ends they seek. The possibilities for establishing correspondences between the symbols of the narrative and the vexed history of the church have long been virtually exhausted; within twenty years of the *Tale*'s appearance this ground had been quite thoroughly covered by Swift or his commentators—friend and foe alike. And whether or not we agree with Swift's detractors that the principal allegorical device was explicitly borrowed from earlier sources,[15] the general outlines of the fiction show little of that wild originality which marks Swift's greatest inventions.

But the apparent frailty of the narrative is quite deliberate and a part of the elaborate jest in which Swift delays the beginning of his actual "tale" with a plethora of introductory apparatus. The prefatory materials and the digressions (both in the chapters so labeled and in those professedly given over to the narrative) suggest to the wary reader, in their magnitude and apparent irrelevance, that the story they surround so elaborately will hardly conform to the mock-author's pretentious view of his own enterprise. The patently anticlimactic quality of the narrative, that is, places a confirming stamp of folly upon the writer who has given such an overblown account of his literary project.[16]

Yet the narrative, when finally we reach it, is no mere dud. Swift, after mountainous labors, may have jestingly brought forth a mouse, but it is a vigorous and engaging creature, with a spirited life of its own. Adopting a leisurely tempo and a conversational manner, Swift is able, whenever he wishes, to turn his tale-telling to direct satiric use, to digress freely, to manipulate and even to suspend the narrative for whatever ends occur to him. The very simplicity of his initial metaphor—the tale of the three brothers and their Father's will—is such that we cannot expect its analogies to be rigorously sustained or thoroughly exploited throughout all of the narrative chapters. As

[15] See Wotton's *Reflections*, p. 327 and the account of various alleged sources for the allegory in *Tale*, pp. xxxi–xliii.

[16] The view of Guthkelch and Nichol Smith (*Tale*, pp. xliii–xlvii) that the allegory was largely written before the prefatory materials and digressions is given substantial support by Davis (*Prose Works*, I, xiv–xv) and Harth (*Swift and Anglican Rationalism*, pp. 6–10). The actual order of composition, however, in no way detracts from the effect—which can hardly be other than deliberate—of a relatively modest narrative, quite disproportionate in magnitude to the length and substance of the materials which precede and accompany it.

the satire intensifies into a punishing assault upon Enthusiasm, the
allegorical basis of the tale disappears, to be replaced by derisive
fantasy and raw, hilarious caricature.

In the role of a tale-teller with slight responsibilities to formal
order, Swift is able fully to indulge his zest and talent for invention.
Above the modest structure of the allegory loom those marvelous
"systems" which impress us not with their satiric force or the significance of the doctrines they convey, but with their imaginative
virtuosity. They are not totally independent of Swift's general intentions in the *Tale;* their genesis is the allegory and their undeniable
satiric overtones ring harmoniously with the principal tenor of
Swift's satire in the work. At the same time, I believe, they are superb
specimens of the way in which the satiric fiction, no longer a mere
vehicle of attack, can assume a transcendent and memorable power
in its own right and serve as evidence that the satirist's permanent
achievement is that of the imaginative artist.

The first of these famous "systems" appears in the initial chapter
of the narrative proper and is the account of the tailor-deity and the
clothes philosophy. In the chapter, the allegory represents the history
of the Church from its inception to the time of Constantine's con-
version. The burden of symbolic meaning is quite uncomplicated:
the dying Father leaves each of his three sons a coat, requiring that
it be properly cared for according to the provisions of His Will.
Succumbing to fashionable pressures, the sons contravene their
Father's wishes by adorning the coats in a succession of foppish
ways. These "embroideries" of primitive Christianity they justify
by unscrupulous sophistry, clearly recognizable as the rationalizing
by which "great Additions to Christianity" have been reconciled
to basic dogma. This is the essence of the central allegory and, as
satire on religion, the chapter goes no further—perhaps because, as
Professor Dargan has said, Swift's worldly symbols "bring down to
their own level things which are of greater real or reputed value and
dignity"[17] and the elaboration of the basic device might be somewhat
dangerous. Whatever the reason, the analogical account of Christian
history becomes the point of departure, the narrative "excuse," for a
catalogue of urban follies and fashionable recreations in which the
brothers' initial symbolic identity is of little importance. In the attire

[17] H. M. Dargan, "The Nature of Allegory as Used by Swift," *Studies in Philology,*
XIII (July, 1916), 161.

of contemporary fops, the youths are plainly representative of highly secular, contemporary foibles. As allegory on religion, the chapter marks the first stage of what Miss Williams has called "a gradual departure from given truth, a steady descent into self-deceit."[18] But dominating this simple narrative is the animated fictional representation of fashionable vices, vices so familiar and persistent that their punitive mockery comes very close to sheer comedy.

The clothes-philosophy is a part of the allegory only because the rise of tailor-worship is what makes necessary the strenuous rationalizing of the three brothers:

> For, about this Time it happened a Sect arose, whose Tenents obtained and spread very far, especially in the *Grande Monde,* and among every Body of good Fashion. They worshipped a sort of *Idol,* who, as their Doctrine delivered, did daily create Men, by a kind of Manufactory Operation. This *Idol* they placed in the highest Parts of the House, on an Altar erected about three Foot: He was shewn in the Posture of a *Persian* Emperor, sitting on a *Superficies,* with his Legs interwoven under him (p. 76).

The account of the tailor-god is whimsically developed with puns and other exploitations of the attributes and apparatus of the tailor's trade. From this simple conceit, there is developed a self-contained, rather elaborate "system," a mock-philosophy which has little bearing, if any, upon the religious allegory. The initial postulate is simply the divinity of the tailor; the consequence of this postulate is that all things may be seen as the tailor's creations, i.e., as clothes. Accordingly, the clothes-metaphysics, based on the notion of the tailor as creator, is used to describe the nature of the universe; the clothes-ethics and psychology proceed from the same assumption. And subsequently, the "subaltern doctrines," a sort of clothes-epistemology and clothes-politics, follow from the same fanciful but consistent premise, since whatever faculties can be attributed to the creations of the tailor-god must be the attributes or adornments of clothes. From the single concept of the tailor as God and hence Creator, there are derived the essentials of most of the traditional philosophic disciplines; and the putative author argues that this is, indeed, what he has demonstrated when he refers to his account as a "short Summary of a Body of Philosophy and Divinity" (p. 80).

[18] *Jonathan Swift and the Age of Compromise,* p. 133.

Within this relatively obvious structure the satiric performance is accompanied by a display of comic art. As in the earlier treatment of the three "machines," the section begins with a figure which violently (but not, for the reader, unsympathetically) distorts reality: the concern for fashionable attire—or for appearances in general— amounts to the deification of the tailor. For a paragraph the conceit is pursued with almost exclusively comic effect; the tailor-god is the excuse for outrageous puns and mock-historic conjectures. Then, with the exposition of a "System of Belief," the procedure becomes something more than playful fantasy:

They held the Universe to be a large *Suit of Cloaths*, which *invests* every Thing: That the Earth is *invested* by the Air; the Air is *invested* by the Stars; and the Stars are *invested* by the *Primum Mobile*. Look on this Globe of Earth, you will find it to be a very compleat and fashionable *Dress* (p. 78).

The putative author is here advancing an "argument" of his own. The rhetorical questions, admonitions, and requests for the admission of "Postulata" make this clear, and it is his assertion that "those Beings which the World calls improperly *Suits of Cloaths*, are in Reality the most refined Species of Animals, or to proceed higher, that they are Rational Creatures, or Men."

Given these premises, it is possible, in the manner of philosophers, to develop them further:

Others of these Professors, though agreeing in the main System, were yet more refined upon certain Branches of it; and held that Man was an Animal compounded of two *Dresses*, the *Natural* and the *Celestial Suit*, which were the Body and the Soul: That the Soul was the outward, and the Body the inward Cloathing; that the latter was *ex traduce*, but the former of Daily Creation and Circumfusion. This last they proved by *Scripture*, because, *in Them we Live, and Move, and have our Being*: As likewise by Philosophy, because they are *All in All, and All in every Part*. Besides, said they, separate these two, and you will find the Body to be only a senseless unsavory Carcass. By all which it is manifest, that the outward Dress must needs be the Soul (pp. 79–80).

The basic invention in these passages, as well as the concepts and images by which it is developed, possess an understandable fascination for those who, in the tradition of M. Pons, are engaged in the pursuit of Swift's "themes."[19] The emphasis upon surfaces and appearances, the endowment of the non-human with human attributes, the grotesque misdirection of religious zeal, the mock-apotheosis of vanity, and perhaps even the questionable piety of the underlying conceit—these and other ingredients of the fiction invite the attention of critics who seek in Swift's writings a consistent fabric of preoccupation and belief. And ultimately, both the satiric assaults of the section and the devices by which they are advanced may be brought into some kind of conformity with whatever we can discover about Swift's fundamental convictions.

Initially, however, we do not search for themes but for the precise satiric character of these pages. The perverse consistency of Swift's preposterous logic may drive us to ask uneasily what is wrong with such a glibly developed world-view and what authentic errors in the thoughts of real men are reflected in its original premises. The immediate context of the allegorical "plot" suggests that the genesis of the system is merely fashionable vice, the substitution of vulgar and totally secular standards for those of piety. Since, however, the ultimate, monstrous manifestations of tailor-worship are represented in theological terms, we are led to suspect that the system is the creature of philosophic error as well as mere frivolity. Here, as elsewhere, Phillip Harth is singularly illuminating and has shown, in my opinion incontrovertibly, that the "error" is materialism.[20] The false premise which makes the clothes-philosophy possible lies as much in the writings of Hobbes as it does in fashionable vanity. When the entire universe can be materialistically explained, "the outward Dress must needs be the Soul." For if, philosopher-fashion, we adhere to traditional terms and thus to the dichotomy of soul and body, but concurrently, man, like all else, consists only of what can be sensorily perceived, then the visible element of man which is not his body can only be his soul.

Though the clothes-philosophy appears to be an "intrusion" in the allegorical narrative, it is thus integrally related to it as a satire on abuses in religion. For this fantastic system must be seen not only as the product of secular follies which blind men to their religious duty

---

[19] Pons emphasizes *"la doctrine esthétomorphique"* and finds in the clothes-philosophy a crucial statement of theme and expression of *"l'humeur swiftienne"* (*Swift: Les années de jeunesse et "Le Conte du Tonneau,"* p. 321).

[20] Harth, *Swift and Anglican Rationalism,* pp. 77, 80–85.

but, in Professor Harth's terms, as "an antireligious doctrine in direct contradiction to Christianity."[21] Even the identification of so
fundamental an error does not exhaust the satiric implications of
Swift's fiction. The solemn inflation of an egregiously mean image
into a universal system is strongly suggestive of more pointed parodic
intention. We know, for example, that easy and unqualified systematizing is a form of error with which the *Tale* frequently taxes
Bentley and Wotton.[22] As Mrs. Starkman has pointed out, moreover, the "great chain" and the macrocosm-microcosm correspondence are concepts which characterize the "Modern" metaphysics and
which, per se, could be regarded only with aversion by the orthodox.[23] And in the gravely confident manner in which manifest absurdity is expounded, it also seems likely that there is mockery of
the uncompromisingly mechanistic modes of argument which,
though their origins may have lain with Hobbes or Descartes, were
to be found in the most current pages of the "new" science and
scholarship.

The reduction of mechanistic theories to a single, outrageously
simple-minded concept may point as well to more popular literary
productions and to works which attempted, by comparably simplistic devices, to make intelligible the doctrines of contemporary science.
A model of this sort of thing is Fontenelle's *Entretiens sur la plu-
ralité des mondes,* which, according to Professor Lovejoy, "no doubt
did more than any other single writing to diffuse these [new cosmo-
graphical] ideas among the educated classes generally."[24] Swift was
thoroughly familiar with Fontenelle: the French writer had con-
tributed to the Modern cause in the famous controversy.[25] Not least

[21] P. 77.

[22] Harth discusses (pp. 64–66), the "reductive systems" which Swift assails as a
species of religious and philosophic error. The claims to possess—or at least to describe—knowledge universally, exhaustively, and systematically with which Swift
taxes Bentley and Wotton may likewise be manifestations of impious arrogance, but
should be seen as learned rather than religious abuses. For examples of Swift's attack
on the latter kind of systematizing, see *Tale,* pp. 69, 125, 145, 169.

[23] *Swift's Satire on Learning in "A Tale of a Tub,"* p. 57.

[24] A. O. Lovejoy, *The Great Chain of Being* (Cambridge, Mass., 1936), p. 130.

[25] Bernard Le Bovier Fontenelle, *Digression sur les Anciens et les Modernes*
(1688). The *Entretiens,* originally published in 1686, was translated into English by
Aphra Behn and appeared as *A Discovery of New Worlds* (London, 1688). Swift's
awareness of Fontenelle is established fact: the French writer shares with Perrault the

important, he was conspicuously adroit at the glib vulgarizing by
which, from Swift's standpoint, doctrinal error was compounded by
corrupt artistic practice. For Fontenelle, there is no problem in explaining the earth's atmosphere. "Thus it is," he says to the coyly
inquisitive Marquise in the *Entretiens,* "that the Earth, which is
very solid, is wrapp'd in a Covering of soft Down of twenty Leagues
thickness, which is the Air that is carried round at the same time
with it."[26]

The satiric implications of Swift's mock-system are undeniable.
But their presence and power are made possible by a self-contained,
brilliantly developed fiction which, however derisively it echoes various manifestations of the new scientific spirit, delights us above all
as a "logical" structure based upon a foundation of utter absurdity.

The complex satiric development which can accompany a fundamentally comic performance is seen climactically as Swift completes
his great clothes-chain:

To conclude from all, what is Man himself but a *Micro-Coat,* or rather a
compleat Suit of Cloaths with all its Trimmings? As to his Body, there can
be no dispute; but examine even the Acquirements of his Mind, you will
find them all contribute in their Order, towards furnishing out an exact
Dress: To instance no more; Is not Religion a *Cloak,* Honesty a *Pair of
Shoes,* worn out in the Dirt, Self-love a *Surtout,* Vanity a *Shirt,* and Conscience a *Pair of Breeches,* which, tho' a Cover for Lewdness as well as
Nastiness, is easily slipt down for the Service of both (p. 78).

The passage, as Professor Harth has pointed out, is, in its style, an
indisputable and highly amusing parody of Hobbes.[27] On other
grounds, too, it doubtless deserves some of the sober attention it has
received.[28] Its gloomy cynicism is arresting, and, in a sense, it adum-

---

distinction of being slain by Homer with a single blow in the *Battle of the Books*
(*Tale,* p. 246); there is some likelihood that his *Histoire de Mréo et d'Eénegu* sug-
gested Swift's basic allegory in the *Tale* (Pons, pp. 304–6 and *Tale,* pp. xxxvi–xxxvii);
and Sir Harold Williams points out that, among French miscellaneous writers in
Swift's library, "Fontenelle easily heads the list"; see Harold Williams, *Dean Swift's
Library* (Cambridge, 1932), p. 65.

[26] Fontenelle, *A Discovery of New Worlds,* trans. Aphra Behn (London, 1688),
p. 38.

[27] *Swift and Anglican Rationalism,* pp. 84–85.

[28] Pons's emphasis upon "L'esthétomorphisme" in this connection is, I think, very
justly questioned by Quintana in *The Mind and Art of Jonathan Swift,* p. 91.

brates the extraordinary analysis of surfaces in the "Digression concerning Madness." In his parody on Hobbes's analogy between the human and the political body, Swift is also providing another debased specimen of the absurd analogies and figures offered by the fable-mongers. But quite apart from the cynical assumptions on which it is based, the passage is a new, ingenious ramification of the clothes-figure in which an assumed view of human depravity is the foundation for a brilliant jest. For the final turn of wit, the comparisons of religion to a cloak, and honesty to a pair of worn shoes are mere preliminaries; it is only when we encounter the description of conscience as a pair of breeches that the series of comparisons acquires its true force—the force which is, above all, that of an indelicate joke.

Neither in this paragraph nor in the succeeding one—in which Swift extends his mock-logic to assert that since what appear to be men are really clothes, what appear to be clothes are really men—is Swift's chief accomplishment that of satiric "exposure." Instead, he has carried out a grotesque intellectual caper, pursuing an initial, fantastic conceit through a series of mutations, each of which is not only related to the whole but involves a new exercise of wit. To the extent that this performance is a caricature of either prevailing "modern" habits or a particular writer, it is parody and effective punitive satire. If we do, indeed, recognize the manner of such a writer, we are prepared to laugh at its straight-faced employment in the exposition of a system which is outrageous from beginning to end. In more fundamental respects, the satire may, in fact, operate persuasively, if we are able to recognize in the clothes-philosophy the somewhat distorted consequences to which the assumptions of materialism may lead. But to the greater extent that the "system" involves extravagant elaborations upon a preposterous thesis, the superb extension of a single grotesque metaphor, it remains a joke— a triumphantly comic artifice.

It is entirely possible that Swift's major purpose in constructing the clothes philosophy was to satirize some such phenomenon as materialism. But the very fact that it has remained for such modern scholars as Mr. Harth to disinter this authentic satiric victim suggests the uniqueness and intrinsic satisfaction which readers have discovered in the fiction itself. Passages like that upon the "Micro-Coat" are not, after all, truly important expressions of Swiftian conviction; the cynicism they invoke is surely not very different from that which must be temporarily adopted to enjoy a great deal of the humor— written and unwritten—which exploits a deep skepticism about human honesty or altruism or chastity. Whatever we conclude about such myths as the vehicles for satire or the expressions of belief, we must remain alert to them as rare imaginative achievements, with a memorable dimension of sheer delight.

This aspect of the satiric fiction is, I believe, even more evident in the latter of Swift's two great systems in the *Tale,* the account of the Aeolists, those demented worshippers of the wind to whom Section VIII of the book is devoted. Like the section on the clothes-philosophy, the Aeolist chapter is, as it were, a "narrative digression," claiming some relation to allegorical plot, since Jack, the Puritan brother, is the founder of the sect. And again like the clothes-philosophy—but unlike most of the frankly labeled "digressions"— the Aeolist chapter cannot be viewed as an essentially satiric excursion. It is an elaborate fiction, originating doubtless from satiric motives which account for much of the *Tale,* but with an ultimate satiric impact that is submerged in the exuberant flood of Swift's comic inventiveness.

Although in this study I am not attempting even a superficial analysis of the *Tale*'s structure in its entirety, it is useful to note the location of the Aeolist section within the book and, in particular, its close relation to the ensuing chapter, the famous "Digression concerning Madness." A connective sentence at the outset of the latter chapter binds the two together as the product of a single, sustained discussion by the author. There is also an obvious "topical" tie, for Aeolism has been founded by Jack, a victim of the madness on which Swift is moved to "digress." Most important, the two chief structural elements in the *Tale*—the narrative itself and the animadversions of its putative author—are climaxed respectively by the account of Aeolism and the "Digression concerning Madness." For in the eighth section, the general course of the historical allegory has led to an elaborate, independent fiction, a myth *sui generis,* of unique humorous power. The ninth section—which I shall consider in my final chapter—involves a parallel and even more memorable expansion of the activities of the *persona* into a discourse from which emerge the principles of belief basic to the entire satiric enterprise.

The Learned *Aeolists,* maintain the Original Cause of all Things to be *Wind,* from which Principle this whole Universe was at first produced, and into which it must at last be resolved; that the same Breath which had kindled, and blew *up* the Flame of Nature, should one Day blow it *out* (p. 150).

Like the belief in the tailor's divinity, the single article of faith described in this first sentence of the Aeolist chapter is defended by conceits and word play and then made the basis for an elaborate mock-system of beliefs and rituals. Swift purports to offer only a few of the "most important Precepts" (although "the *Compass* of their Doctrine took in two and thirty Points"), and he does not here provide the systematic pseudo-philosophy of the section on tailor-worship. We learn of the Aeolist gods (the four winds) and their devils (the "camelion" and the windmill) and are offered an amusing account of the Scottish origins of the chief god, the North wind. But the "Mysteries and Rites" of the Aeolists are described in lavish and unlovely detail. If Puritan "inspiration" is equated with wind, the opportunities for a lewdly imaginative interpretation of Enthusiastic habits are abundant, and Swift's account of Puritan pulpits and preachers, grimaces and mumblings, ecstasies and visitations exploits them without inhibition.

The most obvious satiric object of this fable is, of course, Enthusiasm itself and, more specifically, the religious manifestations to which the term applied in Swift's day. If the text is not sufficiently clear about the dissenting denominations under attack, the fifth-edition notes (with their references to "Seditious" and "Enthusiastick" preachers as well as to the Quakers) make the identification unmistakable—as Swift clearly wished it to be. This aspect of the myth requires no further explanation than do any of the obvious assaults upon Dissent for which, elsewhere in the allegory, Jack is the regular vehicle.

A secondary object of satire in Swift's absurdly mechanistic treatment of the wind as a deity may be considered. Even in this section of predominantly religious satire, the opportunity for attacks on scientific materialism seems not to have been neglected. Pneumatic experiments were common undertakings of the Royal Society's projectors and though Wotton is probably not the satiric victim in a section which develops from the religious allegory, his assessment of modern achievements with respect to air suggests the importance with which such inquiries were viewed. "There is," he asserts, "scarce any Body, whose Theory is now so near being completed as is that of the Air."[29] And in his own pseudo-mechanical account, Swift may be expressing the amusement he feels, as in the case of acoustical experiments, at the scientific language in which invisible phenomena are treated as visible and palpable.

Another possible object of Swift's satire lies in his adoption of the Hermetic jargon in such references as that to "what the *Adepti* understand by their *Anima Mundi*" (p. 150) or to Paracelsus and the *Quinta essentia* (p. 152). In these fugitive references to the "dark authors," however, there are few grounds for regarding hermetic mysticism as the principal satiric target.[30] Though occultism may have been regarded in some quarters as "Philosophical Enthusiasm," it could only have appeared as a disreputable counterpart of the far more formidable religious manifestations of that disorder. Occultism, like Grub-street, or the doctrines of Lucretius, serves Swift, I think, as a kind of ready-made pejorative, the terms and authorities of which automatically discredit the argument in which they are invoked.

[29] *Reflections*, pp. 182–83; see also pp. 243–44.

[30] In a fifth-edition note (*Tale*, p. 127), Swift forthrightly stamps Thomas Vaughan's cabalistic *Anthroposophia Theomagica* as "a Piece of the most unintelligible Fustian, that, perhaps was ever publish'd in any Language." This uncharacteristically direct dismissal suggests that Swift felt no need to discredit occultism satirically but was prepared rather to exploit its general disrepute in stigmatizing more immediate and substantial victims. His interest in the occult (displayed almost exclusively in the *Tale*) seems to have been confined at most to its amusingly controversial or easily readable aspects. Aside from two astrological works, he seems to have owned none of the "dark" writings (see Harold Williams, *Dean Swift's Library*, pp. 85–86) and much of his occult "lore" could have been gleaned directly from Thomas Browne's *Vulgar Errors*, from which, for instance, he appears directly to have derived his knowledge of Paracelsus (see *Tale*, pp. 152, 165, and 351). The controversy between Thomas Vaughan and Henry More seems to have caught his attention only as a long-settled dispute in which More was totally victorious; for an account of this bitter quarrel see Vaughan's *Works*, ed. A. E. Waite (London, 1919), pp. 468–73, and *Conway Letters*, ed. Marjorie Nicholson (New Haven, 1930), pp. 72–73. Well before the writing of the *Tale* the occult philosophers could not have been taken very seriously, for their most famous satiric treatment—Butler's "Hermetic Philosopher"— exploits the occultist as a stock figure of fun, whose eccentricities are obvious; see *The Genuine Remains in Verse and Prose of Mr. Samuel Butler* (London, 1759), II, 225–52, as well as a similar stereotype in *Hudibras*, Part I, Canto I, lines 529–622.

Whatever secondary facets there may be to Swift's satire in Section VIII, therefore, it seems clear that the assault upon Enthusiasm is the chief satiric procedure in the myth of the Aeolists and that what is notable about the section as satire is presumably related to the effectiveness of that assault. It is accordingly somewhat surprising to note that this attack proceeds upon grounds which are far from novel and is directed against aspects of Enthusiasm which were matters of common scorn. In the "Digression concerning Madness" Swift's basic device is a species of "inverted" inspiration so that it is an experience not of elevation but of ugly affliction by madness. In the Aeolist myth he similarly seizes upon the phenomenon of inspiration and reduces it to a kind of nasty, self-induced seizure. This debasing technique—and even the happy play upon the windy connotations of the word "inspiration"—is by no means original with Swift. Inspection of a single earlier, popular book—one familiar, moreover, to Swift himself[31]—will indicate the degree to which Swift's actual assault upon Puritanism had been anticipated.

Henry More's *Enthusiasmus Triumphatus: or a Brief Discourse of the Nature, Causes, Kinds and Cure of Enthusiasm* was first published in 1656 and was reprinted, with separate pagination, in *A Collection of Several Philosophical Writings of Henry More* (London, 1662).[32] In his widely known assault upon Puritanism, More employs a pseudo-clinical approach to Enthusiasm and, as the title suggests, purports soberly to discuss the phenomenon as an affliction with its "Natures, Causes, Kinds, and Cures." Swift and More, furthermore, not only have in common this general derogatory approach to Enthusiasm as a pathological condition but employ, in many instances, strikingly similar images and fictional theories.[33]

[31] Fifth-edition note in *Tale*, p. 127.

[32] I have used the latter edition for all references. It might be noted that the original appearance of *Enthusiasmus Triumphatus* (1656) was as a preface to a new edition of two tracts which More had earlier issued in an attack on Vaughan.

[33] An admirable discussion of the grounds on which Enthusiasm and, linked with it, Imagination were suspect during the seventeenth century can be found in George Williamson's "The Restoration Revolt against Enthusiasm," *Studies in Philology*, XXX (October, 1933), 571–603. This study first called my attention to suggestive resemblances between such devices and ideas as those of More and the later inventions of Swift. I have traced correspondences between the *Tale* and the writings of More and Casaubon with greater detail than the present study permits in my unpublished doctoral dissertation, *Swift's Satire in "A Tale of a Tub"* (University of

Although More initially defines Enthusiasm as "a full but false perswasion in a man that he is inspired," he moves rapidly to a quasi-mechanistic inquiry into its cause—which, it is soon discovered, is Melancholy. More's treatment of this infirmity is extremely suggestive of Swift's, even to his various references to wind and the debasement of wind-images. Thus, after a discussion of the operations of Melancholy and an account of "material causes" conducive to Enthusiasm (wine, the tarantula bite, St. Vitus' dance, etc.), he considers the particular religious manifestations of Melancholy—the Enthusiasm, that is, which Melancholy induces. Of the Enthusiast he observes:

such a *Melancholist* as this must be very highly puffed up, and not only fancy himself *inspired,* but believe himself such a special piece of *Light* and *Holiness* . . . that he will take upon him to reform or rather *anull,* the very *Law* and *Religion* he is born under. . . .[34]

In such people, argues More, it is often common to associate "greatness" (i.e., size) with the presence of God:

Whence it is a strong temptation with a *Melancholist* when he feels a storm of devotion or zeal come upon him like a mighty wind, his heart being full of affection, his head pregnant with clear and sensible representations, and his mouth flowing and streaming with fit and powerfull expressions, such as would astonish an ordinary Auditorie to hear, it is, I say, a shrewd temptation to think that it is the very *Spirit of God* that then moves supernaturally in him; when as all that excess of zeal and affection and fluency of words is most palpably to be resolved into the power of Melancholy, which is a kind of naturall inebriation.[35]

The correspondence between these passages and Swift's description of Aeolist inspiration is clear. One is tempted to substitute "Aeolist" for "Melancholist" in More's arguments, and, in effect, Swift seems to have seized upon the wind, which More uses in a figurative sense, and effectually to have substituted it for Melancholy as the moving cause of Enthusiast antics. Both writers reduce the causes of Enthusiasm to a single monistic source; More asserts that "Fervour,

---

Chicago, 1953), pp. 278–83. In *Swift and Anglican Rationalism,* pp. 60–65, 107–15, Harth carefully discusses More's relationship to Swift, although with an emphasis rather different from my own.

[34] *Enthusiasmus Triumphatus,* p. 11.

[35] Pp. 11–12.

Zeal, and Spirit, is in effect all one,"[36] while for Swift the same thing is true of "Spiritus, Animus, Afflatus, or Anima" (p. 151). And perhaps More comes closest to Swift's conceit and his actual language when he goes on:

The *Spirit* then that wings the *Enthusiast* in such a wonderful manner, is nothing else but that *Flatulency* which is in the *Melancholy* complexion, and rises out of the *Hypochondriacal* Humour upon some occasional heat, as Winde out of an Aeolipila applied to the fire. Which fume mounting into the Head, being first actuated and spirited and somewhat refined by the warmth of the Heart, fills the mind with variety of *Imaginations,* and so quickens and enlarges *Invention,* that it makes the Enthusiast to admiration *fluent* and *eloquent,* he being as it were drunk with new wine drawn from that Cellar of his own that lies in the lowest region of the Body, though he be not aware of it, but takes it to be true *Nectar,* and those waters of life that spring from above.[37]

An examination of *Enthusiasmus Triumphatus* will provide the reader with a number of further, equally striking parallels between More and Swift.[38] It is impossible to establish the extent to which Swift made deliberate use of More's ideas, but, in any case, the question is of secondary importance. What is of greater significance is the fact that the most important aspects of the "system" by which Swift's attack on Enthusiasm proceeds seem naturally to have been invited by Puritan habits and dogmas and, clearly reflected in the

[36] P. 12.

[37] *Ibid.*

[38] More offers interesting resemblances to the "Digression concerning Madness" as well as to the Aeolist myth, in particular in his mechanistic account of the causes of Enthusiasm (pp. 5–9) and his equation of Fancy with madness (p. 38). The relationship of religious zeal with hermetic lore is indicated by More, but again in a manner to suggest that "Philosophical Enthusiasts" need not be taken seriously, since their writings "will sufficiently demonstrate to all that are not smitten in some measure with the like Lunacy," that they are "but Counterfeits, that is, Enthusiasts" (p. 29). Even such a detail as Swift's reference to the Delphic oracle is anticipated (p. 28). And we should note, as well, the general tone adopted by More; for the most part he maintains an air of mock-didactic sobriety, interrupted by occasional vehement denunciations, but the false respect which pervades his writing is illustrated by such passages as his introduction to a long list of Paracelsus' follies, in which he proclaims, "Listen, therefore, attentively, for I shall relate very great mysteries" (p. 29).

writings of Swift's predecessors, had become virtual commonplaces of anti-Enthusiast polemic.[39]

If, therefore, this famous chapter of the *Tale* is considered purely as a new satiric attack upon the Puritans, it must be viewed as the exploitation of a well-established, hostile stereotype through an invention or conceit which, in its basic outlines, is by no means original. More's work alone reveals that, to the extent religious Enthusiasts are abused upon readily discernible grounds, many of Swift's points had previously been made. Thus the attribution of inspiration to a single base and material source, the derisive representation of the Puritans' pathological eloquence, inflated self-esteem, and alternate exaltation and depression, the equation of the term "spirit" with meaner concepts, and even the analogy between inspiration and flatulency all appear plainly in the writings of at least one earlier assailant of Puritan zeal. In a few instances in which assaults on historical manifestations of Enthusiasm in Swift's chapter have not been anticipated by More, the satire is directed to obviously vulnerable matters, such as the Scotch origins of Enthusiasm or the female clergy among the Quakers.

[39] A year before More's work, there appeared Meric Casaubon's *A Treatise concerning Enthusiasme as it is an Effect of Nature: but is Mistaken by many for either Divine Inspiration or Diabolical Possession* (London, 1655). Lacking the pseudo- scientific air of inquiry to be found in More, Casaubon is equally hostile to religious Enthusiasm. Following a distinction between natural and supernatural Enthusiasm, he assigns many kinds of Enthusiastic manifestation, most of which have religious applications, to the category of natural Enthusiasm and hence to "an extraordinary, transcendent, but natural fervency, or pregnancy of the soul, spirit, or brain, producing strange effects, apt to be mistaken for supernatural" (p. 17). His appearance of objectivity is belied by his introductory warning that the reader must not "embrace a Cloud, or a Fogge for a Deitie; it is done by many, but it is a foul mistake: let him take heed of it" (Sig. A1ʳ).

The degree to which such attacks may be said to have become a "tradition" by the time of the *Tale* may be inferred from Williamson's article ("The Restoration Revolt against Enthusiasm," pp. 578–99). See also Oliver Elton, "Reason and Enthusiasm in the Eighteenth Century," in Vol. X of *Essays and Studies by Members of the English Association* (Oxford, 1924), pp. 122–36.

Evidence of the way in which disparate attacks, of varying degrees of seriousness, had, by 1700, crystallized into a firm position under philosophic auspices can be seen in Locke's chapter on Enthusiasm (chap. xix, Book IV), which was added to the fourth edition of his *Essays* in that year. His examination and rejection of Enthusiasts proceeds from a brief and confident characterization of them as "men in whom melancholy has mixed with devotion" (John Locke, *An Essay concerning Human Understanding,* ed. A. C. Fraser [Oxford, 1894], II, 431).

In what, then, does the power and presumed excellence of the chapter consist? Once more, I think, the answer lies in the imaginative development of a fiction which, as it is gleefully expanded, loses its analogic dimension and acquires the character of robust comic fantasy. For the aspects of the Aeolist myth which are most memorable are those whose correspondence with the historical manifestations of Enthusiasm are impossible—and unprofitable—to establish. Thus the bellows-pumping, flatulating, bladder-carrying priests, the argument for wind as a first cause, and the solemn inclusion of superstitions concerning the Laplanders are instances in which the fiction created by Swift has moved along of its own force into conceits which, while eminently amusing and appropriate developments of the fiction itself, are satirically irrelevant with respect to vulnerable aspects of Puritan doctrine or practice. Seen in this light, scholarly concern for the symbolic significance of the "camelion" and windmill devils in the Aeolist system appears somewhat misdirected.[40] These objects, in fact, are perfect specimens of inventions which, though they may reflect in a general way upon Enthusiastic moodiness, represent no authentic phenomena but are developments of the fable itself. A religion which worships wind will abominate the chameleon who devours and the windmill which buffets wind. The "significance" of such conceits cannot be established if we view the section as an exclusively satiric construction, but their appropriateness to the context of a humorous fiction is entirely plain.

The Aeolist system is not an allegory but a scandalous myth. Here Swift deliberately suspends his allegorical account of religious history and embarks, not on an actual "digression," but a new and independent fabrication. His obligations to the satiric story of the three brothers are met by attributing Aeolism to Jack and by the broadly punitive effect of the identification of Aeolism with Enthusiasm. As satire, the fantastic conceits of mutual inflation, eructation, and secret reinflation are extravagant libels in which the merest echo of historical relevance is belatedly and inconsequentially supplied by such references as those to belching through the nose. Swift is largely indifferent to the persuasiveness or even the historical aptness of his fiction. The indifference is justified, for the reader, by the fact that the fiction has taken on a life of its own. It develops (in a manner

---

[40] *Tale*, pp. 159–60. The editors' note at this point reveals the range of serious conjectures which have been advanced to explain the "devils."

reminiscent of the clothes-philosophy) upon self-contained principles rather than upon systematic analogy to authentic aspects of Puritanism.

Here, I think, is the essence of the "playfulness" which has been attributed to the *Tale*.[41] It source is not, in the last analysis, our frustrated expectations, the abandonment or alteration of Swift's presumed "positions," or the apparent shapelessness of the work. It lies, rather, in Swift's willingness to pursue the rich possibilities of his satiric invention, to develop the fiction which, despite its initial introduction as a satiric instrument, soon expands beyond the limits of satiric utility. The germ of the Aeolist myth is undeniably the alleged habits of the Puritans. In its complete and final form it is an exploitation not of Puritan folly but of the deep sources of the comic.

We need not explore the question of what basically produces laughter to recognize the elementary comic formula which provides the humor of the Aeolist myth. Wind, gas, vapor, noise, the most mechanical of man's biological activities: these form one group of Swift's ingredients. Aspiration, inspiration, eloquence, soul, spirit, divinity: these form the other. The purely humorous possibilities inherent in the juxtaposition of the two—possibilities inveterately exploited in the unpublished humor of the ages—require no solemn exposition here. Lechery, blasphemy, and animal inadvertence lie at the core of a huge body of informal humor. To suggest that the appeal of this section is, in large measure, that of successful obscenity, of the dirty joke, is only to underscore its fundamentally comic character. As Aristotle's dictum that "the Ridiculous is a Species of the Ugly" shrewdly points to the reason for the persistence of lewd humor, the same assumption tacitly appears in the more ambitious formulas of other students of the comic. For Bergson, the source of laughter is "something mechanical encrusted upon the living,"[42] and for Monsignor Knox, the sphere of humor is predominantly "man and his activities, in circumstances so incongruous, so unexpectedly incongruous, as to detract from their human dignity."[43] On

[41] "No book on Swift has ever done justice to the infinite playfulness of his mind; the trait is, nevertheless, fundamental in all his works and in all his behavior": George Sherburn, "Methods in Books about Swift," *Studies in Philology*, XXXV (October, 1938), 644.

[42] Henri Bergson, *Laughter: An Essay on the Meaning of the Comic*, trans. C. Brereton and F. Rothwell (New York, 1911).

[43] Ronald A. Knox, *Essays in Satire* (London, 1928), p. 18.

the well-established foundations of anti-Puritan satire, Swift has created a new structure. It has not been created, however, to expose Puritan weaknesses in a new light or ultimately even to exacerbate the contempt in which the Puritans are held. As compared with the works of More or Casaubon or L'Estrange or even Dryden, it is novel and permanent because it is an object of delight, whose appeal is the timeless one of broad and unrestrained comic invention.

III

I have said that the power of the satiric fiction itself is more generally apparent in punitive than in persuasive satire, since our satisfaction with the former species comes largely from the originality and aptness of the satirist's invention. From the specimens we have already examined, moreover, it will be seen that the fictional developments of punitive satire, like those of comedy itself, tend to be more elaborately and obviously fanciful than those of the persuasive species. It is not by accident that the punitive and comic power of *A Tale of a Tub* is found most readily in the gratuitous "systems" and descriptive details which embellish the narrative rather than in the central allegory or the digressive speculations of the supposed author.

Conversely, where the satiric fiction consists largely in the posture assumed by the satiric writer, whether as a totally fictional *persona* or in less extreme degrees of dissimulation, we are not so likely to find a purely punitive form of assault. Effective parody, for example, is ordinarily a genuine type of satiric exposure in which, by *reductio ad absurdum* or some form of distortion, the satirist seeks to heighten our awareness of his victim's infirmities. Merely to reproduce in exaggerated form, for the sake of amusement, weaknesses which are already quite evident to all is, as a rule, a rather puerile form of punitive derision. Parody, whether of manner or substance, if conducted for satiric ends, assumes its most artful character chiefly when, with new acuteness, it underscores or discloses those vulnerable qualities of its victims on which, in effect, the satirist bases his case. This is largely what is achieved by such a complete work as *A Tritical Essay upon the Faculties of the Mind* as well as by such single passages as the parodic assaults upon L'Estrange, Marsh, Dryden, and others which can be noted in *A Tale of a Tub*.

But if we recall Swift's high talent for fantasy together with his zest and capacity for self-disguise, it is not surprising that his fictions of the "first person" will occasionally strike us with the force of those narrative constructions we have called "quasi-libels." Having, that is, assumed the identity of his victim, he may be expected at times to exploit his fictional role not only for the disclosure of his enemy's faults but for a performance designed to delight us by the novel, if rhetorically irrelevant, foolery in which he engages. Thus there are times when, in the postures he adopts as in the stories he tells, Swift seems to succumb to the spirit of playfulness, malicious or otherwise, in relative indifference to the persuasiveness of what he writes.

To some extent this is certainly true of Swift's assumption of the role of Isaac Bickerstaff, in which he succeeded, with a thoroughness granted to few satirists, in discountenancing the charlatan astrologer, John Partridge.[44] In playing the part of a lesser (or perhaps a super) Partridge, Swift was, after a fashion, engaging in parody and carrying, to a memorably absurd extreme, the cautious ambiguity and self-confident particularity which alternately mark the predictions of the fraudulent almanac-maker. It is also possible that, as recent studies have suggested, Swift's assault on Partridge was motivated not merely by the love of a jest at the expense of a culpable victim but by a real desire to discredit activities which he soberly regarded as subversive.[45]

Most students of Swift, while expressing some admiration for the Bickerstaff papers, tend to regard them as relatively "light" productions, implying thereby a difference in degree between these frivolous writings and those satiric attacks which proceed from more weighty grounds against more formidable enemies. What must, I think, be recognized is that here Swift's satire is of a different kind from that which is epitomized in such compelling documents as *A Modest Proposal* or, in fact, in such other assaults upon individual men as *The Importance of the Guardian Considered*. The fact that the Bickerstaff performance was a successful hoax is not directly relevant to its stature as satire. A hoax, to the extent that it depends upon its fiction being taken for truth, does not properly lie within the satiric spectrum, since the fictions of effective satire are always recognizable for what they are. But the Bickerstaff papers have intrin-

[44] *Prose Works*, II, 141–70.

[45] See, in particular, Davis' Introduction in *Prose Works*, II, x–xi.

sically delightful qualities which have nothing to do with the consequences of their publication. In many passages they display a lunatic extravagance which transcends all resemblance to the productions of Partridge. Swift, beginning as a pseudo-Partridge, embarks on his own career as almanac-maker, moving with a kind of spiteful exuberance to ever novel predictions which embrace, at the high point of fantasy, the imaginary death of Partridge himself. Here is literary imagination of the nature if not the magnitude of the great fantasies in *Gulliver's Travels* and the *Tale,* lavished on the playful elaboration of a satiric fiction. The satiric "connection" with reality is often tenuous, but from this kind of writing we do not require it.

The "runaway author" who, properly enough, soon dominates the Bickerstaff papers appears to an interesting extent in the famous *Fragment of a Discourse concerning the Mechanical Operation of the Spirit.*[46] There is good reason, of course, to search for the persuasive ends of this document. In its conception and its title, the "fragment" is rather plainly parodic, reducing to absurdity the mechanistic doctrines of the new science by applying them to that realm which, above all others, is not subject to their rules. There is, moreover, a brilliant plurality of satiric targets achieved by the application of this assumed approach to the phenomena of Enthusiasm. The mechanism, so outrageously applied by the Moderns in their search for universal truths about matters genuinely spiritual, is here turned upon Enthusiasm, which is shown—familiarly and satisfyingly for the anti-Puritan reader—to have its origin in the quite mechanical "corruption of sense." Yet as an "exposure," a convincing assault upon either projectors or Fanatics, the *Mechanical Operation* seems quite unsatisfactory. Such attacks as are made directly proceed upon many of the same grounds and through many of the same devices as those found in *A Tale of a Tub* (which, of course, from its first edition on appeared in a single volume with *The Battle of the Books* and the *Mechanical Operation*).[47] Despite a variety of brief satiric

[46] Printed in the Guthkelch–Nichol Smith edition of the *Tale,* pp. 259–89.

[47] Various views concerning the relationship between the *Mechanical Operation* and, in particular, Sections VIII and IX of the *Tale* are summarized by James L. Clifford in "Swift's *Mechanical Operation of the Spirit*" in *Pope and His Contemporaries: Essays Presented to George Sherburn,* ed. J. Clifford and L. Landa (Oxford, 1949), pp. 141–44. Whatever Swift's original plans may have been, it is very hard to imagine a structural relationship between the "fragment" and those parts of the *Tale* it most resembles. On the one hand, its mechanical scheme is patently different

asides and ingenious sallies, this work would, I believe, be truly a
"fragment"—and a redundant and uninteresting one—were it not
for the lewd, totally fantastic "theory" which it develops.

Here, in a manner not unlike that of the Aeolist section in the
Tale, Swift has begun on firm satiric grounds: the Aeolist myth has
its genesis in the tale of the brothers, while the *Mechanical Operation* begins with the parodic assumption of the projector-victim's
identity. In both instances, however, the ensuing fiction develops beyond any point at which it can be said to reflect upon actuality. Swift
has again, as it were, succumbed to the rich, if obscene, possibilities
of his artifice. In the "fragment" the theory is supposedly that of a
projector, and it is a theory about the workings of Enthusiasm. In its
substance, however, it is based at most on shaky stereotypes and hostile canards; it reflects, however distortedly, no authentic weakness;
it requires from us the barest recognition and no inference or reflection. Our response, whether amused or distasteful, is plainly elicited
by the grotesque and bawdy invention itself.

Any discussion of Swift's use of the *persona* leads inevitably to
that complex and elusive role he assumes as putative author of *A
Tale of a Tub.* As we have already suggested, exhaustive generalizations about the character he has thus created are made virtually impossible by the shifting and often incompatible qualities which we
recognize in him as the book proceeds. He is at times a patent debased caricature of individual satiric victims, at other times a kind of
omnibus representation of various pervasive intellectual infirmities,
at still other times a shrewd if oblique observer, whose convictions
are hard to distinguish from those of the historic Jonathan Swift.
What we must understand about these widely diversified roles is that
they are assumed in the pursuit of equally diversified literary ends
and that the nature of the *persona* changes as he is variously employed in the interests of persuasion, or punitive satire, or of entirely
playful comedy. When he provides us with a mordant but recognizable distortion of Dryden's servility, L'Estrange's self-pity, or Wotton's arrogance, he is drawing new attention to what are, for him,
damning weaknesses in these men. When, in the role of a critic,
projector, or Grub-street hack, he appears to be engaged in some

from the wind-philosophy of Section VIII, but, on the other hand, the objects and
grounds for its attack sufficiently resemble those of the Aeolist myth so that, if linked
to the latter, it would appear to be a thin and redundant addition.

fantastic act of unconscious self-debasement, he is involved in punitive satire. When his playful ineptitude or eccentricity bears no discernible resemblance to the actual follies of actual victims, he is
undertaking a largely comic performance.

But if it is impossible to discover in the *character* of Swift's *persona* sufficient consistency to provide the *Tale* with a comprehensive
principle of order, something of this sort can, I believe, be found in
his *performance*. The informing framework of the *Tale* is one of
true literary parody; its satiric assault is directed not against a set of
moral or intellectual vices embodied in a *man* but against a form of
activity—a literary enterprise, debasingly represented in the entire
gesture of writing "a tale of a tub."

Swift's emphasis on purely literary abuses within the *Tale* has
prompted Herbert Davis to assert that "the real object of Swift's satire in the *Tale* is the corruption he saw in English letters during the
latter half of the seventeenth century, destroying what he felt to be
its finest achievements."[48] While Davis' conclusion calls, I believe,
for severe qualification, it is true that satire on literary habits accounts for the broadest and most sustained posture which Swift assumes, namely the *act of writing* a book in conformity with prevailing literary customs.

In the simplest structural terms, the character of the *Tale* is derived from this fiction. Of the 210 pages which the entire work occupies in the Guthkelch–Nichol Smith edition, well over one-third
are devoted to the prefatory materials. Within this substantial area
of the book, religious issues receive almost no satiric treatment[49] and
at only one point are the problems of parties in the Ancients-Moderns controversy clearly singled out. The huge preponderance of the
satire, on the other hand, is aimed at targets which are of an almost
exclusively literary character—either literary practices so widespread
as to be familiar to every reader or habits of composition which can
readily be attributed to an individual author.

The methods which Swift employs within these pages cover a wide
range of satiric technique, from the simple parodic adoption of an
antagonist's manner by the putative author to the satiric allegory in

[48] *The Satire of Jonathan Swift* (New York, 1947), p. 17.

[49] A conspicuous exception is the treatment of the pulpit as an "Oratorial Machine"
in the "Introduction" (*Tale*, p. 58).

which, as in the tale of the Leicester-Fields mountebank,[50] the narrator's position is of minimal importance and his tale carries the entire satiric burden. Varied satiric procedures, moreover, operate in close conjunction with one another. The list of "living authors" which the writer submits to Posterity (pp. 34–38) is a splendid instance of this: the immediate satiric device is debasement through association, but this is made possible by a fictional situation in which the apologist declares to Posterity the existence of literature which would otherwise be quickly forgotten; and this situation is, in turn, incorporated within the general conceit of an address to Posterity, itself a mockery of the practice of L'Estrange.

What all of these highly diversified materials succeed in doing, however, is to establish a putative author and, more significantly, to suggest something about the basic character of his artistic undertaking. There is nothing very explicit in our expectations; they are, indeed, notable for their very latitude, and the air of digressiveness and even caprice which pervades the introductory pages in a sense prepares us for an assortment of postures and topics which will be unexpected and even inconsistent. We do understand, however, that these early sections have been written in mock-defiance or (what amounts to much the same thing) parody of common literary customs. The most obvious and the most sustained fiction, therefore, is, as it were, the author's pretense that the *act* of writing the *Tale* is colored by the habits and values of his literary milieu.

It is not an accident, in my opinion, that the "Conclusion" of the *Tale* is nominally included by a desire to conform to literary custom. It has been described, in the closing words of the preceding section, as "the Ceremonial Part of an accomplished Writer, and therefore, by a Courtly *Modern,* least of all others to be omitted" (p. 205). As such it returns the reader to the "outermost" frame of the work, to the comprehensive fiction which represents the book as a sober literary enterprise in which fashionable conventions may be observed or defied but must always be taken into account. Thus the *Tale* is enclosed, at beginning and end, by the fiction of an idle story, bearing no direct relationship to attacks upon Modern learning or religious controversy. In the end, as in the beginning, the author of the *Tale* asks primarily that his work be regarded as a

---

[50] In the "Preface" (*Tale,* p. 46).

specimen—now special, now typical—of the literature of the age. In doing so he allows his own character and that of his work to remain sufficiently unspecified so as to permit the detailed satire to move in many directions or to become suspended in the interests of pure comic artifice. Yet the book itself is entirely "in the modern kind," and from it we derive a sustained and shabby picture of the writing, publication, and reception of books in Swift's day. The successful piece of literature, Swift implies, is truly "a tale of a tub." Produced from dubious motives, with its formal adherence to convention concealing a poverty of content, it is published by venal opportunists for the fleeting enjoyment of a shallow, capricious public. The *Tale* purports to be this sort of book. Its author dedicates, digresses, boasts, toadies, and complains not because it is necessarily in his character to do these things but because they are literary habits appropriate to the time. If we seek a *structural* principle for the *Tale* —one which permits, rather than is dictated by, the satiric, expository, and comic procedures which it encloses—we must find it in this very broad parody of literary custom. The model on which the *Tale* is constructed is not to be defined in terms of the beliefs or characters of men but can be found in the literary practices of Swift's day.

Only in terms this general can we say anything very meaningful about the total nature or function of the *Tale*'s supposed author. As we have suggested, moreover, it is the very latitude of the fiction and of the expectation it engenders which permits the remarkable diversity of procedures and effects which are achieved within its limits. Swift has adopted a fiction which commits him to very little; his *persona* is not irretrievably a fool or a knave, although it is more than likely that a book "in the modern kind" will reflect some evidences of folly and knavery. His only responsibility is, as it were, to a tradition of irresponsibility. Yet, on the other hand, if he produces flashes of scornful insight or even of sound common sense, they are not precluded by the character of the literary undertaking.

IV

The subtle uses to which Swift puts the *persona* in the *Tale* defy formulation, but they make themselves abundantly clear whenever we encounter this curious spokesman. Though he may plainly proclaim his identity, associating himself firmly with causes and customs toward which Swift is obviously hostile, it is unsafe to assume that, for any length of time, his arguments will simply be those of a fool or a rogue. His most extravagant gestures—on the surface, gross caricatures of prevailing literary or learned practice—can be accompanied by undisguised insights into human error. His outrageous mock-logical excursions can rest on a foundation of brutal truth. Stylistic parody is rarely more than a partial "key" to his function in any particular passage, for even as, in mock-deference, he apes the manner of Swift's victims, he is likely to display a devastating awareness of their infirmities.

Here, for example, is the voice of the *persona,* plainly identifying himself at the beginning of Section V of the *Tale,* "A Digression in the Modern Kind," whose very title is a signal of parodic intention:

We whom the World is pleased to honor with the Title of *Modern Authors,* should never have been able to compass our great Design of an everlasting Remembrance, and never-dying Fame, if our Endeavours had not been so highly serviceable to the general Good of Mankind. This, *O Universe,* is the Adventurous Attempt of me thy Secretary;

> *—Quemvis perferre laborem*
> *Suadet, & inducit noctes vigilare serenas.*

To this End, I have some Time since, with a World of Pains and Art, dissected the Carcass of *Humane Nature,* and read many useful Lectures upon the several Parts, both *Containing* and *Contained;* till at last it *smelt* so strong, I could preserve it no longer. Upon which, I have been at a great Expence to fit up all the Bones with exact Contexture, and in due Symmetry; so that I am ready to shew a very compleat Anatomy thereof to all curious *Gentlemen and others.* But not to Digress farther in the midst of a Digression, as I have known some Authors inclose Digressions in one another, like a Nest of Boxes; I do affirm, that having carefully cut up *Humane Nature,* I have found a very strange, new, and important Discovery; That the Publick Good of Mankind is performed by two Ways, *Instruction,* and *Diversion.* And I have farther proved in my said several Readings, (which, perhaps, the World may one day see, if I can prevail on any Friend to steal a Copy, or on certain Gentlemen of my Admirers, to be very Importunate) that, as Mankind is now disposed, he receives much greater Advantage by being *Diverted* than *Instructed;* His Epidemical Diseases being *Fastidiosity, Amorphy,* and *Oscitation;* whereas in the present universal Empire of Wit and Learning, there seems but little Matter left for *Instruction.* However, in Compliance with a Lesson of Great Age and Authority, I have attempted carrying the Point in all its

Heights; and accordingly throughout this Divine Treatise, have skilfully kneaded up both together with a *Layer* of *Utile* and a *Layer* of *Dulce* (pp. 123–24).

"A Digression in the Modern Kind" purports to be a rambling, unnecessary affair, "a long Digression unsought for, and an universal Censure unprovoked" (p. 132). As is generally the case with the digressions and prefatory materials of the *Tale,* however, its general structure is perfectly plain. The author is seeking to make clear "the Beauties and Excellencies" of his book. Thus he begins with his discussion of instruction and diversion; he makes it clear that his undertaking is to be "an universal System in a small portable Volume, of all Things that are to be Known, or Believed, or Imagined, or Practised in Life" (p. 125), facetiously citing an imaginary hermetic nostrum which has aided him; he recognizes that Homer may have attempted a similar undertaking but laments, Wotton-wise, the poet's "momentous Defects" in modern learning; and he concludes with a defense of his own self-advertising by deferring to contemporary examples—notably that of Dryden.

In terms this simple, each major portion of this section can be said to involve a putative author whose most egregious foolishness can be seen as a debasement of Wotton's claims for modernity or as mockingly servile deference to prevailing literary habits. But the voice of the *persona,* as it emerges in the detailed movement of each argument, is far more than a distorted echo of Wotton or Bentley or even a generic "Modern." With even greater flexibility than he displays in his allegory, Swift endows his *persona* with a kaleidoscopic diversity of nuances and tones, ranging from near lunacy through the perverse wisdom of a *faux ingénu* to something close to direct, penetrating shrewdness. Even where his performance can be described as parody, it ordinarily involves more than mere distorting mimicry. Again and again, a conceit or image employed by the *persona* captures, with a special aptness, the quintessential folly against which Swift directs his attack. Swift is a superb parodist of manner, entirely willing to caricature the broad, obvious facets of his enemies' style and substance; but almost always he is concurrently interested in the power of particular words and phrases to push the attack one step further, to refine folly to the ultimate point of absurdity.

In the initial passage of the "Digression in the Modern Kind," this satiric complexity is typically illustrated. The author, as a self-styled Modern, seems at once to assume the role of surrogate-victim. His beliefs and mannerisms, we assume, will be those of Swift's victims. Stylistically, the passage displays the sententiousness, pedantry, and self-consciousness which Swift claims to find in his Modern enemies, Wotton and Bentley above all. The quotation from Lucretius is here, as so often in the *Tale*, a further signal of arrogance and impiety; readers familiar with *De rerum natura* may recall its context and the author's claim "to display clear lights before your mind, whereby you may see into the heart of things hidden."[51]

But the image of the "Secretary of the Universe" is something more than an overblown parody of Modern pretentiousness. It represents the preposterous extreme to which mockery of such undertakings as Wotton's *Reflections upon Ancient and Modern Learning* can be pushed. For in his preface to that work, Wotton sets out his vision of the perfectability of human knowledge and his confident and sanguine account of what has thus far been achieved in the pursuit of this extraordinary goal. It is not difficult to detect what Swift, in both his piety and his skepticism, found offensive in such a passage as this:

> In the first place therefore, I imagine, that if the several Boundaries of *Ancient and Modern Learning* were once impartially stated, Men would know better what was still unfinished, and what was, in a manner, perfect; and consequently what deserved the greatest Application, upon the score of its being imperfect: which might be a good Inducement to set those Men who, having a great Genius, find also in themselves an Inclination to promote Learning, upon Subjects wherein they might, probably, meet with Success answerable to their Endeavours: By which means, Knowledge in all its Parts, might at last be compleated.[52]

If we cannot share Swift's disgust with Wotton, we can understand what prompted it: the systematic assessment of all present knowledge, the bland assumption that some of it is, "in a manner, perfect,"

[51] Lucretius, *De rerum natura*, I, 140–45. I cite the translation of W. H. D. Rouse in the Loeb Classical Library edition (Cambridge, Mass., and London, 1924), p. 13.

[52] *Reflections*, pp. i–ii. Wotton's "Conclusion" is equally relevant. Some future age, he believes, "may raise real knowledge upon the Foundations laid in this our Age, to the utmost possible Perfection to which it can be brought . . . and thereby effectually immortalize the Memories of those who laid those Foundations, and collected those Materials which were so serviceable to them in compleating the noble Work" (p. 395).

the confidence that, by the labors of this age and those to come, all knowledge will actually be perfected. These beliefs of Wotton's are epitomized in Swift's "small portable Volume of all Things," the compilation of which is a task for no one but the "Secretary of the Universe." Thus, in his initial parodic performance, Swift's *persona* is not merely distorting Wotton's Modernity; his apparently playful role is designed to strip Wotton's view of knowledge of all extraneous facts and to thrust it before us in its final enormity.

Yet even within this single passage, it is clear that the *persona* serves other purposes than to embody Modern error. From his pinnacle of vainglory he descends to other matters until, toward the end of the passage, he offers assertions about mankind which seem little different from the views of Swift himself. His anatomy of human nature is an interesting adumbration of the "Digression concerning Madness," where emphasis is on the rotten but authentic insides of things and on Reason which comes "officiously, with Tools for cutting, and opening, and mangling, and piercing, offering to demonstrate, that [things] are not of the same consistence quite thro'" (p. 173). His discovery and his argument as to mankind's "greater Advantage by being Diverted" involve a kind of logic which, while it can hardly be taken literally, is certainly alien to the Wotton brand of simplistic optimism. Disdainful, restless, yawning, Mankind is no fit subject for instruction. Whatever *Utile* such a treatise as the *Tale* contains is included out of deference to "Great Age and Authority," rather than from the hope that it will prove effective.

We approach close to genuine Swiftian skepticism at such moments as these. The view that men are not susceptible of instruction and require only diversion is almost antithetical to the fatuous conception of human wisdom implicit in the claims of the "Secretary of the Universe." Almost—but not quite, for if we account for such a passage by talk of "dropping masks" or the abandonment of positions, we imply, I think, a curious limit to Swift's imaginative artistry. The *persona*, however varied the responses he may elicit, never entirely ceases to be a *persona*, and hence a fiction. We may react to him with outrage or sympathy or amusement, but never with completely sober literal-mindedness.

If, in the passage we are considering, we confine our attention only to the spokesman's motives and mannerisms, these can be associated consistently with Swift's satiric targets—largely Wotton, with probably one touch of Dryden.[53] To dissect the carcass of human nature is an undertaking clearly to be labeled as Modern. As in *The Mechanical Operation of the Spirit,* scientific probing of the material world is extended to invade the intangible and universal. The *persona*'s naïve satisfaction with his "new" discovery concerning instruction and diversion, his verbal affectations, and his assumption that the "matter" of learning is virtually exhausted are all in character, to the extent that he has overtly associated himself with the "Modern Authors."

But the Swiftian realities are, so to speak, thrust upon this caricature of a Modern; they are the raw facts to which any inquiry, however fatuous, is bound to lead. The virtuoso of the *Mechanical Operation* is generally a silly man, but he produces a discovery of remarkably complex nastiness; the projectors of Gulliver's Third Voyage are engaged in incredible enterprises, but the noisome facts of organic and physical reality keep cropping up as the only product of their researches. If the ugly actualities are to emerge in the *Tale,* they must obtrude themselves on the awareness of its first-person narrator as the kind of thing which, even in his folly, he cannot ignore. The carcass of human nature, when dissected, inescapably stinks and must be reassembled in neat skeletal form. Modern authors simply do digress upon digressions. And an inquiry into man's "Epidemical Diseases," however motivated and however reported upon, is bound to take into account their essential character.

The emergence of such unlovely realities, even in the vainglorious literary performance of Swift's Modern Author, reveals, I think, Swift's remarkable powers of artistic restraint. Certainly other satirists have made much of characters, "spokesmen" or otherwise, who are persistently deluded or obsessed or wicked and who can, in short, be regularly relied upon to be entirely "wrong" in their response to an actuality which is only the mirror of their own illusions. Quixote, of course, has his virtues, but we are all quite aware of the outlines of an unalterable Quixotic world; the same thing is true, I think, of the great comic "types" of Jonson and Molière, and of such figures as Pangloss or Micawber. The destructive play of reality against their comprehensive illusions is supplied, so to speak, by the author, either through characters who display, in some form or other, a Sancho-

---

[53] Dryden repeatedly asserts that the ends of all poetry are delight and instruction; see, for example, *Essays of John Dryden,* ed. Ker (Oxford, 1926), I, 36, 143, 181, 209.

like practicality, or through their own narrative or discursive insistence upon true matter of fact.[54]

There have been attempts to show that the *Tale*'s nominal author is likewise a complete victim of folly—that he is consistently a "hack" or a "Bedlamite" or, as a "Modern," totally in error about any question of consequence. The inevitable corollary of such a view is, of course, that where the *Tale* indisputably displays authentic insight, where distressing realities are firmly noted, "unmasking" or "string-dropping" must take place; and Swift, unable to manipulate his puppet in the interests of literal truth, strides from the wings in his own angry identity. And this is precisely, I think, what Swift is never willing entirely to do. As I have argued, his commitments to the identity of the Tale-teller, as to Gulliver and Bickerstaff, the nominal Christian or the Modest Proposer, may be minimal—but, such as they are, they are inevitably honored. At the same time, brute fact, a special brand of knotty reasonableness, and the laughable paradoxes of actuality are all so important in Swift's satiric arsenal that he will not long suppress them in the unremitting employment of a single fictional device.

I have, however, mentioned only the two most simple aspects of the uses to which Swift puts his *persona*. For what I have said is merely that, in the latitude Swift allows his spokesman, he can both display unpleasant qualities and detect them—particularly in their grosser aspects. Beyond this however, in even the single, relatively uncomplicated passage we have been considering, we can observe a more complicated performance by the *persona*. This procedure might be described as a kind of "internal logic of error"—a mode of pseudo-argument which, disarmingly leading us through reasonable steps to preposterous conclusions, forces us to examine the terms and assumptions on which the reasoning is initially based.

The passage I have quoted concludes with the writer's profession that his "Divine Treatise" is composed of layers of *Utile* and of *Dulce,* but that he has gone thus far only in "Compliance with a Lesson of Great Age and Authority," a more sympathetic course presumably having been to write for "Diversion" alone. One need know nothing about Swift beyond what has been thus far revealed

---

[54] The problem of the play of illusion and pretentiousness against reality in the performance of the *persona* is given thoughtful attention by Ronald Paulson in *Theme and Structure in Swift's "Tale of a Tub"* (New Haven, 1960), pp. 35–86.

in the *Tale* to recognize how totally alien such conclusions are to his actual beliefs. The sugar coatings and transparent fables, the palatable homilies and easy aphorisms, the flamboyant devices for securing attention and the handy compendia for ready learning are adumbrations of the *"New help of smatterers"* which the *persona* is shortly to advertise (p. 130) and, as such, are the objects of repeated bitter satire throughout Swift's assault on abuses in learning. One is, indeed, tempted to believe that Swift would regard the work of pure diversion as preferable to the course which is allegedly followed in the *Tale*.

But the *persona's* espousal of this obviously distasteful position is more than simple sarcasm or the parodic assumption, by a satiric dupe, of a position which is manifestly untenable. The mock-author has arrived at his conclusion by a process of deliberation and research, and, in our awareness that his conclusion is indeed outrageous in the context of the *Tale,* we are naturally interested in how it is reached. It is based upon two assumptions, one of which is patently false but the other, curiously enough, true—or at least manifestly sympathetic to Swift's actual views. The false assumption is clearly that "in the present universal Empire of Wit and Learning, there seems but little Matter left for Instruction," for no aspect of Wotton's reasonings infuriated Swift and his allies more than the conception of knowledge as perfectible or exhaustible. The true, or at least reasonable, assumption is, of course, that man's "epidemical Diseases" are *"Fastidiosity, Amorphy,* and *Oscitation,"* all characteristics of a bored restlessness which Swift elsewhere finds in the fashionable world.[55] Immediately, therefore, the *persona's* conclusion follows from his sound perception of more or less visible phenomena, on the one hand, and his deluded beliefs concerning intangible circumstances on the other.

But these assumptions themselves are extensions of the earlier discovery that "the Publick Good of Mankind is performed by two Ways, *Instruction* and *Diversion.*" As I have said, this triumphant proclamation of a commonplace has its parodic effect. Beyond this, however, the proposition, on close scrutiny, is, I think, one of those perverse truths which embody the kind of "moral realism" that will

[55] See, for example, *A Compleat Collection of Genteel and Ingenious Conversation* and its Introduction (*Prose Works,* IV, 99–201) in which the idleness and triviality of fashionable life are attacked as severely as is the vulgarity of fashionable language.

be discussed in my final essay. Swift's terms in such propositions are carefully chosen and bear careful examination. We note, for instance, that the end served by Instruction and Diversion is rather modestly defined as "Publick Good." No question, accordingly, is raised about genuine enlightenment or advancement or, assuredly, salvation. And, as the subsequent argument shows, what is "good" for the public is merely what will pander to its temporal infirmities and humor its illusions. Shallowness is to fight shallowness; boredom and disdain—the products themselves of ignorance and superficiality—are merely to be "diverted." For men, in their delusion of wisdom, are no longer susceptible of the instruction which is the only true antidote to these mundane afflictions. It is "good" to write fables, only if the good is defined as whatever pleases man by catering to his weakness and his vanity.

The *persona*'s argument therefore is neither sarcastic nor parodic in any simple meaning of these terms; it is rather a systematic exposition of wrongness. A work "in the modern kind" is, on the surface, silly enough to be exposed by parody of its fraudulent claims to knowledge, its self-advertisement and self-pity, its digressiveness, pretentiousness, and servility. Its layer-cake organization can be seen as the product of unexamined critical clichés, just as its flamboyant manner reflects the author's view of his "universal" stature. But there are graver charges to be leveled against books of this kind— charges which parody alone cannot make entirely clear. Silly, false, and disgusting as such works may be in execution, their motives and consequences are even more disturbing. For their genesis is a kind of realism which takes into cynical account the obtuseness of contemporary man, and they are successful only to the extent that they confirm him in his folly. In this passage, accordingly, Swift's *persona* is his alter ego to a degree, for both recognize the damning facts about the "Publick Good." Where the *persona* becomes a villain and hence a satiric victim is in his shameless willingness to exploit these facts in the conduct of his literary enterprise.

This account of the uses to which the *persona* is put in a single passage is probably not exhaustive by any means, and more ingenious readers may still uncover ambiguities I have not seen. As it is, the remarkable flexibility of the device in Swift's hands should be abundantly clear. The *persona* has served as a vehicle for parody—

and even in this capacity he can range from transparently exaggerated mimicry of the manner we find in Swift's victims to postures which, like his claim to be Secretary of the Universe, carry their pretensions to a point of extreme yet uniquely apt absurdity. He is able, at the same time, to observe certain unpleasant yet indubitably real facts, even as Swift would have us observe them. In addition, he displays a capacity for at least one kind of internally consistent logic; with his premises firmly grounded on demonstrable fact (as both he and Swift see it), he proceeds systematically, but in complete moral indifference, to conclusions which only exacerbate the unpleasantness of the reality.

These, however, are not keys or categories which will do much to illuminate the vast range of satiric purposes to which the *persona* can be put. The passage we have examined, for instance, strikes pretty deep. Its implications are serious enough to provide a hint—not to be truly confirmed and broadened until the "Digression concerning Madness"—of the firm principles which basically direct Swift's assault on the abuses in learning. It is, at the same time, an exuberant beginning to an exuberant chapter, and if its subtleties are not exceeded in subsequent passages, its fanciful aspect is only a modest prelude to what is to come. The *persona* is able to produce —with, to be sure, the excuse that he has found it in the posthumous papers of "a great Philosopher of *O. Brazile*"—a marvelous hermetic recipe for implanting in one's head *"an infinite Number* of Abstracts, Summaries, Compendiums, Extracts, Collections, Medulla's, Excerpta quaedam's, Florilegia's *and the like, all disposed into great Order, and reducible upon Paper"* (p. 127). The satire here is largely punitive, as Swift, succumbing to the playful urge to exploit the possibilities of arcane lore, expands upon the opportunity for fun offered by the single idea of a mystical nostrum.

In the ensuing strictures upon Homer, however, the satire resumes its stinging particularity, although once again the *persona* appears in a novel role. He introduces his subject as a proof that Homer leaves much to be desired in his performance of the same task to which the author addresses himself, namely "A compleat Body of all Knowledge, Human, Divine, Political, and Mechanick" (p. 127). Although an outright caricature of Modernity would presumably involve the contemptuous dismissal of Homer, Swift's author produces some measured praise, seems reluctant to point out Homer's deficiencies, and asserts that the poet is "a Person not without some Abilities, and *for an Ancient,* of a tolerable Genius."

This new posture of half-apologetic criticism is, I think, the most particularized parody for which the *persona* is employed in the chapter. Swift might have found instances of fierce anti-Homerism, particularly among the French defenders of the Modern position.[56] His target—and model—is Wotton, however, and the *persona's* praise of Homer is based on the qualified, reluctant, but withal favorable judgment which Wotton accords the ancient poets. Thus, after suggesting that time and custom color our estimate of ancient eloquence, Wotton confesses, "Yet though due allowance ought to be made for these Prepossessions, one has Reason to believe, that this Reverence for the ancient Orators and Poets is more than Prejudice."[57]

Moderation and candor can hardly be caricatured, and Swift has first to distort the appearance of these qualities into an air of grudging condescension. Adopting such a tone, he exploits a premise implicit in many of Wotton's judgments, namely that the ancients labored under the handicap of being ancients. The *persona* takes Homer to task for his ignorance of various patently modern achievements—a conceit which, as Mrs. Starkman has suggested, reflects the standards of a "scientific Modern" who seeks to remake the past in his own image.[58] This posture, moreover, is employed to produce a list of "important" modern innovations which is ludicrously trivial and foolish. Homer is held to be deficient because he is ignorant of cabalism, hermetic lore, candle-end holders, flies, spittle, the spleen, political "wagering," tea, and venereal therapy. These topics can be variously seen as patently mean modern phenomena, as the subjects of sober reports in the *Philosophical Transactions* of the Royal Society, or as debasements of claims for modern progress made by Wot-

---

[56] Mrs. Starkman in *Swift's Satire on Learning in "A Tale of a Tub"* provides valuable suggestions as to the sources in which we may find evidence of the virulent Homeric controversy in France (pp. 89–91). Wotton's "Reflections upon Perrault" (*Reflections,* pp. 42–52) reveal the extreme nature of Perrault's position on ancient poetry and oratory—from which, it should be noted, Wotton feels compelled to differ sharply.

[57] *Reflections*, p. 21.

[58] *Swift's Satire on Learning in "A Tale of a Tub,"* p. 91.

ton himself.[59] In all cases, the effect is substantially the same: the *persona* has produced a silly, trifling catalogue of evidence for modern superiority. And to the simple parody implicit in a patent distortion of Wotton's manner and his views is added a devastatingly selective list of modern achievements by which the *persona,* for the moment an utterly fatuous idiot, gives away his own case.

These few examples, which do not begin to exhaust the functions of the mock-author within even a single chapter, make clear several facts about Swift's use of the *persona* in the *Tale.* In the first place, he is nobody's fool—even Swift's—for long enough to be regarded as essentially a stock spokesman-dupe. His voice can clearly resemble that of Wotton or Bentley, Dryden or L'Estrange, or even provide an outrageous debasement of these victims of Swift's satire, but it is never safe to assume a priori that his statements are a reflection, direct or indirect, of the beliefs and characteristics which Swift imputes to his enemies. On the other hand, I do not think we can ever say that his voice is literally that of Jonathan Swift. In his closest approaches to the truths most cherished by Swift, he remains—as we shall see in the "Digression concerning Madness"—enough a writer "in the modern kind" to sustain his *air* of ingenuous vanity and to argue in terms which, if unexamined, are in keeping with the learned and literary vogues of which the *Tale* purports to be a product. At such moments, indeed, the *persona*'s language seems quite deliberately calculated to preserve his own non-Swiftian identity. Mankind's "epidemick diseases" may well include, for Swift himself, those which his spokesman claims to have discovered, but the discovery is described in the jargon of pedantry as *"Fastidiosity, Amorphy,* and *Oscitation."*

Between the extremes of the uniquely destructive parodic role and minimally-disguised service as Swift's alter ego lie the countless permutations in which the *persona* can combine shrewdness and stupidity, logic and fancy, fact and falsehood in ever differing proportions. Where he offers mock-argument, rather than the patently fanciful constructions of his nostrums and catalogues and pseudo-histories, he is the infinitely flexible master of an "internal logic of error" in which premises, reasonings, and conclusions are constantly variable with respect to truth and falsehood; if we have detected a

---

[59] See R. C. Olson, "Swift's use of the *Philosophical Transactions* in Section V of *A Tale of a Tub*," *Studies in Philology,* XLIX (July, 1952), pp. 459–67.

particular pattern in one of the *persona*'s quasi-logical demonstrations, we can feel confident that it will not soon be identically repeated.

Where the *persona* merely develops a single conceit—as he does, for example, in his hermetic "nostrum" and, to a large extent, in his condescending assessment of Homer's "modernity"—there is much ingenuity and usually much fun. Such passages are doubtless best appreciated if we recognize in them—as in a narrative myth such as that of the Aeolists—the lavish distortion of a commonly accepted "error" in a context of semi-nonsense. But in the knottier development of such paragraphs as those which open the "Digression in the Modern Kind," we encounter an attack whose full dimensions are covert, obscured by the convolutions of an argument half false and half true, and requiring for their recovery a fairly systematic process of analysis.

Here, I think, is a revealing clue as to the nature of persuasive satire. In his role as Secretary of the Universe, Swift is not content merely to exploit our easy assumptions about Wotton or modernity in general. His argument must be unraveled, his terms examined, his premises questioned in the kind of genuine inquiry which leads, I think, to genuine discovery. If persuasive satire, unlike punitive satire, seeks to impose upon us convictions which are in some measure novel, we can arrive at them only through affirmative acts of the understanding. They are introduced to us as solutions to problems raised by the satirist, as the conclusions to inquiries which we are induced, by the satiric fiction, to undertake. Thus, in his persuasive, as opposed to his punitive, role, the *persona* is deliberately elusive and challenging. His fictional posture, when he is employed for persuasive purposes, is rarely very amusing intrinsically. And it is, at most, only superficially meaningful unless we are prepared to exert our powers of inference and logic and to isolate the literal truth within the fictional fabric which initially claims our attention. In such instances, the satiric fiction is more than a novel and engaging vehicle for the disguise of an attack upon commonplace grounds. For the facts and meanings to which these challenging passages ultimately direct the reader's attention will be of a sort which lends power and credibility to the entire satiric assault.

The *persona* of the *Tale* can serve as a kind of nexus in our discussion of the punitive and persuasive uses of the satiric fiction. He is capable of elaborate and transparent absurdities, of broad parodic mockery, of fantastically exploiting the manifest follies of Swift's victims. But he is capable as well of prodding and disturbing us until, in our search to discover what he "really means," we are at last confronted with the graver and more responsible charges on which we may believe Swift's satire, for all its hilarious playfulness, is finally and firmly based.

V

My earlier discussion of *Gulliver's Travels* was chiefly intended to distinguish between satiric and non-satiric elements in that work, employing for this purpose the view that genuine satire involves attack upon an identifiable victim. Inevitably, however, we were compelled to note the character of Swift's numerous fictions and to recognize that, while at times they serve largely as instruments for the satirist's assault, at other times their appeal is primarily that of original and engaging fantasy.

We have observed as well the difficulty of describing the total achievement of the *Travels* (or what amounts to much the same thing, establishing the "unity" of the work) in terms of a single exclusively satiric enterprise. Not only does the great diversity of Swift's targets discourage such attempts, but the vigor and magnitude of both comic and mythic components in the book produce effects which should not be confused with those of authentic satire. Accordingly, no account of the *Travels* as an exclusively satiric assault, described in terms of its victims and its strategy, can suitably subsume its other, important kinds of literary achievement.

There remains the possibility, however, that in Swift's fiction, whatever the diversity of ends for which it is employed, there can be found a consistency and wholeness which provide an adequate principle of order for the entire work. In *A Tale of a Tub* we have discovered that the notion of a self-conscious literary undertaking, conducted in acute awareness of contemporary habits of writing, publishing, reading, and criticism, provides a single posture to which the supposed author regularly adheres and yet permits a remarkable assortment of satiric and non-satiric procedures within this wide fictional context. Similarly, *Gulliver's Travels* may be—or purport to be—a single kind of enterprise, so simple that it permits (often at the same time as it masks) the pursuit of a great variety of ends, satiric and otherwise.

We have already found reason to anticipate difficulties in such an approach to the *Travels*. They arise very often from Swift's indifference to the preservation of a well-knit fiction in the presence of immediate satiric tasks. Voyage III, as we have noted, presents the most conspicuous instance of this tendency. Lacking a comprehensive fiction in any way comparable to those which embrace each of the two earlier voyages, the third book incorporates a miscellany of experiences in an order which is largely inconsequential. The ingenuity of many of its individual conceits is undeniable, yet none, I believe, has the brilliant originality of the fictions which are central to the earlier works, or is there, for the most part, the kind of reciprocal involvement between Gulliver and his hosts which marks all three of the other books and which endows them, at the level of fiction alone, with a kind of artistic sophistication which is notably absent from Voyage III.

We have observed as well that even the handsomely organized fictional development of the voyages to Lilliput and Brobdingnag is occasionally suspended in the interest of clear satiric attack. The curious (and self-consciously justified) employment of the Lilliputians as Utopian exemplars in Book I, chapter 6, the irrelevant and grotesque (if amusing) defense of Lady Flimnap's chastity, the gratuitous and revolting account of the Brobdingnagian Maids of Honor, and similar satiric excursions arrest, if they do not actually impair, the emerging image of these kingdoms and of Gulliver's place within them. And we have also seen that the particulars of plot in Voyage I gradually divorce themselves from the basic notion of the minuscule kingdom, so that, as satiric intensity grows with the increasing resemblance between Gulliver's plight and that of the outcast Harley administration, the physical stature of his ungrateful hosts becomes a very incidental matter.

These and other difficulties (of which one of the most obvious is the quite arbitrary mixture of the admirable and distasteful among the mythical kingdoms) discourage attempts to generalize about the "world" in which Gulliver finds himself in any separate voyage—and still more about the "world" of the *Travels* as a whole. As was true of *A Tale of a Tub,* much of this apparent caprice is quite possibly deliberate, since, in the tradition of Lucian and the spirit of the

Martinus Scriblerus project,[60] Swift frequently apes the fraudulence, implausibility, and pretentiousness of popular travel literature. Whatever total vision one seeks in the *Travels* cannot be gained by assembling the overt particulars of the lands which Gulliver visits or the experiences he undergoes.

But if the voyages themselves cannot be seen as a single organic fiction, what of the voyager? Certainly Gulliver has been described as Swift's greatest role, a *persona* triumphantly contrived to suit a multiplicity of satiric purposes, the spokesman whose ultimate savage misanthropy is an extreme and unforgettable statement of Swift's own views. If, indeed, Gulliver can be seen in some such light, then his experiences and their significance become secondary and our attention can focus upon the man himself.

But our acceptance of Gulliver as a *persona* must be severely qualified. It is clear that he compels from us, at different points, responses which are extremely varied and even incompatible. Most obviously, he is made to serve both as a vulnerable symbol of folly and as a sensitive judge of the folly of others; as William Ewald points out, "He can criticize as well as illustrate the faults of travel-writers, Englishmen, and human beings generally."[61] We have encountered a similar multiplicity of roles in the *persona* of *A Tale of A Tub.* Unlike such a surrogate-victim as the nominal Christian or the spokesman who expresses, for all its distortion, Swift's true sense of outrage in *A Modest Proposal,* the fictional authors of both the *Tale* and the *Travels* yield to no single satiric formula.

There is an added danger in describing Gulliver as another *persona.* The proposer and the nominal Christian, Bickerstaff, and M. B. Drapier, the Church of England Man who produces the *Sentiments,* and the alleged author of the *Tale* are all essentially engaged in exposition—in arguments, demonstrations, declarations of fact or belief. To the extent that any of these "authors" is a genuine satiric fiction, our first task is the scrutiny of the "position" which is assumed. Whichever one of many possible satiric purposes governs the construction of such fictional figures, we are, as it were, concerned with their states of mind, their habits of thought and expression, the

---

[60] See *Memoirs of the Extraordinary Life, Works, and Discoveries of Martinus Scriblerus,* ed. Charles Kerby-Miller (New Haven, 1950), pp. 101, 200–201, 315–20.

[61] William B. Ewald, Jr., *The Masks of Jonathan Swift* (Oxford, 1954), p. 139.

premises from which their arguments proceed, as well, of course, as with the substance of the arguments themselves.

Gulliver's Travels, on the other hand, has a clear plot, however episodic and disjointed it may be, and Gulliver is accordingly a *protagonist,* in the traditional sense, far more obviously than he is an expositor. It is certainly true that in such passages as the dialogues with the Brobdingnagian king or the Houyhnhnm master, or even more notably the final revelation of his views upon his last return to England, Gulliver provides us with a kind of discourse which is plainly expository and invites inferences as to the actual position which Swift is urging upon us. But the voyages are not mere excuses or motivations for such passages; things *happen* to Gulliver and, narrator though he is, he is above all a *character* whose experiences —rather than postures, beliefs, or literary habits—constitute the major fiction of the work.

If, then, we view Gulliver, initially at least, simply as the "hero" of a fictional plot, his character appears far less complicated and elusive than we might find it if we insist on viewing him as some kind of "spokesman." From the outset we are aware that he is educable and inquiring, resourceful and honorable, possessed, above all, of a species of sound common sense and practical judgment which is rarely, if ever, called into question. Even where he is employed as a comic or satiric dupe, it is largely his knowledge and sophistication rather than his good sense or decency which are found wanting. His sufferings among the Lilliputians are brought about largely by his physical size, his guileless generosity, and, of course, the vice and folly of the Lilliputians themselves. Even the salvation of the queen's palace displays, for all its broad humor, Gulliver's expediential prudence in the service of a benevolent enterprise.

Gulliver's infirmities of character emerge, as we have said, in dialogue with those wiser than himself, in his occasional ingenuously sober acceptance of what is patently ludicrous,[62] such naïve expectations and subsequent disappointments as he encounters among the Struldbruggs, and in the persistence of his belief in man as the meas-

---

[62] Gulliver rarely admires phenomena which are plainly ugly, vicious, or bizarre. When he occasionally loses his human, common-sense perspective and shares in the special values of his hosts, it is generally to comic effect, as in the alleged intrigue with Lady Flimnap (pp. 49–50) or his attempts to vie with the Laputans on such matters as etymology (pp. 145–46).

ure of all things despite the abundant evidence he receives to the contrary. These, however, are limitations of vision, engendered by the society of which Gulliver has been a part, and, of course, are ultimately to be amended by his final terrible discovery among the Houyhnhnms.

When the *Travels* is viewed simply as a tale, Gulliver seems a reasonable and convincing protagonist. His restlessness and curiosity lead him to travel; his understandable frailties precipitate many of his dilemmas; his resourcefulness extricates him from them. He is benign enough to invite our sympathy, honest enough so that, once within the make-believe framework of his story, we are never tempted to accuse him of saying "the thing that is not." His deficiencies and rigidities are plausible, and plausible too are the consequences to which they lead within the plot. His character is, indeed, without peculiarity; whether as narrator, hero, or dupe (and he is variously all of these) he must be taken as one of ourselves.

Nor is there anything inconsistent in the satiric use which Swift makes of the character he has created. Gulliver is not a politician, a projector, a profiteer, pedant, lawyer, or lecher; the assaults upon these and other kinds of person and institution are achieved through what Gulliver sees and tells. He is, on the other hand, a travel-writer, an Englishman, a European, a human being, and where he is employed as surrogate-victim it is in one of these roles. Where he is truly a critic—where, that is, he literally offers judgments which essentially coincide with our own—it is at a level appropriate to his rather commonplace faculties; he is disgusted at whatever is grossly repellent, outraged by palpable cruelty or deceit, puzzled or amused by arrant folly. If, in very occasional passages, he displays an uncharacteristic cynicism, it seems engendered by a kind of blandly uncritical acceptance of evil as a fact of life. Thus, for example, his simple-minded astonishment at the political projectors of Lagado, who sought to instil notions of civic virtue into the conduct of government (p. 170), reveals him as a sort of *faux ingénu*. His naïve dismissal of such reformers as mad, that is, expresses the bitter truth that it is hopeless to expect wisdom and honesty in government affairs. Although these sentiments are somewhat at odds with the glowing account of political appointment and preferment which Gulliver has earlier given to the Brobdingnagian king, they are not incompatible with his general character. The belief that governmental corruption is inevitable is a standard one in the doctrinal equipment of the ordinary man. (Indeed, great numbers of Americans today seem to accept, with a complacency equal to Gulliver's, the presumably inalterable venality and guile which operate within that political system they venerate above all others.)

Thus Gulliver in his several roles—as observer and reporter, as master and victim of circumstance—is a thoroughly flexible agent of Swift's many purposes yet preserves that consistency of character which renders him, wherever necessary, credible and sympathetic. With such a character there are few limits to what a writer like Swift can do, and the *Travels* might well have gone on and on (or, for that matter, ceased earlier), leaving its readers with a rich miscellany of literary experiences, now satiric, now comic, now philosophic, untroubled by questions of unity, development, or total significance. This, in effect, is what is provided by such purely episodic but triumphantly satiric works as Lucian's *True History* or *Don Juan* or even, essentially, *Candide*. And it is, I believe, what is provided by the first three voyages of *Gulliver's Travels*. For despite the brilliant symmetry of conceit which links the first two books, it is Gulliver and what happens to him—rather than any unified satiric purpose or procedure, any coherence of imagery or idea, any singleness of philosophic vision—to which alone we look for organic continuity. What happens to Gulliver, moreover, is presented in a series of basically dissociated episodes, some with the magnitude and complexity of his disgrace, danger, and escape from Lilliput, others as short and simple as his Brobdingnagian encounters with the wasps, the monkey, and the rats. Among these episodes there are few relationships of antecedent and consequent. No character—not even the beloved Glumdalclitch—survives beyond one or two phases of Gulliver's adventures. Gulliver is confronted by no persistent problem, engaged in no compelling inquiry or search beyond the desire to return home (and even this plays little part in the second voyage). With the establishment of Gulliver's character and his propensity for travel, we are confronted with the possibilities for incident on whose substance and magnitude Swift's own wishes and talents impose the only limitation. This is, so to speak, a literary system of "occurrences," each to be relished for its own effect and in its own way, deriving credibility and intelligibility, to be sure, from the presence of a single character and the recurrent use of a voyage as the central activity of each book, but possessed of no further organic quality, whether of structure or of purpose.

All this is abruptly, even violently, changed with the voyage to the Houyhnhnms. This book, too, is above all a narrative, a series of happenings, yet happenings which are profound and startling, which are inseparably linked within the wholeness of a single myth, and which involve Gulliver in a sustained process of inquiry and discovery.

The belief or vision which Voyage IV presumably embodies has, quite understandably, commanded enormous attention. In our final chapter we shall attempt to discuss the philosophic ground from which this extraordinary fable proceeds, but at this moment we should recognize that the most obvious—and certainly a very crucial—way in which Book IV differs from its fellows is in the nature of its plot. However we may be tempted to attribute the singularity of the fourth book to the depth, intensity, or strangeness of its ultimate "meaning," we must also note that the "system of occurrences" by which the earlier books proceed has here yielded to an account of a single though complex experience. And that experience, fantastic though its form may be, is at heart one of the most shocking and powerful of which the human mind can conceive, for it is, in effect, a discovery so profound that a man's total view of life is violently and irrevocably altered.

At the very outset of Book IV Gulliver admits that his five months at home have been spent "in a very happy condition," but adds the qualification, "if I could have learned the lesson of knowing when I was well" (p. 205). The "happy condition" may evoke memories of the "Digression on Madness," for in the light of what subsequently occurs in the Fourth Voyage, one is tempted to define Gulliver's initial state as that of "being well-deceived" and Gulliver himself as a fool among knaves. One need not, however, be particularly sensitive to the Swiftian version of such a term as "happiness" to recognize that Gulliver begins his final voyage in a state of blissful ignorance from which he is drawn only by his characteristic wanderlust, but drawn never to return. For each of a series of shocking discoveries in the Fourth Voyage removes him further from his erstwhile satisfaction, and his ultimate state of mind is very close to the antithesis of that in which he begins his adventure.

For the most part, the "events" of the Fourth Voyage take the form of critical discoveries—but discoveries which, unlike the great majority of those made in the earlier voyages, deeply affect Gulliver's most basic beliefs and are accompanied by great changes in his emotional condition. Like most important discoveries within literary plots, those of Gulliver possess a substantive interest which transcends the inventive context in which they occur and drives us almost irresistibly to grave and persistent problems in the world of reality. But the magnitude and authenticity of such questions must not blind us to the quite extraordinary narrative from which they emerge, a narrative which requires no ulterior significance to exercise upon us a powerfully arresting effect.

For the story of Gulliver's final voyage is one of increasing alienation from the traditional sources of human security. In the course of events which leads ultimately to the destruction of every principle by which Gulliver has conducted his life, the perfidy of his piratical shipmates forms, as it were, a prelude, embodying, in an incident which is entirely compatible with the realities of eighteenth-century life, the themes of the belated discovery of human villainy, of rejection, and of solitude which are subsequently elaborated on the level of myth. Outcast and disillusioned, Gulliver arrives among the Houyhnhnms and stands, unknowing, at the brink of further nightmare discoveries which will dwarf, in their horror, the sufferings he has already undergone. Of these discoveries, the terrible moment of recognition in which Gulliver detects the Yahoos' physical identity with mankind is the earliest, but in some ways the most climactic. Upon it are based the loathing for the Yahoo breed, the admiration for the horses, and the torturing ambivalence of Gulliver's attitude toward himself which constitute the fabric of the subsequent action.

With Gulliver's growing disaffection from his own kind, there develops, of course, an admiration for the Houyhnhnms which, ironically, is to prove the ultimate source of his alienation. For he is damned, as it were, by his own humanity, cast out from those he most admires because they find in him evidence of that which he most loathes. Like the philosopher-kings in Plato's myth of the cave, Gulliver returns, blinking and reluctant, from an immense vision which has been vouchsafed to him alone and which will forever set him apart from his fellows. But unlike the light which Plato describes, Gulliver's vision is twofold, involving the glory of an excellence which is totally unattainable and the wretchedness of a heritage which is inescapable.

If the story of the Fourth Voyage falls somewhat short of true tragic stature, it is doubtless because Gulliver is so entirely a victim of forces over which he has no control, because he has so little opportunity for the kind of choice from which the most powerfully tragic actions traditionally proceed. And there remains with him, too, a kind of solemn naïveté which is assuredly less than heroic. Though Gulliver tends to forget that the Houyhnhnms, after all, are horses, Swift is at pains to remind the reader of this fact[63] and, in consequence, we never entirely share Gulliver's fatuous admiration of his masters.

But there are abundant grounds for compassion in the story, and we are able to participate to a great extent in the horror of Gulliver's discoveries and in the bleakness of his final isolation from men and from Houyhnhnms alike. Moreover, in contrast to his practice in the earlier books, Swift is unwilling to jeopardize the close-knit development of his narrative in order to pursue specific satiric targets or to exploit comic possibilities. Even Gulliver's devastating account of "the whole state of Europe"—incorporating as it does the most purely satiric elements in the entire book—is, unlike his earlier conversations with the Brobdingnagian king, closely related to the central course of the narrative. For the establishment of his own identity and the assessment of the species to which he belongs are problems which lie at the heart of the distressing situation in which he finds himself.

There are things about the Fourth Voyage which have proved controversial when viewed as the allegorical expressions of a Swiftian "faith," but which seem intelligible and proper as parts of an artful, moving narrative. Thus, for example, if the question of what the Houyhnhnms "stand for" is given higher priority in our inquiries than the matter of what they actually achieve in the narrative, there are bound to be troublesome and inconclusive problems. We must find it difficult to admire creatures who are so austere and in-

---

[63] The physical endowments, needs, and implicit limitations of the Houyhnhnms as horses are never glossed over by Swift, although this would be entirely possible if he were seeking literally to depict them as "perfect." Thus, for example, in his "account of the Manners and Customs" of these creatures (pp. 251–54), Gulliver includes references to diet and to physical exercises which are clearly appropriate to horses.

flexible and who remain, whatever Gulliver may make of them, somewhat ludicrous throughout. Their symbolic meaning, their perfection or imperfection, the faculties they exemplify and those they lack are questions which can—and doubtless will—be argued indefinitely. But for purposes of the narrative itself, their role is entirely clear and, viewed in this light, they are not "problems" but, on the contrary, brilliantly conceived creations in an imaginary universe. Swift makes clear what they are: horses whose possession and profitable employment of reason elevates them infinitely above the Yahoos, who lack it altogether, and man, who has abused the vestige of it with which he has been endowed. In this role, they are seized on by the disillusioned and dispossessed Gulliver, and in this role, too, they reject him in a gesture calculated to disclose the final, terrible fact—that his humanity is inescapable.

Similarly, Gulliver's widely discussed encounter with Pedro de Mendez, the humane and intelligent Portuguese captain who effects his return to England, is entirely acceptable when it is regarded as, above all else, an integral narrative incident. It is perfectly true that Gulliver's ungracious response to Don Pedro's generosity is shocking. For those who are anxious to make of Gulliver a Christian hero or a spokesman for Swift—and particularly for those who feel, in general, that what Gulliver has come to believe is what Swift would have his readers believe—the hopeless misanthropy reflected in Gulliver's reaction requires the kind of ingenious explaining-away which has been abundantly lavished upon it. But this is the sort of problem which, as Professor R. S. Crane has pointed out, is not raised by the text itself but which must be read into it by those who insist that the "implications" of the *Travels* conform to an a priori notion of Swiftian belief.[64] Within the actual context of the Fourth Voyage, Gulliver's reaction to Don Pedro's kindness is precisely the one which is called for, and indeed alternatives are virtually unthinkable. This is so, not because the episode fits into some comprehensive "significance" implied by the allegory or because it is a part of Swift's satiric mission, but because it represents an artful, final stage in the plot itself. For in Gulliver's reaction toward Don Pedro is measured—far more strikingly than in the mere account of his general attitudes—the total magnitude of the discoveries he has

[64] See Crane's review of Martin Kallich's "Three Ways of Looking at a Horse" in *Philological Quarterly*, XL (1961), pp. 427-30.

made and the change they have wrought within him. A final en-counter with foolish or evil men—men, say, of the stamp of his erst-while shipmates—would only afford anticlimactic confirmation of the terrible discoveries upon which his misanthropy rests. The su-preme test of his new and agonizing condition, however, can lie only in his exposure to the best of men, and it is the rejection of the be-nevolent Portuguese which makes uniquely clear the depth and per-manence of Gulliver's aversion to all mankind.

In urging that the basic plot of the Fourth Voyage serves as the primary object of critical attention, I am not, of course, denying that the book has a "meaning" which transcends the fictional narrative. In my final chapter, I shall be concerned with some of the assump-tions from which Swift's strange myth proceeds and with the aspects of the human condition about which it inevitably raises questions. I would argue, however, that the imaginative fecundity, artful rigor, and emotional impact of the narrative itself remain, whatever the focus of one's analysis, a primary source of the power which the book exerts. If, that is, the Fourth Voyage is an expression of Swift's own misanthropy, Swift has embodied his views in the magnificently shocking story of how Gulliver became a misanthrope. To insist on the primacy of these facts is, I believe, to clear up some muddy criti-cal waters, although at the expense of frustrating some professional muddiers. The "implications" of the myth may be difficult to square with what Swift believed, or might have believed, or should have believed. But the story is unequivocal. We know what Gulliver feels; the habits and endowments of both Yahoos and Houyhnhnms are bluntly set forth; the status of mankind is made abundantly plain. Even more than in the first two books, Swift displays, in the Voyage to the Houyhnhnms, his high mastery of that art by which satire can transcend the ephemeral character of argument and exposure— the art of the storyteller.

Because, in its depth and intensity and in the magnitude of the change which Gulliver undergoes, the Fourth Voyage is plainly cli-mactic, we may tend to feel it imposes upon the whole of the *Travels* an order that has not been previously apparent. On the level of the fiction alone, however, this is very hard to discover. Although the first three books are full of changes in the character, role, and expe-riences of Gulliver, it seems impossible to say that these form any kind of sustained crescendo. Gulliver's decency and resourcefulness, indeed, emerge most clearly in the First Voyage; in the subsequent two books his personal traits are largely irrelevant. As I have suggested, no persistent problem or need drives Gulliver through his early adventures, and the Fourth Voyage begins, as have the earlier ones, with a protagonist to whom anything can happen. However profound the discoveries which he ultimately makes on his final voyage, they are not made in response to overt questions which have concerned him earlier.

It is possible, of course, to argue that the first three books are a protracted display of Gulliver's human frailty and that, with the Voyage to the Houyhnhnms, he becomes, in Middleton Murry's phrase, "regenerate."[65] Viewed in this light, the *Travels* becomes a kind of tale of intellectual sin and redemption and, in his agonizing discoveries amongst the Houyhnhnms, Gulliver achieves the only possible salvation from the folly to which he has hitherto been prey. There is, as I shall subsequently point out, a great deal to be said for this view of the Fourth Voyage, but it seems impossible to view the three earlier books as primarily "preparing" us for the change which Gulliver will undergo. He is not consistently vain and fatuous, and while he is impervious to the implications of some of his earlier experiences, others, such as his encounter with the Struldbruggs, are plainly enlightening for him. The three early books, moreover, cannot be viewed as a systematic exposure of Gulliver's own limitations. Functioning, as we have said, not only as occasional alien dupe but as dispassionate observer and as critic, he fails to offer a consistent picture of a man whose intellectual redemption is urgently needed.

One may also find in the Fourth Voyage a kind of "thematic" nexus which brings into intense focus those strictures against mankind which have been adumbrated in the earlier books. And it is true that among the Houyhnhnms and Yahoos, those infirmities of which we have seen fragmentary and sporadic manifestations now appear as generic phenomena. Gulliver, for example, becomes aware on his visit to Brobdingnag that the human body, seen under special circumstances, is a loathsome sight; his exposure to the Yahoos, however, makes it clear that, for him, humans are universally hideous. So too, as has often been pointed out, the perfidy of the Lilliputians, the greed of the Brobdingnagian farmer, the bizarre undertakings of the pedants and projectors—all of which as single discoveries

[65] John Middleton Murry, *Jonathan Swift* (London, 1954), p. 342.

might be taken as "accidents" or, at the most, as "symptoms"—must ultimately be viewed as the manifestations of a human depravity which is universal and inveterate. It is, indeed, possible to attribute most of the evil and ugliness which are exposed in the first two voyages to man's congenital state of body and intellect—to his Yahoo nature, as it were—and to discover in the outrageous enterprises of the Third Voyage that perversion of a fragment of rationality which ingloriously distinguishes mankind from its Yahoo brethren.

Such observations as these underscore the climactic and focal character of the Fourth Voyage and confirm the view, offered earlier, that it serves as a kind of universal myth in which the strictures which have preceded it have their ultimate source. Granted that the Fourth Voyage functions in some such fashion, this does not impose any significant principle of order upon the earlier books, nor does it minimize the formidable diversity of ends and means which are pursued in the first three voyages. Indeed, where Swift has been most trenchantly satiric—in his particularized attacks upon men and institutions—the interpretation of his victims' sins as manifestations of universal human weakness would appear to vitiate the strength of his assault. If, that is, all men are vain, stupid, and evil, the vices of a Walpole or Nottingham hardly merit special indignation.

Nor does such a "thematic" approach succeed in reconciling the striking disparities of tone and effect which are achieved in the earlier books. In their many comic aspects, the Lilliputians, various of the projectors, and even Gulliver himself remain patently remote from the savage portrait of the Yahoos. And to suggest that all of the frailties which are exploited, comically or satirically, frivolously or fiercely, are manifestations of a single, comprehensive vice is to conceal the magnificent versatility of Swift's achievement beneath the label of a simple didactic enterprise.

In the final analysis, our scrutiny of the *Travels* as a fictional narrative supplies the minimal unity which embraces the entire book, yet, perhaps paradoxically, forces us to recognize that, beyond this, no unifying artistic formula can be produced. As pure narrative and as philosophic myth, the Voyage to the Houyhnhnms is indeed climactic, but climactic largely by virtue of its contrast to, rather than its development from, the voyages which have preceded it. Against the shifting variety of the first three books, against their appearance of ebullient formlessness, the Fourth Voyage emerges with organic clarity as a magnificent finale. In its orderliness and magnitude, it is unanticipated and independent, and the more powerful for that fact. Yet it casts no retroactive magic over the pages which have preceded it. Their own freedom refuses to be embraced by a single concept of theme or belief, and they resist the boundaries imposed by a single satiric motive or a conventional literary formula. They are informed and sustained by invention; they are the product of a talent which, however varied the uses to which it is put, is unflaggingly and supremely imaginative.

VI

The nature of any satiric fiction must, as we have suggested, be clearly recognized if the satire is to be effective—if we are to understand it properly. We have seen, moreover, that the forms which the fiction may take are limited only by the range of artistic invention —that simple distortion, elaborate postures, and sheer fabrications may all be employed to provide that novel obliquity which is the hallmark of satiric art. Beyond the kind of awareness which is necessary simply if we are to understand what the satirist is doing, the presence of the satiric fiction raises crucial questions in the critical assessment of works which have been called satiric. We have seen that the ingenuity and aptness of the fiction determines, to a large extent, the degree of power which can be achieved in both punitive and persuasive satire. And we have discovered, in works like *A Tale of a Tub* and *Gulliver's Travels,* that the fiction not only can serve to convince or delight us with its treatment of authentic satiric victims, but also can exercise a potent, autonomous ability to satisfy us through sheer imaginative artistry. When this happens, as we have suggested, the work tends to lose its satiric character, either through the diminution of the hostile or critical aspects which constitute the satiric "attack" or because, as is true with most genuine comedy, the objects of assault cease to display the authentic particularity which characterizes the victims of satire. Thus, one might say that when the fiction becomes "excessive" it dominates our interest and understanding and we are no longer concerned with the historical actuality with which, in some measure, the satirist inevitably comes to grips. In such instances we have, as it were, moved beyond the satiric spectrum into the areas of purely imaginative—or, in some cases, generally didactic—literature. And although, as our account of

Gulliver's Travels suggests, the satisfactions and importance of such writing may be enormous, we are no longer confronted with true satire.

We should finally note, at the opposite extreme from the kind of work we have been discussing, those writings which, while they may share motives and seek goals indistinguishable from those of satire— and particularly of persuasive satire—do not employ an overt fiction, in any strategic sense, and should therefore be regarded as polemic rhetoric. It is not surprising that rhetorical writing of this kind is often produced by the same men who are capable of great satire or that their readers are led to regard such products as somehow satiric in intent and effect. The wit, ingenuity, and imagination which operate in the service of satire can be employed to excellent advantage in the service of literal argument, and the same indignation which prompts the invention of the satirist can explode in direct frontal assault.

One of Swift's most famous productions, often cited as a triumphant specimen of his satiric genius, is, I believe, a testimony to his mastery of literal polemic rather than of satire. In the *Drapier's Letters*,[66] though the style and sentiments are inimitably and gloriously Swiftian, we find a work which imposes on us few, if any, of the characteristic demands of satire and for which a mode of inquiry appropriate to satire would be irrelevant and possibly misleading.[67]

Of the miscellaneous documents by Swift which are related to the controversy over William Wood's copper coinage, the four earliest letters from the pen of "M. B. Drapier" appear to be the most important,[68] since, among other things, it was these letters which

---

[66] My references to the text of the *Drapier's Letters* will be found in the edition by Herbert Davis (Oxford, 1935).

[67] Much the same thing might be said about such a work as *The Importance of the Guardian Considered (Prose Works,* VIII, 3–25). Its title is patently facetious and, as Davis points out, "an almost trivial tone is maintained deliberately, as befitting an attempt to expose a rather foolish impostor. . . ." Thise pose, however, is not the manifest invention which marks the satiric fiction but embodies precisely the frame of mind in which presumably Swift wants his readers to view the efforts of Steele. The actual substantive refutation of the *Guardian,* moreover, proceeds along lines which, however trifling, must be accepted quite literally in order to be effective.

[68] Letters VI and VII, whatever their intrinsic interest, cannot claim the historic importance of the earlier documents, for although apparently written during the time of the Wood controversy, they were not published until 1735 in the Faulkner edition of Swift's *Works.* Letter V, to the Lord Viscount Molesworth, is—despite its wit and

achieved a demonstrable political effect seldom surpassed in the history of English literature.[69] As I have indicated, there is much in these four publications which we have come to associate with the satirist's art; their agility and vigor bear the stamp of Swift, and their passionate indignation carries a ring which we have heard before in his most fiercely satiric moments. Moreover, within the terms of our own approach to satire, we discover in the *Drapier's Letters* a bold, unremitting assault upon unmistakable historical particulars, that is, upon Wood and his entire project. But what seems to be lacking, insofar as satire is concerned, is the palpable but vital fiction which transforms polemic into satire and in which ingenious falsehood is indispensable to the disclosure of truth.

It is, of course, obvious that one fiction pervades the whole of these documents: this is the *persona,* the Drapier himself, the humble cloth-merchant in whose identity the Dean of St. Patrick's chose to address the people of Ireland. But this *persona*—unlike any of those whom we have so far considered—is neither a vital device in achieving the persuasive end of the document nor the kind of fictional creation upon whose identification *as* a fiction the power of satire depends. An analysis of the first letter, for example, can be conducted virtually without reference to the feigned identity of its author.[70] If the one passage in which the Drapier announces his own resolutions with respect to Wood's coinage (p. 8) were deleted, the persuasive effect of the whole would not be substantially impaired. What is probably more important is that, even if we were to grant the strategic importance of the *persona,* the effectiveness of this assumed personality lies not in its being recognized as a fictional pose but in its being accepted as genuine! If, that is, the personality of the humble though astute tradesman critically colors these letters, it does so as a successful rhetorical stratagem rather than as a transparent sa-

---

a satiric quality which exceeds those of the earlier letters—by no means as direct an instrument in the controversy over Wood's patent, since it is a relatively frivolous vindication of the Drapier's role in the affair.

[69] The precise historical importance of the letters is nowhere made clearer than in Davis' historical introduction (*Drapier's Letters,* pp. ix–lvii).

[70] An analysis of the *Drapier's Letters,* with special emphasis on the first, is conducted in traditional rhetorical terms in an unpublished Yale doctoral dissertation, Harold D. Kelling, *The Appeal to Reason: A Study of Jonathan Swift's Critical Theory and Its Relation to His Writings* (1948), pp. 133–40.

tiric invention. And finally, it should be pointed out that, whereas the genuine satiric fiction (particularly when it takes the form of a *persona* or putative author) tends to depart from or disguise the satirist's true sentiments, this cannot be said of M. B. Drapier. It is, to be sure, unlikely that readers long believed that a genuine draper had composed the letters—or that Swift intended that this be so[71]— but recognition that the Drapier was a fictional creature would, in no respect, disclose that his position was a fiction as well. For the Drapier is, almost entirely, Swift's alter ego—a politically expedient mask for his identity but, in no respect, for his beliefs. The wrath and the reasoning of M. B. Drapier are undisguisedly those of the Dean himself.

It is possible that in the gross exaggerations and fraudulent arguments which latter-day critics have detected among the Drapier's appeals,[72] there is an inventive device of sufficient importance to mark the writing as satiric. In at least one instance they have indeed been hailed as implicitly satiric, for Professor Quintana exclaims:

Was there ever such exuberant logic? The truth is that the first of the *Drapier's Letters* is, in its peculiar fashion, one of Swift's humorous

[71] It is clear that by the time Lord Carteret had landed in Ireland in October, 1724, almost simultaneously with the appearance of the Fourth Letter, the Drapier had been popularly identified with Swift. The general circulation of the pertinent quotation from the first book of Samuel (with its references to "Jonathan") which occurred at that time can certainly be interpreted in no other way; see Walter Scott's "Memoirs" of Swift in his edition of the *Works* (2d ed.; London, 1883), I, 279; William Monck Mason, *The History and Antiquities of the . . . Church of St. Patrick* (Dublin, 1819), p. 347 n.; and *Correspondence*, III, 220. It is interesting, too, that one of Swift's earliest surviving references to the *Drapier's Letters*, in a letter to Carteret, encloses a copy of the First Letter with the assertion that it "is entitled to a weaver and suited to the vulgar, but thought to be the work of a better hand" (*Correspondence*, III, 191). Swift's pointed and transparent professions of ignorance or indifference to the Drapier in subsequent letters (*Correspondence*, III, 216, 224, 229, 266) are in marked contrast to the silence he preserved with respect to such a work as the *Tale*. To his friend Ford, he showed no reticence whatever concerning the Drapier's identity; see *The Letters of Jonathan Swift to Charles Ford*, ed. D. Nichol Smith (Oxford, 1935), pp. 106, 111–12, 116, 119.

[72] Swift's exaggerations, dispassionately pointed out by Sir Walter Scott (*Works*, I, 268–69), are dwelt on at tedious length by Monck Mason (*History and Antiquities*, appendix, pp. lxxxv–xcvii), who attempts to defend Swift's arguments as respectable and his evidence as literally accurate. Swift's exaggerations—particularly with respect to the actual and anticipated value of Wood's coins—have been regularly noted and alternately defended, condoned, and deplored by scholars ever since. Davis' assessment of the exaggeration as a rhetorical half-truth is characteristically sensible (*Drapier's Letters*, p. 200).

masterpieces, and it is quite unbelievable that all of its readers missed its inspired lunacy—let the English parliament and privy council look to their laurels![73]

Now although Quintana quickly notes that the Drapier's reasoning "is not altogether specious," the passage I have quoted furnishes an excellent specimen of an attempt to regard the Drapier's performance as satiric. In effect, Quintana seems to be arguing that the fictional posture is primary, that the first letter gains its ends not by direct persuasion but by a deliberately and recognizably "lunatic" argument, designed to mock the irrationality of English governing bodies. The Drapier's claims and prophecies, in this view, become not the rhetorical exaggerations of the aroused patriot, but the palpable parody of the manner which Swift attributes to his enemies— the mask which he, as a satirist, has assumed in order to debase, by his discreditable behavior, the reputation of its normal wearer.

This interpretation can certainly not be rejected out of hand. As long as an attack employs a fiction of even the most negligible sort, it is possible to emphasize its satiric quality. But the inescapable fact is that the persuasive power and political consequences of the first letter were not achieved on the basis of its "lunacy" or its capacity to reduce to the absurd. Swift's earliest biographer leaves little doubt as to the way in which the letters were received:

> At the sound of the DRAPIER'S trumpet, a spirit arose among the people, that, in the eastern phrase, was *like unto a tempest in the day of the whirlwind*. Every person of every rank, party, and denomination, was convinced that the admission of WOOD's copper must prove fatal to the commonwealth.[74]

It seems difficult to believe that the response thus described was elicited by a subtle mockery of British administrative unreason. Far more convincing is Sir Walter Scott's view of the matter:

> The first three letters of M.B., Drapier in Dublin, dwell, therefore, upon arguments against Wood's half-pence, derived from their alleged inferiority in weight and value, and the indifferent or suspicious character of the

---

[73] Quintana, *The Mind and Art of Jonathan Swift*, p. 264.

[74] John, Earl of Orrery, *Remarks on the Life and Writings of Jonathan Swift* (5th ed.; London, 1752), p. 49. Like Orrery, Delany treats the *Drapier's Letters* as forthright political argument, and Deane Swift bluntly asserts that they "are all very serious and political" (*Essay upon the Life, Writings, and Character of Dr. Jonathan Swift*, p. 196).

projector himself. These arguments, also, had the advantage of being directly applicable to the grosser apprehensions of the "tradesmen, shopkeepers, farmers, and country people," to whom they are professedly addressed. . . . Whether Swift himself believed the exaggerated reports which his tracts circulated concerning the baseness of the coin, and the villainy of the projector, we have no means of discovering. Once satisfied of the general justice of his cause, he may have deemed himself at liberty to plead it by such arguments as were most likely to afford it support, without rigid examination of their individual validity, or (which is most likely) like most warm disputants, he may himself have received, with eager faith, averments so necessary to the success of his plan.[75]

The satirist's office is plainly neither that of the deliberate deceiver nor the honorably "warm disputant," and if there is indeed, in Quintana's reading of the first letter as an exuberant distortion of parliamentary folly, a third alternative to Scott's suggestions, the reported reception of the letters makes it a most unlikely one.

The most important arguments in the *Drapier's Letters* seem, as a matter of fact, entirely rhetorical. The Drapier anticipates great dangers; he savagely discredits Wood, his patent, and his coinage; he argues from precedent and from public interest; he appeals directly to the emotions and apprehensions of his audiences. If his facts, figures, and prophecies are distorted, these are the falsehoods hazarded by the rhetorician, the falsehoods which will succeed if they are believed. Scholars of a later day, comfortably remote from the turbulence and naïveté of Swift's original audience, have been quick to detect the distortions and errors of logic within these documents. The nineteenth-century students of Swift seem to have been content, for the most part, to designate these elements as "the ordinary and recognized methods of political controversy."[76] In our own time there has been a tendency to impose upon them some pattern peculiar to satire.[77] But it seems safe to say that the immediate effect of these tracts—the effect which won for them a place as one of the most dramatically persuasive literary undertakings in our language

[75] *Works,* ed. Scott, I, 268–69.

[76] The phrase is that of Sir Henry Craik in his *Life of Jonathan Swift* (London, 1882), p. 349.

[77] In addition to Quintana's implication that the letters operate satirically, Davis characterizes Swift's attack on Wood as "political satire and political action," despite a realistic recognition of the purely rhetorical strategy that Swift adopts; see *The Satire of Jonathan Swift,* p. 66.

—was not that of a parody upon anything or of a jesting attempt to reduce Wood and his money to absurdity. The appeal of the *Drapier's Letters* is powerful and direct. The passions and ultimately the action they evoked could only have followed a literal and whole-hearted acceptance of their arguments.

The arguments advanced in the *Drapier's Letters* are not exclusively those of direct polemic rhetoric, for there are occasional passages which clearly fall within our definition of satire. One of the most notable of these, however, should illustrate the manner in which satire performs, albeit effectively, a limited and subordinate function in the context of the letters as a whole. And it should show as well how the change from ordinary rhetoric to satire is marked by a shift from a direct though passionate appeal, to the patently face-tious assumption of a feigned attitude and personality.

The passage in question is found in the concluding paragraphs of the fourth letter (pp. 84–87). In this address "To the Whole People of Ireland" the Drapier has considered in detail the charges brought against the Irish enemies of the coinage project by certain of Wood's allies. The Drapier has been careful, direct, and moving in his ex-amination of most of these charges. What is more, he has deliberate-ly enlarged the scope of controversy to include not only the question of the royal prerogative but the entire nature of Ireland's so-called "dependence." The conclusion of this letter contrasts with the ear-nestness and force of its central portion in an anticlimactic way to which students of Swift have long been accustomed. For here the Drapier ceases to be the forthrightly indignant instructor of his countrymen. His refutation of his enemies has been accomplished; for a moment he can address himself not to the grave topics of royal prerogative and Irish loyalty, but to preposterous, relatively trivial, and satirically vulnerable threats of personal vengeance which are said to have been made by Robert Walpole.[78] For this task, Swift can afford to assume the role of a simple-minded commoner, now elaborately servile, again facetiously and inconsistently arrogant in his anticipation of the day when he will be a "Great Man" and snub Wood. With grotesque ingenuousness, he strives to show the physical impossibility of carrying out Walpole's threat and cram-ming Wood's brass, intact or as "Fireballs" down Irish throats.

[78] The story of Walpole's exasperated warning, whether true or false, seems to have reached Swift through a report in the *Dublin Intelligence;* see *Drapier's Letters,* p. xli.

Plaintively he protests that the incorruptible, wise, and wealthy Walpole would never lend himself to such undertakings, and reassures his countrymen that "we are perfectly safe from that corner" and will "be left to possess our Brogues and Potatoes in Peace, as Remote from Thunder, as we are from Jupiter" (p. 87).

This transient pose provides, as it were, a sensational satiric coda to the direct and powerful rhetoric of the principal arguments. The fatuously literal response of the temporary *persona* invites us to consider the vanity and bombast of the enemy's threats, the real moral stature of Walpole, and the historical facts about such "peace" as Ireland can look forward to. The striking difference between this isolated satiric sally and the fundamental procedure of the letter as a whole is inescapable. When, in 1725, Swift announced, "The work is done, and there is no need of the Drapier,"[79] he was not dismissing the credulous *ingénu* of these last few paragraphs; he was bidding farewell to the painstaking and eloquent leader who spoke, albeit with infinite wit and considerable covert artifice, as a simple and angry man. The stature of Swift's performance in the *Drapier's Letters* is a matter of historical fact. Their success is almost unparalleled in the history of tractarian writing, but it is a success achieved primarily by an adroit rhetorician rather than by a satirist.

VII

Our discussion of many kinds of satiric fiction has taken us far from the traditional notion of the satirist's office. In this chapter we have not been concerned with whatever persuasive or didactic function can be assigned to the art of satire but have dwelt upon those faculties of literary invention by which, no matter what its ultimate purpose, satire must be sustained.

The exploration of Swift's employment of fiction has been conducted with two principal propositions in view. The first of these is that a manifest fiction of some kind is indispensable to the satirist's art. When this fiction is lacking, as we have suggested it is in the central arguments of the *Drapier's Letters,* we may indeed have notably successful rhetoric or exposition, but we do not have satire. When the fiction goes undetected, we may have a triumphant hoax, a satire *manqué,* or even—as in the early history of *The Shortest Way with the Dissenters*—an accidental literary curiosity, but the

[79] *Correspondence,* III, 266.

achievements of none of these are to be confused with those of satire. When the fiction is misconstrued—when, that is, its nature is not clearly manifest—we may or may not discover some sort of satiric effect, but clearly the satirist's intention will be realized accidentally, if at all.

The second proposition, employed somewhat more tacitly than the first, is that the depth and permanence of the satirist's appeal depends quite directly upon the nature of the fiction. Particularly in persuasive satire, the aptness and relevance of the fiction is of obvious importance. The construction or discovery of analogues and symbols which truly sharpen authentic facts and issues, the adoption of postures and the pursuit of arguments which isolate and intensify whatever is vulnerable in the satiric object, the distortions and fabrications which nonetheless disclose true implications and consequences, the exaggerations and inversions which throw into novel focus whatever constitutes the victim's weakness—these are the weapons of satiric strategy, to be assessed in terms of their persuasive success. Yet even where the goal of satire is indistinguishable from that of polemic rhetoric, the virtues of originality, color, wit, intrinsic eloquence—in short, the virtues of sheer literary invention—determine in large measure the magnitude of the satirist's effect. As we have said, the persuasive power of *A Modest Proposal* lies in its exasperated but irrefutable indictment of Irish indifference and folly in the face of injustice and misery, but its initial—and permanent—claim to our admiration is the product of its wildly original imaginative conceit. And what is true of persuasive satiric writing is more clearly so of the punitive kinds, for here the satirist's goal is to provide not conviction, but satisfaction—satisfaction closely akin to that of comedy and, like that of comedy, the product of imaginative artifice.

Common experience, I believe, tends to support this second proposition. The ability of satire to survive its own topicality is a phenomenon which has intrigued many students of the art. Many of the issues to which even the greatest satirists address themselves evaporate quickly with the passing of time; the fashionable follies of one season have disappeared with the next; villains grow old and die, or reform. The permanence which many satiric writings enjoy cannot, it seems, be satisfactorily explained by the rectitude of their motives or the timelessness of the questions to which they are addressed. Such satire continues to delight us largely by virtue of its literary excellence—by the satirist's success with plot and situation and character, by his humor, by his capacity to think and write metaphorically and colorfully and, indeed, to exploit all the resources of diction, in short, by his employment of those skills which mark the successful imaginative writer rather than the tractarian or moralist.

Upon the common reader—that is, upon the intelligent but non-professional reader—the great satires of the past generally exert an effect which has little to do with the purity of their motives, the importance of the issues they reflect, or the immediate consequences which they originally sought to produce. We cannot, I suspect, truly share in the indignation of Juvenal, the partisan commitments of Dryden, the despair of Swift; we are indifferent to the justice or lack thereof in Pope's castigation of his dunces or Byron's ruthless abuse of Southey. But to the glittering novelty of a single epithet of Pope as to the whole miraculous canvas of *Gulliver's Travels* we respond with the satisfaction that is the unchanging signal of artistic excellence. If, in reading the satire of the past, we become adherents of the satirist's cause, it is in much the same spirit as we align ourselves with the heroes of purely imaginative literature and for many of the same reasons. The permanence of satire, like that of the poetic arts, lies chiefly not in universality of theme or topic, but in the universality of its power to delight.

Yet the satirist rarely addresses himself to a universal or timeless audience, and it is here that his resemblance to the poet would seem to disappear. Unlike the purely imaginative writer, he is crucially concerned with *opinion*—opinion to be exploited or altered, as the case may be, yet never to be forgotten in his pursuit of the satiric mission. The poet may, as Aristotle suggests, consider only those universal principles which determine whether a man is better than, worse than, or the same as the generality of mankind, and he may achieve credibility by observing only those broad laws which govern probability in the world as we know it. The satirist, on the other hand, must take into account the convictions and passions, the occurrences and habits and institutions of the immediate moment.

Thus there exists in satiric writing an element quite alien to purely aesthetic expressions and responses—the interplay of the convictions of the author with the opinions of his audience, with respect to issues clearly located in historical reality. When, as I have recurrently pointed out, the satirist's assault becomes subordinate to the artistic fiction which is properly its vehicle, the satiric character of his undertaking diminishes and may even disappear.

With questions of conviction and opinion, we come at last to that great area which has exercised such a constant fascination for students of a writer like Swift. What are the beliefs from which his satiric writing proceeds? Where are they to be discovered? How directly do they govern, and how clearly do they emerge from his satiric enterprise? Is the reconstruction of the satirist's intellectual personality, his faith, his moral convictions merely an exercise in biography, or is it indispensable to an understanding of his work? These are questions with which we shall be concerned in the final chapter.

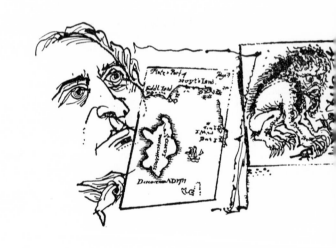

CHAPTER IV

The Satiric Truth

$\mathcal{A}$LMOST EVERYTHING I have been saying about satire has implicitly recognized that, in his own fashion, the satirist must exploit
"truth." Satire cannot be fully effective if we fail to understand what
the satirist genuinely believes and wishes us to believe about the
issues reflected in his work. When we identify his victim, we
establish the "true" direction of his assault, locating his final target in the realm of actuality. Fiction serves a satiric purpose only
when we are aware of the manner and extent of its departure from

authentic fact and belief. The "moment" of satiric recognition, which provided the genesis for my discussion of satire, is a moment of simultaneous awarenesses; we sense that the satiric act or statement is not precisely what it purports to be; it is up to us to supply its "true" meaning from knowledge tacitly shared by the satirist and ourselves.

The truth, for example, which lends sarcasm its entire effect is the uncomplicated antithesis of the scornful superlative which is the form this simple-minded kind of satire usually takes. The satiric truth to be isolated in most appearances of the *persona* can generally be defined in terms of authentic feelings and attitudes of the "real" author. Allegory depends for its effect upon our recognition of phenomena in the world of reality; our knowledge of them converts what would otherwise be pure fiction into an analogical method of discourse. Quasi-slander is redeemed from being outright slander to the extent that demonstrable fact serves as a minimal basis for the satirist's fabrications and distortions.

In this sense—and only, I believe, in this sense—is the truth under all circumstances indispensable to the satirist. It is essential to the satiric art that truth be exploited; it is not essential that truth be novelly disclosed, reaffirmed, augmented, or glorified. In many successful satires—particularly of the kind I have called "punitive"—the only "truth" which must necessarily be apprehended is entirely simple: the identification of a fictional protagonist with an authentic individual, the grasp on manifest actuality which enables us to sense an equally manifest distortion, the recognition of correspondences between the satiric invention and what are often the most commonplace matters of fact.

Since an awareness of the truth, however modestly defined, seems to play this special and indispensable role in the satiric experience, there is a natural temptation to assign some characteristic "truthfulness" to the satirist. It is not entirely easy to disinguish between what I have called the "exploiting" of truth and the "purveying" of it. Yet the distinction must be insisted upon if, as I believe, we are not to lapse into the easy but very dubious generalizations concerning the moral purpose of the satiric office with which both satirists and students of satire have tended to obscure discussions of the art.

Nothing about the minimal definition of satire I have been employing makes it necessary that the satiric work contain an appreciable element of "affirmation." An art whose distinguishing effect is that of attack is almost inevitably more destructive than otherwise. This is not to say that satire cannot elevate, that its consequences cannot be salutary and enlightening, or that, from the assault upon evil, we cannot often expect the enhancement of virtue. On the other hand, it seems entirely possible to me that effective satire can proceed from the most dubious motives, that its result can be purely "negative" from the standpoint of ordinary morality, and that it may even serve, unchecked, as an instrument of skepticism or malice.

The tendency to assign morally benign motives to satire is understandable when the art is seen in the context of historical periods in which the didactic power of any literature was invoked as a principal—if not exclusive—reason for its existence.[1] We can, for instance, sympathize historically with Dryden's proposition (however it may or may not have been borne out in his practice) that the satiric poet "is bound, and that *ex officio,* to give his reader some one precept of moral virtue, and to caution him against some one particular vice or folly."[2] The persistence of such views into our own day, however, is somewhat more difficult to understand. A distinctive tendency of our age's most influential critics has been to dismiss as irrelevant the question of the artist's moral motivation—or at least to refine and manipulate the concept of artistic morality to a point at which it bears little resemblance to traditional notions of benevolence.[3] Yet tacit or explicit assumptions concerning the satirist's decency and altruism continue to color modern discussions both of satire in general and of particular satiric works—conspicuously including those of Swift.

The fact remains, however, that the most memorable satires of Western civilization are not notable for significant affirmations, moral or otherwise. We need not confine our evidence to the most conspicuous examples of indignation or wholesale irreverence—to the satiric elements in Aristophanes or to Juvenal or Swift, *The Dunciad* or *Candide.* Even where we are tempted to describe the satirist's

[1] The familiarity (if not the banality) of Horace's *utile et dulce* in Swift's own day is suggested, as I have pointed out, by his facetious treatment of this doctrine (*Tale,* p. 124).

[2] "A Discourse concerning the Original and Progress of Satire," in *Essays of John Dryden,* ed. W. P. Ker (Oxford, 1926), II, 104.

[3] See, for a recent example, Leslie A. Fiedler, *No! In Thunder* (Boston, 1960), and especially the Introduction, pp. 1–18.

achievement in positive and congenial terms, he remains a satirist entirely by virtue of whatever attack he launches. Horace is "benign" and "good-natured," not because of the benevolence of his observations but because, in comparison with what he might have done (and other satirists *have* done), his strictures are relatively mild; the influence of *Praise of Folly* has doubtless been a wholesome and positive one and Erasmus' tone of voice is often jocular, yet the intrinsic accomplishment of the work lies in its assault upon the weaknesses of outmoded learning. The development of systematic and original beliefs is not the province of satire, and where—as in *The Republic* or *The Vision of Piers Plowman* or, perhaps, *Utopia*—such affirmations must be viewed as the characteristic achievement of the work, then we must recognize that, whatever their glory, they are not the achievements of satire.

Often, indeed, it is precisely at the point where he ceases to attack and reject and seeks to affirm, that the satirist loses his identity—whether in a single work or in his career. Dickens' satire, in such books as *Hard Times* and *Bleak House,* is sacrificed in the interest of elements which, whether we regard them as elevating, fanciful, or merely sentimental, are alien to the art of attack. Mr. Aldous Huxley, however his writing may retain its tartness, has, in his recent works, relinquished the satiric vocation to become a defender of the faith. Changes of this kind may be laudable and welcome; abuse, exposure, and assault are not perhaps an entirely satisfying literary diet—from which it follows that satire may not be either. It is probably quite natural to seek for what is reassuring and constructive from an author we admire; let us only remember that we are not likely to find it in his satire.

The part which truth, then, plays in satire is inevitable only to the extent that we must understand what the satirist is "really talking about," by the fact that his "subject matter" must lie partially in the domain of historic fact—provided his work is genuinely satiric. This is a basic conception of satiric "truth" as it is proper and indispensable to all satire. But our insistence on a limited role for truth in providing a bare, working definition of satire need not automatically outlaw the possibility of assessing satiric works in such terms as their ultimate truth or usefulness—of treating them, as it is any critic's right to treat any work of art, as moral or social or philosophic documents. One has the same "right" to reject a satirist whose premises or arguments or conclusions are unsympathetic as to condemn the work of lyric poets or novelists on similar grounds. Such judgments of essentially "aesthetic" productions are, to be sure, offered in defiance of critical pluralism, and appeal to some single standard of excellence (usually moral) which transcends the peculiar character of the artistic undertaking. But satire, precisely because its characteristic subject is some element in the world of actuality, often appeals to us chiefly and properly because it creates new beliefs, emphasizes and reshapes old ones, or confirms and applies convictions we already hold.

Now, however, I am speaking of values and "truth," however defined, as criteria for judging satire rather than as hallmarks for distinguishing it. It is in this connection that we must consider a further quality on which the effectiveness of satire, though not its irreducible essence, clearly depends. Our *understanding* of satire rests solely on our recognition of the minimal "truth" we have been considering, on our awareness of the satirist's referent in the world of reality and our realization of the scope and nature of his fiction. Our *acquiescence* and *satisfaction* in the satire, however, are strongly conditioned by—if they do not solely depend upon—the sentiments we entertain with respect to its implicit values.

This requirement seems very obvious when considered in connection with the conclusions of persuasive satire. Clearly, if we remain unsympathetic or incredulous throughout the satiric performance, the satirist has, in some measure, failed. Similarly, the punitive satire in which the opprobrium visited upon its victim seems disproportionate or unjust is to some degree unsatisfactory. But these ultimate responses proceed inevitably from the premises which the satirist and his audience earlier share, from common values and convictions, from a normative substratum indispensable to any communication which elicits sentiment or judgment.

In pursuing the normative sanctions of satire, we are again likely to encounter the view which assigns a high moral purpose to the satirist's office. One does not destroy, it is argued, unless one is prepared to build anew. Sensitivity to evil is invariably accompanied by commitment to good. If we are to "agree" with the satirist, he must be agreeable, and the rectitude of his strictures can impress us only in the degree to which they follow from affirmative conviction. And once again we are tempted by quasi-psychological speculations, to the effect that abuse satisfies us only when it is directed to constructive ends and that the satirist is bound to disaffect us unless we sense some "higher purpose" in his apparent lack of charity.

These assertions, metaphorical and otherwise, are all very well; but, once more, satiric writing itself does little to confirm them as fact. The satirist's positive assertions are likely to be unobtrusive and difficult to isolate. Our own pleasure in pursuing his work is rarely, if we are to be quite honest, accompanied by a sense of affirmative conviction. Where, indeed, the satirist too openly rationalizes in arguing a moral foundation for his art, he is likely to sound self-righteous and irrelevant.[4]

The fact is that effective satire can proceed from very minimal commitments to very general values. Some normative basis is indispensable to the satiric performance, but it need be no more clearly specified than that involved in tragedy, comedy, or indeed any art whose effect depends, to some extent, upon an audience's capacity for more or less uniform judgments of gross moral questions. The range of phenomena to which an author can confidently anticipate our responding with praise or blame is, after all, enormous. There is accordingly no reason why the values to which the satirist commits himself cannot be as uncomplicated and transparent as those of other literary artists.

When, as is likely to happen, the satirist views his audience as special or ephemeral, when the standards by which his performance is to be judged involve particular insights and sympathies, he is confronted by a situation in which his normative values may be drawn from sources other than universal predispositions and beliefs. When this occurs, he may well be less satisfactory than otherwise to those who seek to cast him in the role of moralist. For, in such instances, he is likely to exploit dogmas and prejudices or the implicit notions of what is fashionable, attractive, or decorous within his society.

In effect, the normative moral ingredient of satire follows from the fact that culpability has no meaning outside some context of rectitude or propriety. The satirist's choice of that context, however, is governed entirely in terms of its persuasive or artistic utility. He

---

[4] Swift is, of course, no exception. His "apology" in "Verses on the Death of Dr. Swift" (*Poems*, II, 571–72) is his most direct statement about his own satiric practice but cannot be taken seriously by any reader moderately familiar with Swift's best-known satires.

can err in that choice; he can, that is, select standards which his audience—or a large part of it—refuses to share. And the satire which does not rest upon broadly accepted premises is, at best, restricted in its appeal to an elite group of the initiate.

In consequence, the most successful satirists have strongly tended to be conservative, at least with respect to issues relevant to their satire.[5] Certainly, the voice of the satirist is rarely revolutionary. Where his conclusions are unorthodox, unfashionable, or even iconoclastic, they tend to be based on a plea for the "restoration" of what is traditionally sensible or virtuous or good. In America, the true "reformers" in the early twentieth century wrote fiercely mirthless novels of the "case history" kind; but in the satiric enterprises of Sinclair Lewis or Mencken, the rawness and vulgarity of the growing nation were exposed primarily against a background of order, taste, and moderation. At the heart of Evelyn Waugh's most merciless satires, as at the heart of Juvenal's, is an image of traditional decorum, against which extravagance, materialism, and depravity can be judged. Even in the "radicalism" of Voltaire, the basic sanctions invoked are eminently acceptable to men of sense and restraint; the world of *Candide* is objectionable because it is essentially crazy—inconsistent, cruel, inexplicable, excessive, a violation of every rule of sanity and good faith.

"Reforms" are revolutionary to the extent that they are fundamental, and the ultimate revolution overturns or radically alters the basic premises by which men conduct their activities. Thus, though the satirist is often, in some sense, a "reformer," he is rarely, as we have said, a true revolutionary. More often than not, his charge is likely to be leveled at "corruptions" and "abuses," suggesting, tacitly or otherwise, that there has been a falling-away from, or a perversion of, some originally sound and laudable condition. Satirists concerned, for example, with literary problems generally assail scribblers, literary vogues, or the pernicious habits of writers, publishers, and readers; but the greatest of these assaults—those of Pope or Gay or Byron or Swift—proceed by invoking a traditional (if popularly

[5] See Robert C. Elliott, *The Power of Satire: Magic, Ritual, Art* (Princeton, 1960), pp. 266–74. Elliott asserts that the satirist "claims to be conservative" and suspects that politically, "a large majority" of satirists "are what would be called conservative" (p. 273). In my own view, it is the most natural—and hence the easiest—course for any satirist to proceed from "conservative" premises in whatever areas, political or otherwise, he chooses to do battle.

neglected) standard of literary excellence.[6] Indeed, what is "fashionable" in many areas of human life is a common object of satiric attention, precisely because it is held to be ephemeral, excessive, and a departure from older and sounder modes of behavior and belief.

Our recurrent problem, the survival of the satirist's appeal, emerges in this connection again. The approach to satire we have been pursuing would lead one to believe that in the satiric artifice, the conception and execution of the satiric fiction, we are likely to find those elements which lay permanent claim on our admiration and interest. The substantive originality, or truth, or complexity of the satirist's doctrines—both his normative assumptions and the actual conclusions to which they lead him—appear, in most instances, to play a very secondary part in determining his stature. Certainly many (and probably most) of the satires of lasting distinction embody views which lie quite comfortably within the broadest context of belief which marks the character of their age. Such studies as Professor Jack's illuminating discussion of Augustan verse satire tend strongly to support this view as it concerns literary traditions and values,[7] and historians of ideas in general are likely to use even the most outspoken satiric productions of a period as confirmation and exemplification of widely held beliefs rather than as maverick crosscurrents of dissent.

Robert C. Elliott has brilliantly discussed the relationship of satire to the society from which it emerges. While recognizing the "conservative" tendency of the satirist that has been noted here, he has suggested that the satiric power persists by transcending, or at least enlarging, the scope of its original impact so that, at some unspecified stage, both its topicality and its "conservatism" disappear and the satirist "may be revolutionary in ways that society cannot possibly approve, and in ways that may not be clear even to the satirist."[8]

In reconciling the satirist as a "dangerous" or at least uncomfortable presence in society with the conservative fashion in which he ap-

[6] Byron, for example, in *Don Juan* (Canto I, stanzas 201–5), facetiously cites the "rules" of Aristotle and Longinus and declares his own individuality, but he is clearly assailing the misuse of classical authorities by his own contemporaries and he proceeds to urge the commandment, "Thou shalt believe in Milton, Dryden, Pope."

[7] Ian Jack, *Augustan Satire: Intention and Idiom in English Poetry, 1660–1750* (Oxford, 1952).

[8] *The Power of Satire*, p. 275.

pears to exploit the most basic values of society and to argue for their preservation, Professor Elliott asserts that "an attack by a powerful satirist on a local phenomenon seems to be capable of indefinite extension in the reader's mind into an attack on the whole structure of which that phenomenon is a part."[9] This process is described as "magical," functioning by "synecdoche, which is one of the foundations of magic," and, accordingly, whatever the satirist's intent, the assault upon "abuses and perversions" (presumably acceptable to the original satiric audience) becomes an assault upon the total institution. The process by which original intention and effect undergo such radical alterations may, indeed, be a mystic social phenomenon. One is tempted, however, to recognize that many literary works of a kind very different from satire undergo comparable changes of interpretation in the course of history, attributable in some instances to sloppy readings, hearsay reputations, or "influential" critics and, in others, to the wishful thinking by which congenial if inaccurate interpretations are imposed upon the works of one period by the readers of a subsequent one. And one wonders how frequently the subversive dimension of satire is, in fact, thus augmented with the passage of time. Indeed the satirist's invocation of standards which are basic and permanent strongly suggests that the outrage he may originally court with his assault upon particular, cherished institutions is rather likely to diminish with the passing of time and the restoration of his position to historically acquired perspective.

What is, in my opinion, particularly interesting about Professor Elliott's discussion, however, is his choice of the "powerful" satirists who, ultimately or immediately, can be considered "antisocial," whose presence may, with some justice, be judged dangerous to the fundamental values of their society. For here he mentions Lucian, Molière, and, most conspicuously, Swift!

The question that occurs is whether there are not a few peculiarly "powerful" satirists, powerful above all else in the survival of their satiric impact, who reject, from the outset, the essential conservatism of their calling, who are not content to rely upon commonly accepted norms, whatever their source, but who, in the very foundation of their satiric structure, are at odds with common beliefs and values. In other words, when (and it is, I think, far more rarely than Professor Elliott would have us suppose) a satiric work continues to

[9] *Ibid.*, p. 271.

impress us as fundamentally alien or threatening to accepted beliefs and to the common good, it seems probable that the satirist has deliberately rejected the normative values at his disposal and sought to advance his own particular and doubtless unpopular ones as the basis for his attack.

If indeed there is such satire, it has certainly been created at enormous cost. The satirist whose moral or political assumptions are of his own forging not only courts misunderstanding and disapproval; he is faced with the task of constructing, within the context of his own work, the premises which are, as it were, *donné* in the performances of most of his fellow satirists. He refuses, that is, to rely upon an audience which brings commonly accepted values tacitly into play in the judgments which his work invites. Rather, he must, in the very conduct of his satiric enterprise, develop and enforce the principles by which his persuasive or punitive mission will ultimately succeeed or fail.

This task, difficult enough in a context of literal exposition, is incredibly hard within a satiric structure. The obliquity or invention which we have called satiric fiction is certainly not hospitable to the development of firmly stated principles. If the premises from which the satirist operates are not implicit, if they are, moreover, likely to encounter incredulity and resistance on the part of his reader, assuredly they call for the most carefully systematic statement—a statement which has the power to overcome the reader's predispositions and enlist him, as it were, as a sympathetic partner in the satiric undertaking. And a statement of this sort—calling, as it would appear to, for logic, tact, and unequivocal good sense—is precisely what seems most alien to the usual satiric production.

I am, nonetheless, inclined to believe that, in the case of some of Swift's most notable writing, something of this sort actually occurs. If, that is, *A Tale of a Tub* and *Gulliver's Travels* continue to be at odds with some of mankind's most cherished notions about its own dignity and destiny, this is, I think, the product of Swift's deliberate intention. In a limited but important respect, these works are now— and always have been—assaults upon the most fundamental convictions and beliefs; rather than exploiting basic assumptions about the human condition in order to "expose" particular abuses, they have been directed to the assumptions themselves. And, in consequence, Swift can be said to have abandoned "ordinary" satiric practice to the extent that he deliberately refuses to invoke and exploit the moral preconceptions of his audience in the pursuit of particularized satiric assaults. The normative matrix in which his satire is undertaken, the principles which lend sanction to his specific strictures are, as it were, of his own making, advanced, if necessary, in defiance of that substratum of opinion on which we may expect the ordinary satirist at least minimally to rely.

The development of singular premises is, in a sense, not properly a satiric undertaking at all, but is rather the function of that "philosophic" element in some satiric works which, as we have noted earlier, is sometimes confused with authentic satire. And exactly because this element is non-satiric, we must recognize the extraordinary difficulty of incorporating it successfully within an essentially satiric product.

Even in Swift's writing, this "philosophic" production of special premises is very much the exception rather than the rule. Like almost all satirists, Swift is generally content to appeal to the principles of orthodox piety, of cultivated taste, of ordinary sense and restraint in his exposure of contemporary follies. The *Bickerstaff Papers* call into play only a normal, hardheaded capacity to sense what is ludicrous. The *Directions to Servants* invokes only a simple understanding of what, at least in the eighteenth century, a servant should properly be; the *Tritical Essay*, "Polite Conversation," and the various jocular correctives of social habits proceed from a tacit kind of patrician austerity, in the light of which carelessness and vulgarity are plainly culpable. A distaste for what is squalid, incongruous, pretentious, or hypocritical is all that is needed to respond to the satire in most of Swift's verse; an understanding of (if not necessarily an acquiescence in) the political principles of Harley's brand of Toryism provides the premises for the political tracts of Swift's *Examiner* period. And even in the *Tale* and the *Travels,* we are generally asked to do little more than to recognize—and deplore—manifestations of vanity, venality, dirt, dishonesty, and other unmistakable vices and frailties.

II

It is entirely possible to regard *A Tale of a Tub* as the systematic "exposure," on tolerably acceptable grounds, of a formidable diversity of "modern" habits and institutions. Our previous discussion of the work has, indeed, suggested that this approach to the *Tale,* with its insistence upon identifying the particular objects of the satire at each juncture, is greatly preferable to speculation about the "unity" or "thematic structure" of this complicated book. Now, however, it is appropriate to ask whether the *Tale* is not, in its most fundamental character, a far more singular and unsettling work than our previous discussion has suggested. Do its individual strictures, that is, derive sanction only from the "normative" predispositions of the ordinary reader—or can they be seen as applications and embodiments of some more fundamental and disturbing doctrine, peculiar to the *Tale* itself?

There is, as we have suggested, enough good sense and amusement in many of these assaults so that we can regard them as intelligible and effective in their own right. Even in the absence of special premises, of a special "philosophic" dimension, the *Tale* can probably be regarded as "successful" satire and, as I have noted, its essentially comic qualities alone can doubtless account for much of the satisfaction which readers continue to find in it.

But to accept the book at this level alone is to ignore the most compelling and unforgettable element in its pages—the strange, perplexing, yet uniquely arresting "argument" which appears in the ninth section, the famous *"Digression concerning the Original, the Use and Improvement of Madness in a Commonwealth."* The complexity of its development, the unorthodoxy of its views, and the curious intensity of its tone all serve to set the chapter somewhat apart from its context and to justify the term "climactic." More than in these respects, though, the chapter—or at least its central section—seems to me singular in serving precisely the difficult end I have been discussing—the establishment of a comprehensive system of convictions which, while they frustrate ordinary expectations and reject common values, lend sanction and authority to the satire they are designed to support. Moreover, the chapter makes clear how such a statement of belief can emerge without the abandonment of the satiric fiction, in the context of the dubiously motivated literary project which the entire *Tale* purports to be.

By the time we arrive at Section IX, a rather remarkable number of objects have been exposed to satiric attack. Although we subsume them, as I think we can, under the major categories of abuses in religion, in contemporary letters, and in "Modern" learning and science, their variety remains great and their satiric discussion fugitive and somewhat fragmentary. Under the first of these headings has fallen much of the "three brothers" allegory, with its intensifying attack upon Enthusiasm, brought to a memorable plateau of sustained derision in Section VIII, the account of the Aeolists. Under the second we have encountered such literary practices as addiction to prefaces; an exaggerated belief in fables, symbols, and allegories; public lamentation, self-pity, and self-advertisement; and the stylistic vices, with their putative origin in Grub-street, which are attributed to such figures as Dryden and L'Estrange. And we have, finally, noted the many scholarly sins of Wotton and Bentley—their lack of decorum, their devotion to systematizing, deciphering, and index-learning, their ostentatious addiction to learned lumber, and their allegedly inordinate veneration of modern achievements in a number of areas.

What, if anything, would be missing from this diversity of satiric assaults if the "Digression concerning Madness" had been omitted? I do not think they would lose in intelligibility; nor need the lack of "unity," as conventionally defined, concern us. What, in my opinion, is called for is a certain basis of conviction. From the outset, to be sure, the posture of Swift's *persona* has been playful, his formal and substantive commitments slight, his satiric attention wide-ranging and easily diverted. If we feel any uneasiness, it may be on the ground that some at least of his satiric targets are rather more formidable than he will allow—manifestations, however absurd, of habits and doctrines which are puzzling and dangerous. Fun, we may argue, is fun, but in this lengthy treatment of very real abuses, is there no more than fragments and fooling? And we may also entertain, by this point, certain questions about Swift's selection of particular satiric victims. Why does he recurrently address himself to fables and "emblems," certainly rather innocuous forms of literature? What is inherently "wrong" about a systematic assessment of human knowledge? And are there no more vulnerable grounds on which to attack the Enthusiasts than the mechanics of Enthusiasm themselves? Certainly there are clear doctrinal fallacies, if not heresies, of which they are guilty and which would tempt the satiric defender of the Establishment to attack them, however obliquely. And, more significantly, is the memory of the Commonwealth grown so dim that the satirist can ignore the authentic political dangers ever present in Puritanism? One wonders, in fact, at the omission of virtually all political matters from the wide range of "abuses" to which the book has been directed. We have, in short, grounds for deriving much amused satisfaction from the book, yet the same air of playfulness which has thus far provided much of its charm may also, in the face of the tangible and sometimes grave issues it treats, be just a bit dissatisfying. Swift, for all his irresponsible air, has chosen to do certain things and not to do others. Is there no principle to which these decisions can be traced?

It is possible that I am overstating what are, at most, subtle dissatisfactions and that it is precisely because the "Digression concerning Madness" is totally unexpected and, in a sense, uncalled-for that its impact is so extraordinary. Climaxes, however, do not exist in vacuums, and it is not the least of Swift's accomplishments that what Professor Quintana has called "the consummate statement of that moral realism which directed Swift's entire intellectual life"[10] is a firmly integrated part of a gay, frankly diffuse, and largely playful work the size of the *Tale*.

We should recognize, at the outset, that Section IX is, indeed, focally located from the standpoint of the *Tale's* superficial but indispensable structure. It brings together, even more closely than does the preceding chapter on the Aeolists, the narrative allegory and the deliberations of the mock-author which dominate the prefatory materials and the digressions. It is the first of the "digressive" chapters (since strictly speaking, the Aeolist myth has been part of the narrative allegory) which purports to be a direct comment upon the narrative proper. Accordingly, the topics proper to each of the two structural elements in the book (literary and learned abuses in the digressions, religious abuses in the narrative) can appropriately be incorporated within a single chapter. The "excuse" for the section, its *raison d'être,* is consistent with what has preceded it; the author appears to defend what the extended discussion of the Aeolists implies is a uniquely important aspect of his story. This aspect is madness. And it is the defense of madness—transformed ultimately into a plea that the virtues of madness be recognized and exploited— which provides the section with its overt principle of order.

It is indeed characteristic of the *Tale* that the basic structure of the digression actually reflects the three principal topics with which the

---

[10] *The Mind and Art of Jonathan Swift,* p. 96.

title announces the chapter will be concerned—"the Original, the Use and Improvement of Madness in a Commonwealth." Initially, the author defends madness on the ground that the greatest imperial, philosophic, and religious revolutions can be attributed to it. In the course of this "argument," however, he assigns the "original" of madness to mean physiological sources, the "lower Faculties," i.e., those of excretion and generation. In his second major section, the author essentially discusses the "use" of madness by arguing that it is, above all other things, conducive to the "happiness" of mankind. And finally he offers a demonstration that the reforming powers of madness within the state are far greater than has yet been acknowledged by political thinkers and urges (in one of the few passages in which the *Tale* touches on political matters)[11] that madmen be chosen for important public offices.

For our immediate purposes it is the second, central portion of the chapter which alone is crucial. We should, however, note that the critical character and scope of this section are anticipated by the earlier pages of the digression. For, beginning humbly and jocularly enough, with the avowed intention of showing how logical it is that the Puritan brother, Jack, should, as a madman, have created a great religious revolution, the author rapidly develops his argument to incorporate a number of satiric assaults. Again, in his coarsely mechanical explanation of psychological phenomena, he is mocking both the manner and substance of scientific materialists, and at the

[11] The intrusion of a purely political touch in the author's deferential suggestions to Seymour, Musgrave, Bowls, and Howe (*Tale,* pp. 175-76) seems sufficiently alien in this context to merit some attention. I am inclined to regard the passage as a product of the same motives and the same period as the "Dedication to Lord Somers" (which can be dated, by a reference to the "late Reign" of William III, as no earlier than March, 1702). Speaking of Somers, Macaulay says, "Such men as Howe and Seymour hated him implacably," and not only these two but Musgrave as well played leading roles in the impeachment of Somers in 1701; see Macaulay's *The History of England from the Accession of James II* (New York, 1849-61), V, 461, 488-93, and Narcissus Luttrell, *A Brief Historical Relation of State Affairs from September 1678 to April 1714* (Oxford, 1857), V, 33, 39, 51, 53, 61-63. These are doubtless the unnamed enemies referred to in the dedication (*Tale,* p. 26). The inclusion of Bowls, likewise a Tory but not known to have been involved with Somers, seems to be prompted by the fact that he went mad while on the bench at the assizes; see editors' note, *Tale,* p. 176, Luttrell's *Historical Relation,* IV, 482, 545, and 592, and Burnet's *History of His Own Time* (London, 1838), p. 683. That this fugitive political satire, doubtless included in deference to Swift's patron, should appear so unobtrusively is suggestive of the latitude which "a tale of a tub" permits.

same time stigmatizing philosophic and religious Enthusiasm as manifestations of madness—a madness in turn engendered by the very
opposite of "inspiration."[12] In view of Swift's later implications concerning the universal tendency toward delusion, it is significant that
he considers not only the madness of the "conquerors" but the reason for their success in gaining disciples (p. 167). For, by a bogus-
mechanical account drawn from the field of harmonics,[13] he makes
it clear that the success of Enthusiasts depends upon the capacity of
common men to share their madness. And even this point is further
developed for the purpose of a final thrust at Wotton, who, it appears, is mad enough, yet a "conqueror" *manqué* who has misap-
plied to "vain Philosophy" the lunacy which qualifies him well for
"the Propagation of a new Religion" (p. 169).[14]

The movement from this complex but fairly obvious satiric development to the profound and disturbing exposition of the famous
central paragraphs is achieved by a playful Swiftian device which,
even in this crucial position, transiently supplies the air of solemn

[12] For a detailed discussion of these passages, with particular reference to their relationship to Henry More, see Harth's *Swift and Anglican Rationalism*, pp. 101–27.

[13] "And, I think, the Reason is easie to be assigned: For, there is a particular *String*
in the Harmony of Human Understanding, which in several individuals is exactly
of the same Tuning. This, if you can dexterously screw up to its right Key, and then
strike gently upon it; Whenever you have the Good Fortune to light among those
of the same Pitch, they will by a secret necessary Sympathy, strike exactly at the same
time" (*Tale*, p. 167). Harth (pp. 119–20) finds a model—if not a parodic object—
for the passage in Glanvill's *Scepsis Scientifica*, in which, using the analogy of musi-
cal strings, Glanvill mechanically explains "the power of one man's imagination
upon another's." The concept of sympathetic vibration may have been suggested to
Swift from another source as well, for the phenomenon is the object of one of Narcissus Marsh's two published scientific essays, a discourse on the *Sympathy of Viol or
Lute Strings* in Robert Plot's *The Natural History of Oxfordshire* (Oxford, 1677),
pp. 289–99.

[14] For all its crucial character, the chapter permits *ad hominem* satire with a vengeance. Damned with the madness of the philosophic imperialist, Wotton is doubly
damned as a philosophic imperialist who has failed. And to suggest that Wotton,
an ordained clergyman who had produced the *Reflections* in the defense of Anglican
orthodoxy (see his "Preface" to the *Reflections* at pp. iv–xvi), might have been more
successful in "the Propagation of a new Religion" is a further direct insult. Moreover, Swift, in implying that even as a representative Modern, Wotton has failed,
refers to his victim's "Brother Modernists" who whisper against the *Reflections*. If,
as I believe, the Digression was written in whole or part as late as 1698, this may well
be a pointed reference to the disapproval of Thomas Rymer who, though ranked by
Swift as a Modern, dealt very harshly with Wotton in his *Essay concerning Critical
and Curious Learning* (London, 1698).

irresponsibility which marks the entire *Tale* as a parodic enterprise. Seeking to explain how the same vapor can produce effects so different as *"Alexander the Great, Jack of Leyden,* and Monsieur *Des Cartes,"* the author strains his "Faculties to their highest stretch," calls for his reader's devout attention, and produces—a hiatus in the manuscript!

Yet even before this frivolous intrusion, there is a strong suggestion that the reader should expect more from the chapter than the consistent satiric development of a single brilliant conceit. For in extending the influence of madness from imperial and philosophic conquests into the area of religion, Swift offers a general proposition concerning its powers:

Of such great Emolument, is a Tincture of this *Vapour,* which the World calls *Madness,* that without its Help, the World would not only be deprived of those two great Blessings, *Conquests* and *Systems,* but even all Mankind would unhappily be reduced to the same Belief in Things Invisible (p. 169).

The sentence serves as a kind of transition between the open facetiousness and inversion, which is the chief mode of the *Tale* in its satiric and comic aspects, and the very different technique in which the substance of the argument is an almost literal Swiftian truth with only its emotional tone—the implications of perverse praise and blame conveyed by particular words—preserving the fictional "wrongness" of the author. Thus, in the sentence I have quoted, the chief propositions are to be taken as fact: if it were not for madness, the world would lack conquests and systems and men might, indeed, adhere "to the same Belief in Things Invisible." As apologist for madness, as an inhabitant of the mad world, Swift's spokesman errs not in his statement of the propositions but in the judgment he attaches to it. This error emerges only in his "weighted" words (for "deprived" Swift would have us read "relieved"; for "blessing," "curse"). There is, moreover, an adumbration of the pivotal use which Swift will make of the term "happiness" in the ensuing paragraphs. For it is doubtless true that men would "unhappily" undergo a return to the sanity of pious belief; and where governed only by concern for their own happiness, they will, indeed, regard madness as a "help" and conquests and systems as "blessings."

Here is not mere "obliquity," but again, in a new form, the

"internal logic of error." The caprice of the author has largely disappeared; and if the wrongheadedness he shares with most men persists, it is in the value which he attaches to facts that are in themselves undeniable. And this new capacity to state things as they are emerges at the same point at which intellectual systems, political conquests, and religious error are firmly linked by their common cause, madness. The stage is set for the great discourse on deception which occupies the central part of the chapter.

Having therefore so narrowly past thro' this intricate Difficulty, the Reader will, I am sure, agree with me in the Conclusion; that if the *Moderns* mean by *Madness,* only a Disturbance or Transposition of the Brain, by Force of certain *Vapours* issuing up from the lower Faculties; Then has this *Madness* been the Parent of all those mighty Revolutions, that have happened in *Empire,* in *Philosophy,* and in *Religion.* For, the Brain, in its natural Position and State of Serenity, disposeth its Owner to pass his Life in the common Forms, without any Thought of subduing Multitudes to his own *Power,* his *Reasons* or his *Visions;* and the more he shapes his Understanding by the Pattern of Human Learning, the less he is inclined to form Parties after his particular Notions; because that instructs him in his private Infirmities, as well as in the stubborn Ignorance of the People. But when a Man's Fancy gets *astride* on his Reason, when Imagination is at Cuffs with the Senses, and common Understanding, as well as common Sense, is Kickt out of Doors; the first Proselyte he makes, is Himself, and when that is once compass'd, the Difficulty is not so great in bringing over others; A strong Delusion always operating from *without,* as vigorously as from *within.* For, Cant and Vision are to the Ear and the Eye, the same that Tickling is to the Touch. Those Entertainments and Pleasures we most value in Life, are such as *Dupe* and play the Wag with the Senses. For, if we take an Examination of what is generally understood by *Happiness,* as it has Respect, either to the Understanding or the Senses, we shall find all its Properties and Adjuncts will herd under this short Definition: That, *it is a perpetual Possession of being well Deceived.* And first, with Relation to the Mind or Understanding; 'tis manifest, what mighty Advantages Fiction has over Truth; and the Reason is just at our Elbow; because Imagination can build nobler Scenes, and produce more wonderful Revolutions than Fortune or Nature will be at Expence to furnish. Nor is Mankind so much to blame in his Choice, thus determining him, if we consider that the Debate meerly lies between *Things past,* and *Things conceived;* and so the Question is only this; Whether Things that have Place in the *Imagination,* may not as properly be said to *Exist,* as those that are seated in the *Memory;* which may be justly held in the Affirmative, and very much to the Advantage of the former, since This is acknowledged to the *Womb* of Things, and the other allowed to be no more than the *Grave*. Again, if we take this Definition of Happiness, and examine it with Reference to the Senses, it will be acknowledged wonderfully adapt. How fade and insipid do all Objects accost us that are not convey'd in the Vehicle of *Delusion?* How shrunk is every Thing, as it appears in the Glass of Nature? So, that if it were not for the Assistance of Artificial *Mediums,* false Lights, refracted Angles, Varnish, and Tinsel; there would be a mighty Level in the Felicity and Enjoyments of Mortal Men. If this were seriously considered by the World, as I have a certain Reason to suspect it hardly will; Men would no longer reckon among their high Points of Wisdom, the Art of exposing weak Sides, and publishing Infirmities; an Employment in my Opinion, neither better nor worse than that of *Unmasking,* which I think, has never been allowed fair Usage, either in the *World* or the *Play-House.*

In the Proportion that Credulity is a more peaceful Possession of the Mind, than Curiosity, so far preferable is that Wisdom, which converses about the Surface, to that pretended Philosophy which enters into the Depth of Things, and then comes gravely back with Informations and Discoveries, that in the inside they are good for nothing. The two Senses, to which all Objects first address themselves, are the Sight and the Touch; These never examine farther than the Colour, the Shape, the Size, and whatever other Qualities dwell, or are drawn by Art upon the Outward of Bodies; and then comes Reason officiously, with Tools for cutting, and opening, and mangling, and piercing, offering to demonstrate, that they are not of the same consistence quite thro'. Now, I take all this to be the last Degree of perverting Nature: one of whose Eternal Laws it is, to put her best Furniture forward. And therefore, in order to save the Charges of all such expensive Anatomy for the Time to come; I do here think fit to inform the Reader, that in such Conclusions as these, Reason is certainly in the Right; and that in most Corporeal Beings, which have fallen under my Cognizance, the *Outside* hath been infinitely preferable to the *In:* Whereof I have been farther convinced from some late Experiments. Last Week I saw a Woman *flay'd,* and you will hardly believe, how much it altered her Person for the worse. Yesterday I ordered the Carcass of a *Beau* to be stript in my Presence; when we were all amazed to find so many unsuspected Faults under one Suit of Cloaths: Then I laid open his *Brain,* his *Heart,* and his *Spleen;* But, I plainly perceived at every Operation, that the farther we proceeded, we found the Defects encrease upon us in Number and Bulk: from all which, I justly formed this Conclusion to my self; That whatever Philosopher or Projector can find out an Art to sodder and patch up the Flaws and Imperfections of Nature, will deserve much better of Mankind, and teach us a more useful Science, than that so much in present Esteem, of widening and exposing them (like him who held *Anatomy* to be the ultimate End of *Physick*.) And he, whose Fortunes and Dispositions have placed him in a convenient Station to enjoy the Fruits of this noble Art; He that can with *Epicurus* content his Ideas with the *Films* and *Images* that fly off upon his Senses from the *Superficies* of Things; Such a Man truly wise, creams off Nature, leaving the Sower and the Dregs, for Philosophy and Reason to lap up. This is the sublime and refined Point of Felicity, called, *the Possession of being well deceived;* The Serene Peaceful State of being a Fool among Knaves.

These two paragraphs are quite possibly the most arresting ever written by Swift. They have received abundant critical attention, interpretation, and paraphrase, beside which our scrutiny may appear rather pedestrian. I think we should recognize that, in addition to its intrinsic qualities and to the part which it plays in furnishing the substratum of doctrine which informs and enforces so much of the satire in the *Tale,* the passage is a rare instance of Swift's writing at a level of abstraction which transcends the particulars of either satire or comedy. With a few famous passages from his *Correspondence,* the Fourth Voyage of Gulliver, and a few fragments from his poems (notably, of course, the *Verses on the Death of Dr. Swift*), it constitutes the source of whatever fundamental beliefs with respect to morality and metaphysics we can attribute to Swift.

We have already suggested that this, the central division of the three into which the whole section may be said to fall, is integrated into the total context by contributing to the alleged purpose toward which the chapter is directed. In a sense, it too defends madness by urging its importance for the "happiness" of mankind. Beyond this, however, the passage is not essentially satiric—for it is more than satiric. Undeniably bleak in its doctrine, if it is an attack, it is directed against an object even more general than the generic representations of vice and folly which, I have argued, are properly the objects of comic treatment. Mankind, or a universal disposition of mankind, is the object of Swift's attention here. Moreover, the "fiction" of the passage is singularly difficult to locate in such a device as a false posture, narrative invention, or selective distortion. Despite the claims of some critics that Swift "ironically" assumes—and then abruptly drops!—a patently false position,[15] it appears that, through-

---

[15] I have discussed some of the difficulties of this interpretation in a review of Robert C. Elliott's "Swift's *Tale of a Tub*: An Essay in Problems of Structure," in *Philological Quarterly,* XXXI (1952), 302–3.

out the passage, the non-literal element consists at most in an ambiguity (derived from the ambiguity of words themselves) of the
kind we have already noted in an earlier passage.

I have mentioned the generous latitude allowed the putative author of the *Tale*. One thing, however, that such latitude will not embrace is the abandonment of all fiction, the entirely "sincere" statement, in fact, the very appearance of the author *in propria persona*
which certain critics have purported to find in the passage under
discussion. Whatever generalizations may be dubious about the *Tale,*
it seems clear that its "author" must be consistently suspect, that he
cannot, certainly at this belated stage of his performance, ask us to
accept his argument as a literal, authentic statement of sober belief.
The book, that is, cannot cease to be "a tale of a tub," and it is within such an apparently frivolous framework that even so profound
and genuine an argument as that in this passage must be viewed.
Thus, although we cannot regard the discourse on deception as a
"fiction," but as a forthright though very subtle argument, we must
recognize that the passage is complicated by overtones designed to
suggest that the author remains irresponsible and vulnerable to sober
criticism. These overtones are compatible with the nominal purpose
of the entire chapter (the defense of madness), and they provide the
minimal conformity with the pervasive "wrongness" or caprice
which we have come to expect of the putative author.

The first of the two long paragraphs begins with a summary statement about madness, as it has thus far been quite consistently described: its presence leads to the "mighty revolutions"; its absence
permits men to adhere to "the Pattern of Human Learning" and
lead their lives in "the common Forms." This beginning adheres to
the alleged topic of the entire chapter and invites the reader to consider the ensuing discourse merely as an additional exposition of the
character of madness. The madness is ostensibly of the same sort
that has been attributed to the lunatic Enthusiast, Jack, and to the
wind-demented Aeolists. Swift seems to assert, with a kind of wild
sagacity, that the whole of self-deluding, superficial mankind is
mad. But his true discussion is directed to another, more universal
infirmity than pathological madness—an infirmity for which the
label "madness" may be an apt pejorative but which inherently
needs no such damning appellation to appear uniquely shocking.

This infirmity is "delusion," the delusion engendered by the overcoming of reason, by *irrationality* seen not only as the privation of reason but as an "affirmative" quality in the sense that it can (as the previous part of the section makes clear) engender and enforce evils of immense magnitude. "When a Man's *Fancy* gets *astride* on his reason" is more than an arresting figure. It is a description, and for Swift's original audience, a quite intelligible one,[16] of the irrational; it applies to madness, but it applies to a great deal more besides. From this metaphorical definition of the irrational, Swift addresses himself to a threefold task. He must, first, firmly discredit irrationality, and do so in the face of a fact of which he has previously made much, namely the attractiveness of irrationality, in its operations and effects, for mankind. He seeks, second, to stigmatize as irrational vast areas of human activity normally considered in quite an opposite light. And finally, as a kind of synthesis of the two former propositions, he concurrently strives to point out that although irrationality leads to falsehood and delusion, it leads also to what men *consider* to be happiness. To achieve this final, comprehensive formulation, he proceeds, systematically in my opinion, through a series of stages, each of which treats, in progressively expanding contexts, new aspects of irrational delusion, suggests their essential folly, and, at the same time, indicates how they operate toward what the run of mankind considers "happiness."

Thus the argument begins on an almost ludicrously simple plane, with tickling, a phenomenon which, in the grossest sensory area, embodies to perfection the qualities of delusion, folly, and superficial pleasure. From this we move to *"Cant and Vision,"* and Swift progresses so carefully that, in this initial phase, his analogy is very modest and refers to these delusory activities only as those which "Dupe and play the Wag with the Senses." The touch, the eye, and the ear, therefore, provide the basis for the crucial proposition that happiness is "a perpetual Possession of being well Deceived." This is not, of course, a literal assertion; Swift plays upon the ambiguity of "Ear and Eye," for it is to neither organ alone that the powers of Cant and Vision are ultimately directed. These initial illustrations are plainly humble ones, in view of the sweeping conclusions to

[16] The definition of madness as the overcoming of Reason by Fancy or the Imagination is a central point in More's *Enthusiasmus Triumphatus*. Passages from More which closely parallel Swift's "psychology" are cited in my unpublished doctoral dissertation, *Swift's Satire in "A Tale of a Tub"* (University of Chicago, 1953), p. 310, as well as in Harth's *Swift and Anglican Rationalism*, pp. 122–24.

which they finally lead; it is precisely in this sort of understatement that the misleadingly unperceptive character of Swift's invented *persona* is preserved throughout the whole powerful passage.

From his definition of happiness, the author moves on to produce evidence that what has been asserted applies both to the senses and the "Mind or Understanding." With respect to intellectual powers, his contentions are, at this intermediate stage, still rather restrained, being limited to the question of imagination as opposed to memory, of "things past" versus "things conceived." With human "satisfaction" as the sole criterion of judgment, Swift asserts that the "imagined," as opposed to the historically demonstrable "remembered" is again desirable and—from the standpoint of those who succumb to the powers of the imagination—deals with what "exists"; with its "nobler Scenes" and "more wonderful Revolutions," it conduces, as does tickling, to human happiness. And the area in which delusion operates has now been enlarged to incorporate the products—one is bound to think largely literary—of pure imagination.

In moving to re-examine his definition of happiness "with Reference to the Senses," the author may appear to be repeating a demonstration he has already concluded. But in this new context, "Sense" is plainly a mere metaphor, and appearance and reality, in the full breadth of their traditional philosophic implications, are what are being considered. The "artificial Mediums" are largely figurative; for "weak sides and Infirmities" are clearly more than objects of vision.

The position of the author continues to appear somewhat ambiguous at this point, particularly with respect to his apparent disapproval of the fact that "Men . . . reckon among their high Points of Wisdom, the Art of exposing weak Sides. . . ." One wonders whether this is a bogus disparagement of the procedure which, Swift is ultimately to reveal, is the only true pursuit of wisdom or whether it is a more direct attack upon a species of exposure (possibly maliciously or frivolously motivated) which actually enjoys too high an opinion in society. I think it is neither, but again a statement which can be read almost literally *except* that we must view with suspicion the author's professed concern for human happiness. To expose weak sides and publish infirmities is (like unmasking, in which previously concealed ugliness is brought to light) no "high point of wisdom"—if, that is, wisdom consists in what will insure human felicity. Such exposure is simply the revelation of truth. As such, it is not productive of happiness, nor can it win the approval of those to whom happiness is everything and truth a matter of indifference.

At this point, the argument moves, properly enough, to its highest level, with the beginning of the second paragraph. As previously, the distinction between "wisdom" and "pretended philosophy" need not confuse us. Assuming that the end of both activities is happiness, then the "truly wise" man seeks to confirm a "Peaceful Possession of the Mind," while whatever subverts that peace is merely fraudulent.

From tickling we have moved to the eternal problems of human contentment and human wisdom, the province of philosophy, the matrix of most ideas governing thought and conduct. The new ingredient in the paragraph appears to be the much discussed matter of the inner and outer aspect of things, the "surface-depth" distinction on which so much critical attention has been lavished. But I think it is a mistake to view as the *major* proposition of the paragraph the assertion that things which look pleasant on the outside are unpleasant at heart, that beguiling exteriors conceal inner corruption. This point, a simple one, has been delightfully made in Swift's account of the clothes-philosophy (Section II); it receives playful adumbration in the Introduction; it is implicit in the attacks upon systems and index-and-preface learning in such sections as the "Digression in Praise of Digressions."

Now, Swift's examples disclose an unmistakable intention to imply that "happy" *externals* are, in themselves, calculated to appeal to what is base and trivial about man's nature. His premise, that is, has been that delusion conduces to "happiness" and his argument has followed rigorously from this assumption. And before he arrives at his ultimate, astonishing conclusion—before, that is, he confronts us with the recognition that we must choose between the incompatible objects of truth and happiness—he casts a devastating glance at happiness itself, through the two examples of "external" attractiveness which he offers for our inspection. The "Woman *flay'd*" would, for eighteenth-century readers, be recognizable as someone who deserved flaying, quite probably a whore. The *"Beau"* could not be regarded as presenting more than a superficially attractive spectacle, even unstripped. That surface appearances conceal disagreeable realities is only part of Swift's conclusion—and an obvious part which has been thoroughly supplied by demonstrations earlier in the *Tale*. The central propositions remain those with which the passage began: delusion leads to happiness; delusion is nonetheless inherently false, more vicious than the distasteful truth it conceals, its appeal directed to no higher sources of pleasure than are "Varnish and Tinsel," the flaunting beauties of the harlot and the finery of the Beau. The "Sower and the Dregs" are harsh terms, and the entrails of sinners and fops are doubtless unpleasant spectacles; but their authenticity is undeniable and they remain, in this respect, preferable to the "films and images," the "superficies," the sinful lives and fraudulent trappings which conceal them.

In the light of this analysis, the conclusion of the argument can hardly come as a surprise, as a "reversal," or as an "unmasking" of the author's moral identity and purpose. A "Man truly wise, creams off Nature, leaving the Sower and the Dregs for Philosophy and Reason to lap up. This is the sublime and refined Point of Felicity, called *the Possession of being well deceived;* the Serene Peaceful State of being a Fool among Knaves." The final phrase, for all of its abrupt, vehement conciseness, follows firmly from the whole of the preceding argument. The term "truly wise" reveals that what is conducive to human happiness persists as the criterion of "wisdom" until the end of the argument; the opposition of "philosophy" and especially "Reason" to "true Wisdom" is consistent with the initial Fancy-Reason dichotomy and "true Wisdom" is thus patently false, even for those who may have remained belatedly confused up to this point.

The evil power of deception has been made clear. It is the tickling of cant and vision, the whole-cloth fabrication of imagination, the fraudulent tinsel and varnish of outward show; it is, in short, all attempts, under any guise whatever, to offer pleasurable reassurances and induce complacent satisfaction at the expense of truth. The "knaves" are the revolutionary "conquerors" of the earlier argument. The conquest-metaphor assumes greater clarity; as creators of imperial "systems," the intellectual and religious imperialists stand doubly indicted for their enslavement of their fellows and for their corrupt perpetuation of man's irrational desire for security and illusion. Their triumph is, indeed, the triumph of madness, of unreason; to succumb to them is to succumb to folly, to fall victim to knavish deceit.

The argument is complete. Whether the greatest evil is the act of deception, the condition of self-delusion, or the irrational pursuit of satisfaction is never entirely clear, but Swift's ultimate point is that they are as one—their source unreason, their consequence the triumph of falsehood. The distinction between the illusory surface and the genuine inner reality, long apparent in the *Tale,* provides, as it were, the premise for this conclusion. It forms the foundation of Swift's doctrine; for because the superficies of things are not the things themselves, delusion consists in imagining that they are. But it is with man and not with the ultimate nature of reality that Swift is finally concerned. In their universality and depth, the truths with which Swift here concerns himself are philosophic—but they are moral and epistemological truths, rather than the propositions of metaphysics. Man's incapacity to detect truth, his weak surrender to the forces of delusion, his susceptibility to fraud, above all his hedonistic urge for serenity at the expense of reason are the ultimate objects of Swift's exposure.

The crucial function of the "Digression on Madness" should now be apparent. It is more than an amalgamation of "themes" and more than an elevation of satiric targets to a level of universality. It is a statement—as close to literal as is permitted by the pseudo-frivolity of the *Tale*—of the principles from which the most important satiric assaults in the entire work proceed. In literature, the easy summaries of preface and digression, the readily evaded general satire, the doctrine of a wide-ranging, unhistorical imagination, the banal truths wrapped flimsily in the flamboyant disguise of fable and hieroglyph —even critical carping, that ill-humored substitute for judgment— can be seen as embodiments of delusion. The truth is not attractive, nor is it easy to come by. It cannot be embodied in cheery generalizations, extracts, and indexes; it is alien to the spirit of glib apologies or comforting addresses to present patrons and future audiences. The smug maxims, brisk epitomes, and emotionally beguiling flights of fancy are alike tempting—and false.

In science and scholarship, the same principle applies. The facile systems, pious self-congratulations on modern progress, visionary doctrines of intellectual advance toward certain perfection are similarly attractive—and untenable. Here, on these broadest grounds— rather than in the detailed substantive refutation for which we look in vain throughout the *Tale* and the *Battle*—rests the burden of

Swift's assault upon Wotton and Bentley, upon contemporary science and criticism. Blandly indifferent to "the Sower and the Dregs," the Moderns impose upon their fellow men a sanguine and orderly assessment of human knowledge and achievement, offering, in their "true wisdom" a glittering inducement to arrogance and self-congratulation.

And yet again, in religion, the nimble perversion of ancient and rigorous doctrine for ephemeral and selfish ends (the repeated pattern of the "three brothers" allegory), the surrender of orthodox reason to the irrational urges of Enthusiasm, the flashy adornment of man's thankless religious duty with the baubles of eloquence, factional zeal, and "inspiration" epitomize the triumph of fancy over reason. Man's desire for temporal satisfaction here too drives him to folly at the expense of morality and truth.

The three great classes of Swift's antagonists in the *Tale* are those who have "Ambition to be heard in a Crowd"—men who profess to know the truth and seek to impose that knowledge upon others.[17] Preachers, poets, and pedants alike lay claim to the truth. Each claims his special source of truth—inspiration, fanciful invention, scholarly insight. It is little wonder, in view of Swift's attitude toward authentic knowledge, that these sources of reassuring "wisdom" are major objects of ridicule. Inspiration is merely wind; invention is the phantom product of empty heads and empty stomachs; scholarship is an arid and trifling performance, conducted in ignorance. From the same point of view, the media for the dissemination of false wisdom are equally odious. The stark austerity of Swift's doctrine reduces Enthusiastic preaching to demented babble, the scholarly systematizing of learning to arrant deception. The fable created for "painless" instruction, the book written in idle moments to meet the demands of an occasion, the satire which assails all men and no one man, and the cryptic symbol masking a frail commonplace are alike vicious in their fraudulent, comfortable "wisdom." And finally, the success, the "conquests" of these false prophets can be attributed to the fatuous and myopic ordinary man who, seeking only what passes for happiness and entirely contented

---

[17] Swift's initial disdainful treatment of "proselytizing, of people who wish to force their opinion upon others" is noted, in its relationship to the "Digression concerning Madness," by George Sherburn in "Methods in Books about Swift," *Studies in Philology*, XXXV (1938), 650.

with reassuring surfaces, lauds the pedants and projectors, stands gaping before the eructations of the Enthusiasts, and drifts aimlessly and uncritically in the current of literary vogue.

On the basis of the "Digression on Madness" alone, it does not seem wrong to say that Swift's satire rests on a foundation of profound moral conviction. In the thinly veiled forthrightness of this chapter, there are the premises for virtually all of the particular hostilities which emerge in the *Tale,* from its contemptuous dismissal of the popular scribbler to the virulent assault upon Wotton's ambitious systematizing. Hedonistic in their motives, illusory in their appeal, false in their conclusions, the fables and prefaces, Modernist claims and summaries, Enthusiast cant and vision are, in the final analysis, damned on common grounds. Here, rather than in the notion of "modernity" or of undifferentiated "misanthropy," is the lowest common denominator of Swift's satiric principles. It is a mistake to substitute, even at this juncture, the sin for the sinner; the discourse on delusion is a huge bulwark for the satire, but it is not the satire itself. It is, however, designed to make fully and terribly clear the vice of which the individuals and institutions, Swift's satiric victims, stand accused. And it thus makes equally clear that Swift's particular attacks, far from being wanton or irresponsible, proceed from firm and persistent conviction.

The truth, for Swift, is bitterly won, often repellent, rarely conducive to the serenity of the flabby and incurious mind. To pursue, whether in the name of literature, learning, or religion, the easy path of deceptive generalization, satisfying fancy, or diverting eloquence, is a sin against the truth and ultimately against man's capacity to know truth and survive that knowledge.

III

From the central section of the "Digression on Madness" there emerges the definition of the Swiftian "hero." Rejecting the "truly wise" example of Epicurus, he will refuse to content himself with "creaming off Nature"; aware that Happiness, as commonly conceived, is "a perpetual Possession of being well Deceived," he will refuse to allow happiness to serve as his goal, devoting himself to the austere and often painful pursuit of the truth which only reason can uncover. Security, comfort, and the common forms of benevolence play no part in the moral universe of such a man. As the traditional sources of mortal satisfaction, they are also the inevitable sources of delusion.

And thus the ultimate heroic act is an act of discovery, the ultimate heroic stature to be measured only by the clarity of vision and the steadfastness of a man's adherence to it, though in that adherence he lose what the world may regard as his soul. Moreover, it is difficult to assert that the truth is, in any definable way, ultimately ennobling, a "high" Platonic insight into quintessential virtue. At the core of Swift's doctrine lies a view of true knowledge as a goal rarely and painfully attained, terrible and violent to contemplate, remote from worldly standards of conduct or satisfaction, desirable only because it is uniquely real. For those who seek and find true knowledge, there is no promise of mundane power or pleasure but only the prospect of spiritual alienation from their fellows.

Such a doctrine is, in a sense, familiar, however we may resist it. It is echoed wherever knowledge is viewed as the forbidden fruit, wherever man is fearful lest much learning will make him mad, in every argument that ignorance is bliss. Such maxims confirm our doubts about the virtue of pursuing knowledge for its own sake, particularly where that knowledge is untranslatable or, worse, inhuman and savagely destructive. In conventional terms, it is hard to say what is "heroic" about such a search; at most one may discover some perverse brand of courage, of supreme indifference to approval and disapproval, of a willingness to encounter the dreadful solitude of the realm which lies beyond good and evil. This is, I suspect, the curious heroism which we discover in Kurtz, the tormented, corrupted, yet strangely triumphant figure of Conrad's *Heart of Darkness*. In a sense, a savage travesty of the "pursuer of wisdom" as most of us (including the Moderns of Swift's day) would glowingly define the role, Kurtz penetrates, with agonizing suffering and humiliation, to the heart of a vast physical and spiritual jungle, progressively losing in the process whatever claim he may have had on the approval of his fellow men. And at the end of his search, at the heart of darkness, lies not light, but the quintessence of darkness itself, moving him only to savage sentiments and to the final devastating account of his vision: "The horror! The horror!"

Marlowe, Conrad's narrator, is incapable of fully sharing Kurtz's experience and his stature, although he can trace, and, in some measure, understand Kurtz's solitary journey into knowledge. Although

Marlowe draws back, at the moment of real challenge, from embracing and speaking the terrible truth (to Kurtz's *fiancée* he provides, on his return, a lie about her lover's death which is clearly the only benevolent and "sensible" account to offer), he reveals, in his own terms, an insight into the strange, inhuman heroism which he senses in the other man:

I was within a hair's breadth of the last opportunity for pronouncement, and I found with humiliation that probably I would have nothing to say. This is the reason why I affirm that Kurtz was a remarkable man. He had something to say. He said it. Since I had peeped over the edge myself, I understand better the meaning of his stare, that could not see the flame of the candle, but was wide enough to embrace the whole universe, piercing enough to penetrate all the hearts that beat in the darkness. He had summed up—he had judged. 'The horror!' He was a remarkable man. After all, this was the expression of some sort of belief; it had candor, it had conviction, it had a vibrating note of revolt in its whisper, it had the appalling face of a glimpsed truth—the strange commingling of desire and hate. And it is not my own extremity I remember best—a vision of grayness without form filled with physical pain, and a careless contempt for the evanescence of all things—even of this pain itself. No! It is his extremity that I seem to have lived through. True, he had made that last stride, he had stepped over the edge, while I had been permitted to draw back my hesitating foot. And perhaps in this is the whole difference; perhaps all the wisdom, and all truth, and all sincerity, are compressed into that inappreciable moment of time in which we step over the threshold of the invisible. Perhaps! I like to think my summing-up would not have been a word of careless contempt. Better his cry—much better. It was an affirmation, a moral victory paid for by innumerable defeats, by abominable terrors, by abominable satisfactions. But it was a victory.[18]

Couched in language of passionate intensity, Kurtz's achievement is nonetheless that of Swift's "pretended Philosophy which enters into the Depth of Things, and then comes back gravely with Information and Discoveries, that in the inside they are good for nothing." He is as far from the Grub-street fable, triumphantly digging out the "fox" of truth, as he is from the incurious victims of the world's delusion. Like Swift's beaux and harlots, the "externals" of Kurtz's world are so shabby and spurious that one hopes that penetration beneath them will discover some core of sustaining and ennobling

[18] *Heart of Darkness* in *Youth and Two Other Stories* (New York, 1910), pp. 171–72.

"truth." But this is not the nature of truth or of man's encounter with it; at the end of one's search there may lie only the supreme darkness and horror. Experience with the inner actuality is superior to the surface appearance on one ground, and one ground only, namely that knowledge of any kind is superior to ignorance. Conrad's Kurtz is thus a hero in only one sense—but it is a sense which makes clear the uniqueness of his heroism. He has learned what other men cannot and will not learn.

Swift's Lemuel Gulliver is such a hero. In his final state, he offends against every canon of benevolence and decorum. Like Kurtz, he suffers a spiritual exile almost entirely of his own making, rejecting the claims of conventional piety and love, adhering only to the truth of a vision which lends him neither strength nor dignity and only exacerbates his anguished isolation. If we are to judge Gulliver by the ready-to-hand "norms" exploited by the conventional satirist, he is indeed the dupe or villain or worse which recent critics have made him.[19] His knowledge has not even made him educable in any respectable way; against the spiritually wholesome encounter with the worthy Don Pedro de Mendez he reacts with the aversion of ineradicable prejudice—offering to us less reason for admiration than the intractable Kurtz affords his rescuer, Marlowe. Small wonder, then, that healthy-minded readers, reluctantly concluding that there is literally nothing to admire in Gulliver's ultimate condition, seek to reconcile their response to the unfortunate man with some notion of Christian benignity and hence conclude that Gulliver is himself the surrogate for some lamentable satiric target, in whose plight and attitude we can find only a grim object-lesson.

In *Heart of Darkness,* appropriately, the horror remains pretty much unspecified or, to the extent that it is linked with the personal depravity of Kurtz, appears as the intensely individualized invention appropriate to a fictive and darkly lyrical context. Our "understand-

[19] The "villainy," or something remarkably close to it, is urged by Samuel Holt Monk, who argues that, in his final stage, "Gulliver is himself the supreme instance of a creature smitten with pride." See Monk's "The Pride of Lemuel Gulliver," originally published in *The Sewanee Review,* LXIII (1955), 48–71, and subsequently reprinted in, among other places, *Gulliver's Travels: An Annotated Text with Critical Essays,* ed. Robert Greenberg (New York, 1961), pp. 281–99. The most singular—although doubtless not the final—variation on the "dupe" theme is, I suspect, to be found in James R. Wilson's "Swift's Alazon," *Studia Neophilologica,* XXX (1958), 153–64.

ing" of Conrad's story, that is, does not hinge upon our capacity to understand, in any appreciable way, the nature of Kurtz's final overpowering vision, but rather to recognize the grounds for Marlowe's tortured recognition of the other man's perverse heroism.

Gulliver's Travels, on the other hand, is not a novel nor is it, in any meaningful sense of the term, a lyric construction. Though, as I have previously argued, its purely fictional aspect is not without power to move us, we are left in no doubt as to the substance of Gulliver's discoveries; what Gulliver learns, we learn as well, and it is to his "discoveries" that we look if we, too, are to discover and grasp the doctrine on which the book is ultimately based.

In *A Tale of a Tub,* the "Digression concerning Madness" appears as a kind of nexus, in which the disparate courses taken by the satire are brought together and the multiplicity of satiric targets are taxed with a common kind of error and vice. The digression serves, that is, to state principles which illuminate and reinforce the particularized satiric assaults, revealing the premises on which Swift finds his victims culpable, and providing those normative canons which, in more orthodox satires, are supplied by the predisposing convictions and values of the reader. Yet, for all its compelling singularity, the "Digression" is largely a confirmation of the principles on which particular assaults have been based. Swift's victims have, for the most part, stood self-convicted, for we are prepared to recognize in many of them the folly, arrogance, or deceit which are plainly culpable in terms of ordinary intelligence and morality. The digression, then, lends strength to the satire by offering grounds for attack which are peculiar to Swift and which establish a collective basis for his hostility to the rather mixed bag of enemies which his satire pursues.

To some extent, the basic doctrine which emerges from *Gulliver's Travels* serves the same purpose. The final terrifying disclosure of man's bestiality, irrationality, and pride supplies a fundamental charge which can be leveled against the specific objects of Swift's satire, for what he learns among the Houyhnhnms formulates, in gross and relatively direct terms, the vices which have been displayed by the Walpolites, the pedants, the projectors, the statesmen, the Maids of Honor, the Dutch, and the other particular victims who have previously been assailed with some satiric obliquity. And, reciprocally, the individual satiric assaults lend, as it were, documentation to the view of generic human depravity which is fundamental to Gulliver's ultimate discoveries; he has, that is, gathered no evidence in his voyaging which negates, in any way, the conclusions to which his Houyhnhnm adventures remorselessly lead him.

At the same time, a fundamental doctrine, a philosophic (if negative and destructive) attitude toward universal problems, is developed far more centrally and systematically in the *Travels* than in the *Tale*. Gulliver's critical discoveries in the Fourth Voyage are adumbrated throughout the earlier books. The "truths" which he learns, and which move him radically to alter his previous attitudes, are concerned not with the particulars under satiric assault, but with "that animal called man" in that universal aspect which is the province of the moral philosopher. In its violence and idiosyncrasy, the myth of the Fourth Book may come as a shocking surprise, disproportionate in both its breadth and its strange and terrible earnestness to much of the playful comedy and apt but limited satire which have preceded it. Yet whatever Gulliver seems to have learned—what he has been able to formulate in propositions about mankind as a species—as a result of his previous experiences, tends, with clear relevance, toward the damning assessment of man which his final discoveries produce.

Thus, for example, although the exploitation of the "relativism" involving human stature in the first two books is intricate and shifting, it is unremitting in its exposure of what is awkward and unlovely about the human physique.[20] Gulliver's own size, whether as a giant among the Lilliputians or a pygmy among the Brobdingnagians, is almost invariably a source only of discomfort and embarrassment (the one exception, perhaps, being his exploitation of his stature to defeat the fleet of Blefuscu—in itself, an uncongenial and ultimately unprofitable enterprise). And, ingeniously enough, the size of Gulliver's hosts does not, by contrast with their visitor, offer

---

[20] In "Relativity in Gulliver's Travels," *Philological Quarterly,* XXXVII (1958), 110–16, Edward Wasiolek argues interestingly that the relativist experience with physical phenomena may lead us to question "the basis of reality of certain objects which from our gross ignorance we have assumed to be important." Gulliver's encounters may prompt the reflective reader (particularly if, like Wasiolek, he has Berkeley in mind) to re-examine his own broadest convictions about the nature of reality. Gulliver's own discoveries and reappraisals are piecemeal matters. He may generalize—as, for example, he does on the reliability of "Princes and Ministers" (p. 61)—but, at least in the first three voyages, he is not concerned with the kind of abstraction that would lead to pervasive skepticism with respect to moral or metaphysical questions.

them advantages, but is used, instead, to expose their own folly, ugliness, or ineptitude. The Lilliputians' stature underscores their arrogance and ingratitude; the "microscopic" view of the Brobdingnagians reveals their horrifying blemishes.

In the overtly didactic passages of the first three books, as in his earlier discoveries about man's physical endowment, Gulliver gains insights into constant facts about human nature. And we must note that, however "philosophic" these discoveries are, they offer few traces of redeeming "affirmation," few hints of the way in which folly can be avoided or of the satisfactions which accompany wisdom and rectitude.

Where Gulliver is granted glimpses of sensible and virtuous modes of life, it is under circumstances which stress the inaccessibility or impracticality of such conduct. The Utopian origins of Lilliputian education, law, and domestic organization have long since fallen into neglect and exert not the slightest influence on Lilliputian society. The spare outlines of Brobdingnagian learning and polity are "sensible" enough, but are viewed by Gulliver (here in his role of ordinary man) with incredulity.

The individual characters who exemplify reasonable behavior are, uniformly, represented as suffering in consequence. The "great Lord," who is related to the king of Laputa, is an object of universal condescension; Lord Munodi is an outcast, on the brink of financial ruin; the professors in Lagado's school of political projectors are plainly mad. In the satiric enterprise of which each of these figures is a part, they may be said to serve a limited "normative" function, but their primary purpose can hardly be viewed as the exemplification of an "affirmative" course which Swift literally advocates. On the contrary, each of them is plainly an additional instrument of assault—indicating the incredulity and disapproval which await those who pursue a course of reason and thus reflecting, ultimately, the inveteracy of folly.

The unrestrained, almost literal condemnation of western civilization by the king of Brobdingnag is a blow at the roots of Gulliver's pride in his human identity. The encounter with the Struldbruggs elicits what is probably the most direct and literal series of reflections in the whole of the *Travels;* Gulliver's response to what he has seen is proportionate to the experience that has produced it. The myth of the Struldbruggs embodies a very direct assault upon cherished sources of human satisfaction which, we are now asked quite expressly to believe, are illusory and pernicious. In many ways, the Struldbrugg episode is a lesser myth than that of the Houyhnhnms, but it is also almost equally unsettling. Directed though it may be against the vanity and evil of seeking immortality, it strongly implies that human life is a very questionable possession.

In the first three voyages, satire and comedy are, as we have pointed out, only sporadically transcended; there is no progression of systematic philosophic argument, and Gulliver's discoveries, whatever their intrinsic significance, cannot be said to have permanently enlightened or profoundly altered him. When, however, the discourse is directed, by whatever device, to the constant questions of human morality and human intelligence, the emphasis is inevitably destructive, the import invariably unsettling. While the intermittent emergence of "doctrine" can hardly be said to "prepare" us for the Fourth Voyage, it is sufficiently consistent in its principles and direction so that we are, in a sense, already aware of the bleak and terrible assumptions implicit in Swift's assessment of human works and ways. The reader himself can, that is, construct—with no very sophisticated calculus—a fairly accurate account of the beliefs which, presumably, underly Swift's remorseless emphasis upon the vanity of human achievements and values.

But Gulliver himself, even at the outset of the Fourth Voyage, has achieved no such "wisdom." He has yet, that is, to make the final voyage into the heart of darkness, to encounter truth, and to learn the terrible consequences of its acquisition. We have already noted that Gulliver, at the beginning of the Voyage, has spent five months at home "in a very happy Condition, if I could have learned the Lesson of knowing when I was well" (p. 205). As I have said, this is a reasonable point of departure for the violent series of discoveries and changes which mark the action of the final voyage. But the singular definitions of happiness and knowledge provided by the "Digression concerning Madness" endow Gulliver's assertion with peculiar meaning. To "know" when one is well, to recognize the sources of contentment and thus continue happy, is precisely the kind of knowledge which will not do, for the Swiftian hero. Perversely but characteristically, however, Gulliver, the incurable traveler, sets out to sea, refusing to "learn the Lesson" which will, in its fraudulent reassurance, secure his happiness, and drawn instead toward a knowledge which will bar him forever from the ordinary forms of contentment.

In its most fundamental sense, the myth of the Voyage to the Houyhnhnms is a myth about true knowledge. At this level it is the fictional exemplification of the argument presented in the "Digression concerning Madness," for Gulliver, aware that "Credulity is a more peaceful Possession of the Mind, than Curiosity," persists in entering into "the Depth of Things" and comes back gravely—indeed tragically—with the knowledge that "in the inside they are good for nothing." The truth he has learned—any truth worth learning—indeed cannot set him free—free, that is, from misunderstanding, insecurity, anger, despair. It can set him free only from illusion. But in that truth alone rests his terrible triumph.

At a second level, the myth also operates philosophically in that the substance of Gulliver's discovery, in all its bitterness, is communicated to us. The facts about humanity which are made plain to Gulliver are not lies or distortions or the fabrications of the satiric fiction; in their entirety they form a doctrine, directed to the gravest questions and offering the most profound judgment on human achievements and hopes.

Yet Swift is not a philosopher and the *Travels* is not directed, in the final analysis, to the exposition of philosophic belief. I would suggest that the myth of the Houyhnhnms and Yahoos is designed to move and to persuade—that its ends are precisely those which the great majority of readers have always recognized, the awakening of shocking, uncomfortable new awarenesses within its audience. In it we discover Swift the *preacher*—preaching not to expound belief or to offer affirmations of faith, but preaching, as clergymen immemorially have done, to instil in his listeners a heightened consciousness of their own vanity and unworthiness.[21] Raised to a plane of timeless and universal application, Swift's performance remains largely that of the satire which may be called homiletic or, in Pro-

---

[21] A very early defense of the Fourth Book as the work of a preacher can be found in Deane Swift's *Essay upon the Life, Writings, and Character of Dr. Swift*, pp. 219–20. Professor Landa, asserting that Swift's "pessimism is quite consonant with the pessimism at the heart of Christianity," makes it clear, I think, that the bitterness of both the *Travels* and the Irish tracts is entirely compatible with the doctrine and practice of an Anglican divine of Swift's time; see Louis A. Landa, "Jonathan Swift," originally in *English Institute Essays, 1946* (New York, 1947), pp. 20–40, and reprinted in *Studies in the Literature of the Augustan Age: Essays Collected in Honor of Arthur E. Case* (Ann Arbor, Mich., 1952), pp. 177–97.

fessor Sams's phrase, "satire of the second person."[22] It is the kind of attack which is embodied in both the *Argument against Abolishing Christianity* and *A Modest Proposal,* in the non-satiric pages of some of Swift's most powerful sermons, in the admonitions of *The Sentiments of a Church-of-England Man,* and which is directed against the folly or lethargy or even the wickedness of his "congregation."

The heart of this attack lies in the discoveries which Gulliver makes in the Fourth Voyage. And I should argue that Swift's rhetoric requires that we fundamentally concur in the substance of all of his discoveries, however they are come by, but *not* in the extravagance of Gulliver's response to them.

The first and most arresting of these discoveries is, as I have said, Gulliver's shocking recognition that man, in his brute nakedness, is indeed a Yahoo, his ugliness vainly disguised by civilized artifice, his animal powers merely vitiated by "refinements" which are actually corruptions. The second discovery emerges largely in Gulliver's dialogues with the Houyhnhnm master; it is simply that those systems which we regard as the hallmarks of civilization—law, military science, government, "breeding," medicine, and the rest—represent the "institutionalizing," the elaboration of our animal inclinations toward hatred, avarice, and sensuality. What is notable, moreover, is that at this stage Gulliver has assumed the ultimate posture of Swiftian "heroism" with respect to true knowledge. For enlightenment is no longer imposed upon him, but becomes the sole end of his own, deliberate concerns. The "exposure" of human depravity, that is, is actually achieved through Gulliver's own account of civilized society; under the Houyhnhnm influence he views "the Actions and Passions of Man in a very Different Light" and is able to assert that *"Truth* appeared so amiable to me, that I determined upon sacrificing every thing to it" (p. 242).

Gulliver's own account of western society produces a third discovery, unequivocally advanced by the Houyhnhnm master himself, who defines mankind as "a Sort of Animals to whose Share, by what Accident he could not conjecture, some small Pittance of *Reason* had fallen, whereof we made no other Use than by its Assistance to aggravate our *natural* Corruptions, and to acquire new ones which Nature had not given us" (p. 243). Between them, these

[22] Henry W. Sams, "Swift's Satire of the Second Person," *ELH,* XXVI (1959), 36–44.

discoveries have produced, with devastating clarity, a "definition" of man which incorporates both his natural endowments and the uses to which he has put them. This is the "truth," the doctrinal center which both supports and is confirmed by the particulars of Gulliver's many experiences, the final, normative assessment of mankind by which, if at all, the posturings and pretensions of civilization are to be exposed in their vanity and folly.

Yet there remains Gulliver's fourth discovery—that involving the vexed question of the Houyhnhnms themselves. And here it is vital that we remember the ultimately homiletic character of Swift's undertaking. His task, as I have suggested, is to implant not affirmative conviction but an agonizing awareness of inadequacy and false pride within the minds of his audience. Thus, although Gulliver's evaluation of Houyhnhnm virtues is somewhat fatuous and certainly extravagant, we are not required to accept the horses as "ideals" or indeed even as the affirmations of the standard to which mankind could, or should, or must attain. The representation of what is exemplary, the advocacy of what is "right" or noble, the paradigm of our own salvation are not germane to Swift's persuasive mission within the Fourth Book. I am convinced that the superiority of the Houyhnhnms is discovered by Gulliver as proof of the fact that a horse—*even* a horse—could, if endowed with that genuine reason on which man falsely prides himself, achieve a serene, benign, and cleanly prosperity which is the opposite, in every important respect, to the present state of civilized man. Endowed with authentic reason and employing it properly, this stock example of animality and irrationality is, as it were, a metaphorical rebuke to mankind. For man, victim of the bestiality he vainly attempts to disguise, fraudulent vaunter of a rational faculty with which he is slightly gifted but has systematically abused, thus learns—through the patently impossible image of a truly rational creature—how miserably he has fallen short of the mark. And accordingly, Swift asks us to admire the Houyhnhnms only to the extent that recognition of their virtues produces revulsion for our own infirmities.

Gulliver's own view of the Houyhnhnms as "ideal" is part of that excessive response which we need not share in order for Swift to achieve his design. Our awareness of the Houyhnhnms' imperfections is in fact part of that design—the uncomfortable nature of their "superiority" additional evidence that, in all of the terrible truth which is the total Swiftian vision, no single element can be seized upon for reassurance, for affirmation, for the slightest suggestion that there *is* a way, if poor wandering man would only follow it. Many of the horses' infirmities arise, I believe, from Swift's deliberate effort to keep before us their humble animal identity—to make sure, so to speak, that we never lose sight of their horsiness and hence of the particular dimensions of Swift's rhetorical figure. If the Houyhnhnms were to cease, in our eyes, to be animals who are inexplicably and rather humorously rational and were to become instead ideal embodiments of virtue (or on the other hand, satiric surrogates for some dangerous phenomenon) the whole point of Gulliver's discovery (even a horse, given true reason, could put mankind to shame) would be lost—at least upon us. It appears, in fact, that Swift is careful to discourage our forgetting the horses' identity at precisely those points at which there is some danger of our doing so. At strategic intervals we are reminded that these paragons are only the familiar quadrupeds. Swift's comic gift is delightfully exploited as we see the Houyhnhnms traveling on their Yahoo-drawn sledges, decorously consuming their hay and oats (with warm milk for the aged horse), threading needles, and—at the crucial and potentially tragic moment of Gulliver's departure— plaintively whinnying farewell with the words, *"Hnuy illa nyha maiah yahoo."*

Of the Houyhnhnms' graver deficiencies, there are few, if any, that are not manifested exclusively vis-à-vis the Yahoos, or Gulliver as a quasi-Yahoo. Even the inflexibility of Houyhnhnm habits is the inflexibility of fixed principle and permanent order. In their alleged cruelty to Gulliver, the Houyhnhnms act reluctantly, from an aversion to the Yahoo breed and a low opinion of humanity which are enforced by every substantive particular of Gulliver's discoveries. If the achievements and condition of civilized man are revealed, throughout these discoveries, to be loathsome, then it is only consistent for the rational Houyhnhnms to respond to the Yahoo and the human breeds with loathing.

Thus, in its ultimate power, the Fourth Voyage is a savage indictment of mankind, based, to be sure, upon the vision of human depravity, the damning measurement of the unbreachable gap between man's systematized Yahoodom and the life of reason—as, hypothetically, even a horse could live it. The entire myth is the instrument of one who, in hatred of what he saw about him, set out to "vex the world" (and not a particular fragment of mankind) in order to heighten our alertness to our own folly and failure. Swift's account of our condition need not be taken literally in order for it to achieve this purpose, any more than we must share in Gulliver's uncritical admiration of the horses or his implacable aversion to Don Pedro or his own family in order to sense with him the essence of the truth which has led him to such extremes.

It is neither accident nor "irony" that Gulliver's final observations are devoted to man's pride. Granted that they show no traces of charity or moderation, that they show no sign of a "serene peaceful state"; granted that in his contempt and inflexibility Gulliver may himself be guilty of a special kind of pride. They claim our attention not because the man who speaks them is sympathetic or admirable but only because, unlike the rest of us, he has seen the truth. And because Gulliver has seen the truth, the pride of man—pride in the face of the "Deformity and Diseases both in Body and Mind" which are his actual condition—is the single manifestation which "breaks the Measure" of that patience which, in his unalterable knowledge, is Gulliver's sole means of reconciling himself to his species.

The ultimate, inescapable sentiment in the Voyage to the Houyhnhnms is, indeed, savage indignation. But man's condition, in all its dirt and bestiality, deceit and avarice, is not the final object of that indignation. To these facts about the human state, Swift, like Gulliver himself, responds with various degrees of revulsion and contempt, sometimes horrified, sometimes amused, sometimes with the bewilderment of the *faux ingénu*. Poems like *The Beasts' Confession* or *The Day of Judgment* display no more flattering an assessment of human habits and attainments than does the Fourth Voyage, yet they, like even the damning speech of the Brobdingnagian king, lack the savage intensity which dominates Gulliver's final response to what he has seen.

Nor is the ultimate object of this wrath delusion itself, however earnestly Swift may deplore the mere fact of self-deception. "Happiness," as he recognizes in the oblique argument of the "Digression on Madness," is indeed a natural goal of all save a few solitary seekers for authentic knowledge; the man who knows when he is "well" is, in his "true wisdom," a victim of delusion, but he enjoys a kind of false contentment unworthy of Swift's ultimate level of outrage.

In a universe of appearances, there is much that is laughable, lamentable, even terrible, when viewed in the light of actuality, yet within
its limits it is a universe in which even a Gulliver may live in an
uneasy sort of peace.

Thus it is not even man's *failure* to achieve more, to attain true
rationality which elicits Swift's deepest indignation. Professor Sherburn has explained Swift's "misanthropy" as the product of agonized
disappointment in man's accomplishment and sees the *Travels* as
written by "one who had the highest ideals for human achievement
and who despaired of the achieving."[23] It may be hard to settle upon
the nature of Swift's "highest ideals" (they would presumably be
supplied by the kind of "affirmation" which is precisely what is lacking in *Gulliver's Travels*), but of the despair there can be no mistake.
Swift's attitude is, indeed, beyond despair—an icy compound of
resignation and cynicism—and hence beyond indignation. For if
we assume that his "ideals" in some way embody a life led according
to reason, he has represented such a life, as we have noted, in contexts which stress its inaccessibility, its temporal dissatisfactions, and
its grotesque incompatibility with most of the values from which
man derives dignity and solace. The "ideal" indeed plays little part
in Swift's rhetoric throughout his writings. The measured "practicality" of his arguments in *The Sentiments of a Church-of-England
Man* and the *Project for the Advancement of Religion* make no
claim upon absolute sentiments of piety and virtue; the *Argument
against Abolishing Christianity* deliberately rejects the possibility of
restoring that "real" Christianity of primitive times which must be,
if anything is, Swift's personal "ideal"; in the whole of his English
and Irish political tracts, he rarely if ever invokes principles higher
than national self-interest and common material well-being.

The true *saeva indignatio* is memorable in Swift's writing because
it is rare, and it is rare because it is seldom the response which even
the most indefensible of human infirmities arouse within him. What
alone elicits this terrible passion is neither what men have achieved
nor what they have failed to achieve, but the pride which is a sin
against the truth of their achievements. Whether Swift believes man
might ultimately attain rationality or whether he views reason as a

---

[23] George Sherburn in *A Literary History of England,* ed. Baugh (New York,
1948), p. 866. See also Sherburn's "Errors concerning the Houyhnhnms," *Modern
Philology,* LVI (1958), 92–98.

goal far beyond his reach, the fact is that man has thus far egregiously rejected even the first steps along the way to rational existence.
But—and it is this which accounts for Swift's violence—reason is
precisely the faculty on which man most prides himself. In his folly
and arrogance, he has identified himself as that which, of all things,
he is not. In *A Tale of a Tub,* it is not the mere fraudulence of intellectual systems, fables, symbols, divination, and inspiration which
—ridiculous as these phenomena may be—awakens Swift's deepest
anger. It is the fact that, in their manifest frailty and falseness, it is
precisely these "attainments" which prompt man to assert that he has
mastered truth, transcended his natural state, ordered the universe,
and received the direct inspiration of God.

I do not think the crucial concepts in *Gulliver's Travels* are "man"
or "animal" or "rational," for all the obvious importance of these
terms. In the *Travels,* as in the *Tale,* Swift's most profound intellectual commitments hinge, I believe, upon his conception of knowledge and of pride, and upon his insistence that each of these has
both a true and a false aspect. False knowledge is delusion and
superficiality, the slick and sanguine aphorisms and arguments and
systems by which man finds life supportable in the face of his
meager endowments and his corruption even of them. It is the
sarcastically labeled "true wisdom" of the "Digression concerning
Madness," the reassuring semblance of the truth acceptable to all
save those few who ask for the truth itself. It is the basis of rationali-
zation, of fraudulent appeals to fraudulent notions of benevolence,
of the "systems" and "empires" whose very success attests the degree
to which false knowledge is a universal and "perpetual possession."
It is the root of that complacency which Gulliver encounters in all
of the societies he visits in the first three voyages and in which the
Struldbruggs alone, having, as it were, passed beyond the power of
false knowledge for good or evil, do not offer the illusion of
contentment.

False knowledge, in many of its various manifestations, is readily
vulnerable to the assaults of the satirist, the superiority of his per-
ceptiveness, sophistication, and common sense. Mere fragments of
authentic wisdom can suffice to expose flagrant delusion, disguises,
silliness, and knavery. The temporal canons of consistency, demonstrable matter-of-fact, and general benevolence can be successfully
invoked when the task is merely to display abuses, to demonstrate

the inadequacy of means to ends, the discrepancy between what is professed and what is practiced, the vanity or extravagance or destructiveness of many kinds of mundane enterprise.

But false knowledge is merely the genesis of the infinitely greater sin of false pride. Ignorance alone can bring bliss of sorts; to err is, indeed, human. But when, in the face of error, man *congratulates* himself upon his rationality, his superiority to those creatures with which he is linked in bestiality, his mastery of that truth to the avoidance of which his life is devoted, his exploitation of a unique power which he has in fact only neglected and abused, he sins, as it were, "gratuitously," and outrageously. His arrogant self-image is not a product of "those Vices and Follies which Nature hath entitled" him to. It is not developed in the course of that natural, if deluded, quest for happiness which is his normal inclination. In its claims to knowledge and power impossible to man, it is more than "the thing which is not"—it is the thing which cannot and must not ever be.

True knowledge, in its essence, is merely the ability to see without delusion. What is seen may thus be, in fact, "fading and insipid"; the message with which we return after penetrating "into the Depth of Things" may be nothing more than the solemn information that "at the inside they are good for nothing." We find true knowledge in the Brobdingnagian king's assessment of man's physical and moral stature, in the lonely skepticism of the "great Person at Court" and Lord Munodi, in the Luggnagians' awareness that the immortality of the Struldbruggs is a curse. And for all their implications, Gulliver's discoveries on his final voyage are marked by a terrible simplicity. Man in his physical endowments is a lesser Yahoo; man has perverted his pittance of reason to exacerbate his Yahoo nature; a truly rational society, even if its citizens are horses, is impossibly alien to all man is, or wishes to be. The great vision which constitutes Gulliver's final discovery and Swift's final indictment is not the product of special insights or involved reasonings, but of a simple capacity to see things as they are. This capacity is the most unprofitable of possessions, labeling its owner as the gull or lunatic or misanthrope which so many readers have found Gulliver to be, "mad in pursuit and in possession so" when viewed as a possible source of worldly satisfaction.

Having seen the false pride of ordinary mortals, we do not find its opposite, at least in the Gulliverian universe, to be an attractive pattern of humility. Instead, as false knowledge engenders false pride, so true knowledge begets, inevitably, a "true pride" which is the final and, for some, infuriating key to the character of Lemuel Gulliver. And, however kindly our intentions, I do not think we can dissociate Jonathan Swift from this same species of pride. To the devastating portrayal of humanity which brings Gulliver to his final state Swift has offered no mitigating suggestion. Man's ugliness and depravity, his false knowledge and false pride, are only underscored by the grotesque remoteness of the Houyhnhnms' truly rational standards. Don Pedro de Mendez is no more an affirmative reminder of true benevolence than are Gulliver's wife and family; both serve to show the extremity of Gulliver's alienation, the rejection of love, charity, and human society which is the price at which true knowledge is won. If we cannot share Gulliver's adulation for the Houyhnhnms, we cannot deny their bizarre superiority to the Yahoos and to ourselves, as Swift would have us believe we are.

It is a proud man who can represent our state with such relentless scorn, who can unremittingly assail the entire fabric of our happiness and self-respect. It is a strange preacher who makes no concession to our sense of dignity and moderation, who pleads no benign redeeming motive for his strictures—or, indeed, any motive save the passionate conviction of one who believes he speaks the truth. His is a pride which is utterly unapologetic, unlovely, solitary. It is fierce and implacable—and as uncomplicated as anger itself. It is, in fact, *saeva indignatio*.

IV

There is much to be said for the common assertion that what is important to discover in *Gulliver's Travels* is not whether Swift is a misanthrope, but whether Gulliver is a misanthrope. And what is, perhaps, more important than either question is what the reader is to make of Gulliver's "misanthropy" (or lack thereof) and the extent to which he concurs in the truth of Gulliver's discoveries. When we recognize the doctrine from which Gulliver's conclusions must be viewed, we are not necessarily advancing a biographical proposition about Swift, any more, for example, than an appeal to "constitutionality" in a modern political debate justifies our declaring the debater to be a firm believer in the sanctity of the Constitution.

Moreover, the exposition of "belief" in a largely satiric work, however indubitably "sincere" it may be, does not necessarily serve to explain the satirist's true motives or the conviction which determines the entire character and direction of his satiric attack. Swift's attacks on Walpole, in the *Travels* and elsewhere, are plainly the product of partisan zeal and personal aggrievedness rather than of a moralist's desire to display, in Walpole or any other individual, a specimen of the vices which are the true object of his hostility. The strange doctrine of the "Digression concerning Madness" lends new dimensions to Swift's assault upon individual manifestations of Modernity, yet the motive for much of the *Tale* certainly lies in such specific facts as Swift's loyalty to Temple rather than in his generic views concerning human knowledge. Thus the presence in a largely satiric work of a substratum of philosophic values, however comprehensive and arresting it may be, should not lead us to substitute the sin for the sinner as the true object of satiric attack.

In the actual satiric enterprise, furthermore, the power of persuasion and delight depends, far more often than not, upon values which are readily intelligible and acceptable—and, even more commonly, upon values which, since they are held by the majority of men, do not require overt statement or the reader's conscious acceptance. Our encounter with most even of Swift's satire does not involve any very serious suspension or alteration of our ordinary standards. The first three books of the *Travels,* the huge preponderance of satire in the *Tale, A Modest Proposal,* or *Verses on the Death of Dr. Swift,* all in some measure "startling," call, nonetheless, for judgments which invoke very common notions of morality and logic. If, as I have earlier suggested, such satire truly shocks us, it is generally because of the satiric fiction itself which, in its forms and fabrications, does some violence to our notion of orthodoxy or decorum. We recoil, perhaps, from the idea of infant cannibalism, but the satiric "argument" of *A Modest Proposal* is addressed to principles no more bizarre than self-preservation, national integrity, and common-sense economics. It is not, that is, Swift's "misanthropy" which prompts his choice of a mode for Ireland's salvation, nor is it to any sense of cruelty—indeed, quite the contrary—that the essay makes its basic appeal. In fact, to stake the ultimate success of a satiric work upon the audience's acceptance of values which are alien, obscure, or unsympathetic would run counter to every rule of satiric practice. And in Swift's most robust and effective assaults, he proceeds on grounds which are transparent; there is nothing elusive or novel about the basis for his attacks on Wharton or Nottingham, Dryden or Walpole, Puritanism or freethinking.

Hence, even in *Gulliver's Travels,* we must regard with some caution Swift's own account of the "great foundation of misanthropy" upon which "the whole building of my Travels is erected." In his exposure of contemporary men and institutions and even in his revelation of universal frailties—man's physical ugliness and ineptitude or the vanity of wishing to live forever—we can find conviction which depends in no way upon a recognition of the misanthropy from which such attacks are ultimately seen to proceed. Even the earlier portions of the Fourth Voyage, the beginning, as it were, of Gulliver's total discovery, might have been the product (as, indeed, some critics have argued about the entire voyage) of a lofty and affirmative view of man's rational faculty or a passionate but hopeful plea that we reject our animal natures.

On the other hand, such "truth," in its fundamental and universal sense, as Swift's greatest writing provides is only to be found in the critical passages we have been considering. Gulliver's misanthropy cannot be dismissed as the mere posture of a fictional character or even as a premise which invites the suspension of our disbelief in an "autotelic" encounter with the *Travels*. In the final voyage, as in the earlier, more thoroughly satiric sections, Swift requires the exercise of our judgment and belief. And far more than in most satiric writings, he challenges our sense of the just and credible. For not only is the final myth directed to problems which are historically authentic; it is directed to ourselves. We must take Swift seriously, or not at all.

One can accept the misanthropy with varying degrees of reservation; one can reject it in horror (as some critics, from Orrery on, have done); one can deny that it is a view which Swift actually holds or which he would want us to share (as much recent critical ingenuity is employed to argue); but it is clear that questions of belief inevitably condition one's response to this last, crucial section of *Gulliver's Travels*. It remains largely irrelevant whether we regard the historical Swift as a misanthrope; it is supremely relevant whether in this instance we believe he is speaking the truth. Philosophic expositions are not, I suppose, judged in the last analysis solely by the degree to which one concurs in their conclusions. We do, however, expect that their ideas be vigorous and arresting, their arguments intelligible and responsible, their ultimate propositions advanced in conformity to the state of affairs presented in their context. And if their final effect upon us is one of falsehood, subversion, or irresponsibility, they are, as statements of doctrine, failures—no matter how we may rejoice in their ingenuity, charm, eloquence, and other qualities quite irrelevant to the task of the moralist or philosopher.

This is the principal reason why I believe that we must face up to Swift's brand of fundamental truth in the Voyage to the Houyhnhnms—as we must with Plato or Lucretius or Erasmus or others whose communication of belief has taken engaging imaginative forms. If Swift's conception of reality, as it emerges from the Fourth Book, is insupportable and repellent, then the book has failed in that function to which it is, above all others, addressed. Of course it has other excellences; we have spoken of the extraordinary aptness and power with which it concludes the purely fictional account of Gulliver's adventures as well as of the firmness with which the myth and the satiric elements of the total book lend each other reciprocal support. But in the Fourth Voyage, Swift's primary commitment is neither to comic fiction nor to particularized satiric attack; it is to a comprehensive, mythic statement of moral reality. We may accept the statement; we may reject it; we may deliberately look elsewhere in the *Travels* for our satisfaction. But we must take it into account in any serious discussion of Swift's total achievement, for in this, the most famous of all Swift's writings, such a statement is what he sought to achieve.

If Swift's "misanthropy" is not, in any literal sense, the foundation on which the whole of the *Travels* rests, still less can it serve as a "key" or "cornerstone" to his satiric canon in general. It offers few answers to the kind of question which, I have argued, is raised by the presence of a particular satiric work; it would be misleading to seek in Swift's basic doctrines of morality for any particularly helpful insight into the specific goals or procedures of his individual satires—or even for those normative beliefs on which the judgments invited in such works are based. Belief in universal human depravity, indeed, would tend to mitigate the guilt of the individual offender; in a world of illusion, fraud and deception, guile and pretense, can hardly be branded as vicious departures from the norm. It is possible that the central doctrines of the "Digression concerning Madness" and the Fourth Voyage of the *Travels,* produced more than a quarter-century apart, reflect, in their similarity, a single, sustained moral belief which, during the whole of his adult life, may have lain at the bottom of Swift's personal assessment of humanity. It is clear, however, that, agile and prudent satirist as he was, this is not a belief he was anxious to impose upon the audiences of his most polemical satire or on which he depended for his humor, however broadly the latter may have exploited human folly.

Yet there are, I believe, ways in which the particular predispositions and sensitivities, the choices implicit in Swift's roster of satiric victims and modes of attacking them, even the principles he invokes in the course of his satiric appeal, are illuminated by his fundamental conception of the human state. In his few discussions of his own satiric art we cannot find—any more than in his practice of that art—much of the pseudo-benevolence which the satirist so often offers as his *raison d'être.* Even the relatively mellow *Verses on the Death of Dr. Swift,* written many years after the *Travels* and as close to an *apologia* as anything Swift ever produced, are comparatively moderate in their claims:

> As with a moral View designed
> To cure the Vices of Mankind:
> His Vein, ironically grave,
> Expos'd the Fool, and lashed the Knave.[24]

Against even this measured claim to have exercised the satirist's power in the interests of spiritual therapy, we have the overt skepticism which Swift expresses with respect to satire as a generally applicable instrument of reform, both in the Preface to *A Tale of a Tub* and his famous introductory remarks to *The Battle of the Books.* Unlike both Dryden and Pope, Swift never, to my knowledge, justifies his career as satirist in moral terms any more lofty than the modest claims to honorable candor and loyalty which he advances in the *Death of Dr. Swift.* As has been suggested, his most benignly motivated satiric undertakings rarely, if ever, profess to exhort men to what, in any absolute sense, can be called a higher level of morality. The *Argument against Abolishing Christianity* progresses by facetious concessions to expediency and comfort, but, when it is

[24] *Poems,* II, 565.

stripped of this fictional disguise, it urges on its readers no formulas for salvation or improvement beyond those of duty to the established Church. And it enforces its claims by invoking principles no loftier than common welfare, domestic order, and the obviation of manifest heresy and folly.

It is not, perhaps, going too far to suggest that the unpretentiousness of Swift's preaching and his non-satiric religious tracts—what Professor Landa has called "a conservative adherence to simple and indisputable orthodoxy"[25]—is produced as much by fundamental skepticism as it is by a humble conception of the preacher's function. Swift's practice in his sermons, as in such a document as *The Sentiments of a Church-of-England Man,* follows almost invariably his own precept that a "reasonable Clergyman . . . will be at the Pains, to make the most ignorant Man comprehend what is his Duty; and to convince him by Arguments, drawn to the Level of his Understanding, that he ought to perform it."[26]

In the concessions he makes to the "understanding" of ordinary men, Swift seems willing to exploit the world of appearances and to appeal to man's urge, however fundamentally deluded it may be, for serenity and order. Because the only truth which is ultimately "sacred" to him must be revealed as bitter and comfortless, he contents himself, both as preacher and satirist, with the exposure of manifest evil, invoking no more transcendent principles than those of social order, common probity, dignity, and prudence. In the world of appearances there remain for him relative degrees of truth; the course of political action or of religious belief which flies in the face of common interest is plainly a greater folly than the systematic pursuit of that interest, however illusory the contentment yielded by such a pursuit.

But although, in his "practical" roles, Swift generally refrains from pressing his own dark view of moral reality, that view imposes limits upon the promises and persuasions which he has to offer, even for "the most ignorant Man." He is careful in his talk of "errors" and "abuses," for men, in the Swiftian view, do not slip or stray from a condition of inherent dignity and wisdom. The concept of an easy restoration to some prior state of virtue is entirely alien to

[25] *Prose Works,* IX, 101.

[26] *A Letter to a Young Gentleman Lately Entered into Holy Orders (Prose Works,* IX, 70–71).

Swift's thinking. Where his satiric quasi-histories suggest an original
condition of innocence or nobility—in the religious allegory or the
history of criticism in the *Tale,* in Lilliput's erstwhile Utopian institutions, or speculations as to the "pittance" of reason which initially distinguished men from Yahoos—the past is represented as quite
irrecoverable. The Sermons regularly urge that man do his duty—as
that duty is defined in terms of common piety and social usefulness;
but they do not suggest that, through the performance of his duty,
man will approach closer to an absolute model of wisdom or virtue,
for in Swift's conception of moral reality such a model lacks meaningful existence.

   It is this skepticism concerning man's "restoration" to nobility
which also accounts, I think, for the clearly unapologetic and unqualified character of Swift's satire. Dryden, with an appearance of
fairness, takes rueful account of Shaftesbury's past achievements;
Pope's "Atticus" portrait—in itself the supreme specimen of damna-
tion with faint praise—feigns sorrow rather than anger. For Swift,
however, men are not victims of the forces that contend against their
better selves, nor are decent instincts subverted by a ruling passion.
Only in the tenderness of a verse to Stella does Swift assume the role
of the "Friend" who

> ... in Kindness tries
> To shew you where your Error lies

and suggest that a passion which is a fault when improperly directed
may be redeemed by exploitation for "nobler Ends."[27] When, as
satirist or preacher, Swift castigates his audience or, even more, a
victim not associated with his audience, he makes no pretense of
reluctance or of a righteous anger which follows only from a "higher" principle of rectitude. The "bitterness" attributed to Swift is a
very real quality in almost all of his satire. This is not because the
final damning conclusions of the Houyhnhnm myth are directly
reflected in the satire—they rarely, if ever, are. It is because these
conclusions implicitly prevent Swift's employing satire as a genuine
"corrective," from assailing vice and folly as aberrations, from wist-
fully lamenting what might have been and holding out benevolent
lures for the restoration of former glories. For such motives cannot
be professed by one whose view of human weakness stems from the

[27] "To Stella, Who Collected and Transcribed His Poems" (*Poems,* II, 730).

proposition that mankind has in fact employed a modest endowment of reason for the aggravation of his natural corruptions.

Swift's satiric "bitterness" can also be related to another aspect of the Houyhnhnm myth—the final expression of indignation against pride as the human sin to which, alone, Gulliver cannot begin to reconcile himself. Within the conceptual structure of the myth, it is plain why pride is the most terrible of human offenses; it is no part of man's natural endowments, but as a gratuitous, utterly groundless, utterly ugly acquisition, it is the epitome of the "new" corruptions which nature has not given us. Its manifestations within the social order, moreover, are those revolutions and conquests, systems and symbols and inspirations, by which knaves enslave fools and the simplest rules of common sense are overturned.

But pride, at least in Gulliver's outraged conception of it, cannot be countered with benign counsels of humility, nor, since it is totally irrational, can it be reasoned away. Man's myopic complacency can be fought only by devastating attacks on the very foundations of his self-esteem. Without the benefit of reasoned argument, without nuances, he must be shown raw fact about his origins and endowments. From his fraudulent pinnacle of self-admiration, he must, in truth, be "turn'd to that dirt from whence he sprung."[28]

Even the bitterest controversialists feel bound, for the most part, by the rules of decorum and fair play, based as they are upon some concession to human dignity and the right of one's antagonists to be wrong. Such scruples, however, play little part in Swift's conduct of the satiric attack. Properly to assail pride, it is apparently necessary for him to destroy whatever vestiges of self-respect, whatever frail bases for confidence are ordinarily left intact, and to engage, sometimes with questionable relevance, upon *ad hominem* assaults whose power lies largely in the passion by which, transparently, they are motivated. He is likely to neglect the immediate issues of a controversy in order to sneer at the presumption and vanity of an antagonist. His contemptuous account of Steele's qualifications as a writer has little to do with the Dunkirk affair in *The Importance of the Guardian Considered.*[29] *The Author upon Himself* is so filled with brutal vilification and irritable disparagement that very little sym-

---

[28] "A Satirical Elegy on the Death of a Late Famous General" (*Poems*, I, 297).

[29] See the "Account of this Gentleman's Importance" in the opening paragraphs of the tract (*Prose Works*, VIII, 5-7).

pathy can be engendered by the poem's final image of the wronged and weary Dean.[30] The Wotton-Bentley caricatures of the *Tale* and the *Battle of the Books,* apt and sardonically amusing though they may be, are manifestly unfair attacks upon the claims of these men to serious respect. Such satire is designed neither to argue nor to refute, but to bludgeon away at the very foundations of dignity. It is aimed at men rather than at men's vices, and it is carried out with the fierce satisfaction of one who destroys men by destroying their pride.

Swift's bawdiness, his insistence on raw, unlovely physical fact, his coarseness of language and metaphor, can be seen as a more direct reflection of his relentless hatred of pride. I have already attempted to indicate how readily our creature habits and needs lend themselves to the humorous requirements of the comic writer and hence of the satirist. Beyond these uses, however, the facts about our physical endowment are a superlative instrument for the kind of assault on pride which is dictated by Swift's angry view of this moral infirmity. Pride, for Swift, cannot be checked by logic or devout exhortation. Humility, as he conceives it, is suspiciously close to self-contempt and is a state which can best be induced by shock and revulsion, by the inescapable discovery that the grounds for pride are false—and, worse than false, the basis only for disgust and self-loathing. This end can be achieved, as Swift sometimes seeks to achieve it, by an exposure of human institutions, by the satiric demonstration that war and religious controversy, our litigiousness and political maneuverings, our projects and systems, are irrational, self-defeating, and mere extensions of our primordial bestiality. Such undertakings, however, are difficult and controversial; they require reasoning, and they run counter, moreover, to our instinctive tendency to view wars as sacred enterprises, lawsuits as the pursuit of absolute justice, and "projects" of every kind as lofty intellectual crusades.

But the facts of squalor and filth, lust and physical ugliness, require no involved demonstrations and admit of little equivocation. For Swift, these irrefutable realities are the basic antidote to pride, the all-purpose weapon for the assault on man's false estimate of his own beauty, power, and importance. The exposure of this actuality, which takes its most comprehensive form in the Yahoo episodes, is

[30] *Poems,* I, 191–96.

plainly embodied again and again in the "dirty" poems—*The Prog-ress of Beauty; Phillis, or the Progress of Love; The Progress of Marriage; The Lady's Dressing Room;* and others—but it is also employed in the dozens of writings, in verse and prose, in which the object of his satire is "vulgarized." Whether he addresses himself to the pretensions of literary forms (as he seems to do in the *Description of the Morning, Description of a City Shower, A Pastoral Dialogue,* and others) or, as he does countless times, to the pretensions of particular enemies, his emphasis on coarse language, mean objects, odious sights, sounds, and smells, sexual appetites and animal needs is constantly employed to represent the hard core of reality by which illusion and vainglory can alone be discountenanced. Professor Quintana has summed up Swift's moral realism with the phrase, "It is not as you think—look!"[31] We cannot evade the nature of the spectacle, the unwelcome truth, to which Swift thus mercilessly redirects our attention. It is not enough to say that this spectacle is unorthodox and upsetting. Far more often than otherwise, it is ugly and base, compounded of the squalor and vulgarity, the brutality and stink of our Yahoo nature.

In the poems and topical satires, there is no Lemuel Gulliver who can be conveniently dissociated from Jonathan Swift as a fictional creature with his own perverse conception of reality. The raw facts of physical nastiness and human depravity cannot be mitigated by conjectures as to what they truly "stand for." They stand only for an actuality against which to measure the fraudulence of custom, the pretensions of individual men, the vanity of the human self-image which fails to take them into complete account.

At least two recent writers have argued that the persistence of this repellent conception of reality in Swift's works is attributable to an "excremental vision," a vision so basic that no aspect of human affairs could, in Swift's mind, be entirely divorced from it.[32] If this is so, the question remains whether the vision is merely the pathological survival into adult life of small-boy pruriency, an unhealthy fascination with the biological facts which mature men integrate

---

[31] *The Mind and Art of Jonathan Swift,* pp. 96, 364.

[32] The title of one of the most flamboyant chapters in John Middleton Murry's *Jonathan Swift* (London, 1954), pp. 432–48, has been borrowed, with acknowledgments, by Norman O. Brown for his brilliant and upsetting chapter on Swift in *Life against Death* (Middletown, Conn., 1959), pp. 179–201.

into a more wholesome and cultivated view of reality, or whether, as Professor Norman Brown believes, it triumphantly reflects Swift's "insight into the universal neurosis of mankind."[33] In either case, man's pride would be, as it were, only a final turn of the screw, a particularly acute symptom of his folly and impediment to his self-knowledge. If, though, as I prefer to believe, the "excremental vision," while authentic enough, proceeds from a more firmly moral response to human problems and values, it is, in the last analysis, an instrumentality in Swift's relentless assault against pride and illusion. Excrement is an unworthy object of *saeva indignatio;* so, indeed, are the Yahoos. The terrible wrath of this supremely gifted man was not, I feel, directed against the raw facts, revolting as they are, but against the groundless passion of pride which drives man to ever new manifestations of ignorance and arrogance. Swift's mode of assailing pride is possible only to one who, indeed, recognizes an "excremental vision," and his campaign against pride depends vitally upon this deadly weapon, a conception of truth which is capable of destroying self-love and illusion. But as I have tried to suggest, the vision, for all its importance to Swift, is exploited overtly for an attack ultimately directed against the present condition and conduct of mankind—against what man has made of man rather than against the qualities with which he was originally endowed. Even more appropriately, this vision—or the most immediate aspects of it —serves as the instrument of the embattled satirist in his exposure of particular manifestations of illusion and vanity. The relish with which Swift often appears to introduce topics of scatology and beastliness does not, I think, argue a positive satisfaction in these matters themselves; one detects in Swift a more familiar, although perhaps no more laudable, delight in the knowledge that he is producing shock, assailing complacency with the one weapon most perfectly calculated for its destruction.

I would finally suggest that the Swiftian view of moral reality, quite apart from the kinds of substantive preoccupation to which it leads, is rather clearly reflected in the most notable aspects of Swift's style, both in prose and verse. The outspoken enemy of "Artificial *Mediums,* false Lights, refracted Angles, Varnish and Tinsel" cannot be expected to display these devices in his own art. And the dominant qualities of Swift's style—lucidity, unpretentiousness, rig-

[33] *Life against Death,* p. 185.

orous economy—are so obvious that attempts of critics to generalize upon them have a conspicuous sameness. Coleridge's observations are as perceptive as any, when he writes:

Swift's style is, in its line, perfect; the manner is a complete expression of the matter, the terms appropriate, and the artifice concealed. It is simplicity in the true sense of the word.[34]

What is remarkable about such generalizations is the consistency with which they survive the most careful scrutiny of Swift's writing. Except where Swift engages in parody (and here, unlike some writers, the consistency of his own habits of writing makes his deliberate departure from them abundantly clear),[35] his choice of words and his syntactical construction seem constantly to adhere to his own belief that "when a Man's Thoughts are clear, the properest Words will generally offer themselves first; and his own Judgment will direct him in what Order to place them, so as they may be best understood."[36] But unlike the "simplicity" applauded in certain writings of our own day, the unpretentiousness of Swift's style is not the product of manifest calculation; it does not depend on the systematic reduction of thoughts to simple declarations, the deliberate abandonment of "literary" style for "conversational," or the assumption that short words, proper nouns, active verbs, and the absence of modifiers are the infallible hallmarks of true simplicity.

Swift's clarity lies rather in the positive avoidance of whatever is affected, unnecessary, or banal. The appearance of effortlessness in his writing is, I think, entirely genuine. He does not seek for words, images, or metaphors on grounds other than their immediate utility for his purpose. The quest for novelty, allusiveness and connotative richness in language is alien to his conception of the writer's art (and the object of repeated, contemptuous attention in his parody). His "concealed artifice" is contained within the total context of passages or entire works and rarely in single words or images. When, as in *A Tale of a Tub*, a word like "happiness" acquires a special,

[34] *Coleridge's Miscellaneous Criticism*, ed. Thomas M. Raysor (Cambridge, Mass., 1936), p. 220.

[35] For a brilliant application of Swift's manifest stylistic qualities to the text of *Gulliver's Travels*, see Herbert Davis, "Aspects of Swift's Prose," in *Essays on the Eighteenth Century Presented to David Nichol Smith* (Oxford, 1945), pp. 27–32.

[36] *A Letter to a Young Gentleman Lately Entered into Holy Orders* (*Prose Works*, IX, 68).

pejorative meaning, this is provided by the nature of Swift's argument rather than by any inherent ambiguity in the term itself. Even the perverse definition of "truly wise," in the same pages, follows from the demonstration that a kind of wisdom, based upon deception, is indeed exercised in the misguided pursuit of happiness.

The demands of utility and truth prompt Swift to reject not only extravagance and ambiguity but also the pat, familiar, and traditionally authoritative sources on which persuasive writers are ordinarily tempted to rely. His distaste for banality and jargon provides the chief motive for the *Tritical Essay, Polite Conversation,* and the delightful *Meditation on a Broomstick* as well as for some of the most memorable parodic passages of the *Tale* and the *Travels.* For all his adherence to the Ancient cause, in both the *Tale* and *The Battle of the Books,* his employment of classical allusions and invocation of ancient authorities are usually marked by strong suggestions of irreverence. When classical sources, precedents, and conventions are employed in the mocking attack upon various contemporary victims, they too are likely to become plainly "vulgarized" in the process. Similarly, for Swift, the classical tag or proper name, the judgments of antiquity, have little magic in their own right; when he inroduces them it is likely to be in implicitly heavy quotation marks or with a destructive intention to which the reader had better remain alert.

Sir Harold Williams has summed up the quality of Swift's verse, and indirectly his prose, with this remark:

The ideal Swift consciously pursued in the writing of his prose he followed in his verse. The very conciseness, clarity, and directness which lend to his prose a deceptive simplicity, seemingly so easy to imitate and so impossible to attain in practice, fetter him as a poet and confine his range. The scepticism of enthusiasms, pretentions, and cant which underlies his counsel in the *Letter of Advice to a Young Poet,* in his 'Directions for a Birth-Day Song', and in his rhapsody 'On Poetry' confined a natural genius within self-imposed barriers. His poetic vesture was too small for him.[37]

It is only to be expected that the skepticism, whatever its character and ultimate foundation, which pervades his prose should be equally apparent and "confining" in his verse. Nowhere does Swift offer a distinction between the office of the poet and that of the prose writer —or, indeed, between the basic responsibilities of any writer and

[37] *Poems,* I, xiii.

those common to mankind. We look in vain in his works for any conception of art as serving a "mimetic" function, as devoted to ends which can be distinguished from those of ordinary communication. It is hard to imagine the direction to which Swift would turn in defining an artistic "object of imitation." Certainly not to a reassuring conception of "nature"—either in the pristine universality of which, Pope tells us, the "Rules" remain *mutatis mutandis* so true a reflection, or in the happily generalized tulip of which Johnsonian criticism urges that the poet produce a "just representation."

The "self-imposed barriers" within which Swift works, both in poetry and prose, are inevitable for one who attaches to his art no more ambitious a purpose than to communicate effectively what can be seen and known. In the absence of a priori commitments as to what is the "proper" end of the art which he practices; without the slightest illusion that the genuinely "instructive" can, at the same time, prove "delightful"; with reality, as he sees it, as the only appropriate matter for the writer to discuss; and with a view of reality totally devoid of grounds for hope, diversion, or "elevation," it is clear that he has cut himself off from most of the traditional sources of "poetic" power.

If, that is, the conventional notions of lyricism, the tranquil recollections of emotions or anything else, the power to see, feel, or speak as it is not given to other men to do, or even the capacity reassuringly to formulate "what oft was thought but ne'er so well expressed," are offered as the special province of poetry, then Swift as poet does, indeed, work within a "poetic vesture . . . too small for him." But the refusal to recognize a unique poetic office also has its advantages and offers its own kind of latitude. As Swift's own verse shows, the absence of a self-conscious poetic identity encourages the poet to work within the same great range of occasions and purposes as is open to the writer of prose. The same common-sense, temporal issues which elicit prose satire can also call forth the unapologetic display of satiric verse; the jocular spoofs, ill-tempered assaults, transient moments of mirth, anger, or even idle curiosity which appeal to any man of nimble wits can be exploited for the exercise of poetic talent. And so, too, without the slightest nod in deference to lyricism or inspiration or elevation or serenity, such a poet may provide, in his verse, the corrosive and unsettling truths of his prose-myths, his expositions of basic belief and disbelief.

Precisely because the requirements of prosody alone impose upon

Swift's verse the only restriction, his poems are perfectly calculated to reveal the consequences of his most basic attitudes and beliefs in the details of his style. In the compact economy of rhyme and meter the pattern of his stylistic choices becomes entirely clear. The technique of shock-treatment emerges at every level, from shamelessly outrageous rhymes to the climactic insertion of ugly words. The metaphor is sparingly used, and then almost inevitably for pejorative purposes. Wit does not take its form in crystalline perceptions, in titillating but basically agreeable paradoxes, in the elegant union of opposites or halving of wholes by which so many of the world's memorable aphorisms are achieved. Swiftian wit emerges from incongruities left unresolved, from the unexpected introduction not of neat conclusions but of blunt facts, from the inescapable commonplaces of time and place, mean objects and action, raw language, base sentiments—played off against a background of pretensions and fancies and illusions which, almost inevitably, suffers by its juxtaposition with harsh reality. "Poetic" forms, conventions, and diction are either neglected or shamelessly spoofed and exploited. *The Satirical Elegy* assails both the character of the late Duke of Marlborough and the fatuous employment of the elegiac tradition itself. Quite apart from its substance, *On Poetry* is a mocking parody of the "rhapsodic" air and its attendant devices.[38]

Coupled with a concern for the truth in Swift's view of the literary arts is a concern for communicability. Adornments and affectations are not merely departures from the plain truth; they are impediments to understanding. The same kinds of expression which he assails as fraudulent are likewise vulnerable on the score of their unintelligibility—whether they are fables and signs, arcane mysteries, or the inspired snufflings of Enthusiasts. It is interesting to note that the "rules" laid down in the *Letter to a Young Gentleman*[39] are almost entirely based upon a simple principle of intelligibility. The letter is colored by the acute awareness of an audience which may well include the "most ignorant man." To the "acquired" weaknesses of such an audience—their intellectual sloth, desire for entertainment, and self-esteem—Swift makes few concessions; characteristically, he is intensely scornful of vulgar colloquialisms and easy commonplaces. His concessions to the varied limits of

[38] *Poems,* II, 639–60.
[39] *Prose Works,* IX, 61–81.

human intelligence, however, largely dominate his injunctions to the young preacher; learned quotations, affected wit, philosophical jargon, and gratuitous attacks upon heresy are not assailed, in this instance, on the grounds of fraudulence or impropriety, but exclusively in terms of the manner in which they affect the "understanding" of a congregation.

And, whether deliberately or not, this same concern for total intelligibility is plainly displayed in the language of Swift's verse as well as in his comic, satiric, and rhetorical prose. In few of his verses will he traffic with the ambiguities, nuances, allusions, and overtones which, for some, are the essence of poetic diction.[40] The "cruxes," if any, of his poems are the products of historical accident, the particularities of meaning and reference which have eluded us only with the passage of time. And the uncertainty engendered by even the most controversial of his prose writings can never be attributed to the inherent "mystery" of the words and images he employs. When, as I have suggested, he endows terms or figures with "special" meanings, these are acquired through a systematic construction which yields neither to speculation nor symbolic associations but only to close scrutiny and common-sense analysis. If we are left in doubt, if our response to such writings as the Fourth Book of the *Travels* is, in some sense, ambiguous, it is because we are not quite certain where Swift stands, or where we are to stand. The "problems" of Swift's writing itself arise because he resists not our understanding but our belief.

Swift's style, then, is not merely the manifestation of a superlative talent, however plainly it reflects his extraordinary adroitness in the manipulation of words and sounds or the acuteness of his ear for the rhythms and chimes, the similarities and differences of speech. The inimitable clarity of his writing is, in addition, the product of a sustained awareness of audiences, on the one hand, and, on the other, of an unwavering conception of human reality to which any literary quality save utmost clarity would be alien. As preacher, pamphleteer, and satirist, he works always in the arena of opinion; his audience

---

[40] The obvious exceptions to any assertion about Swift's unaffected poetic style are to be found in the four pindaric odes and two "addresses" in couplets which are the product of his years in Sir William Temple's household; see *Poems,* I, 3–55. I am inclined to believe that close reading of even these "exercises" in essentially uncongenial modes of versification will reveal sporadic traces of Swift's special wit and tough-mindedness.

must be educable or entertainable, or his mission is a failure. In the exercise of the satirist's art, he must take into constant account the preoccupations and beliefs which, in the conduct of his satire, must either be exploited or altered. Above all, he must recognize the limits upon the intelligence of his readers and auditors; if he is unintelligible, he is nothing.

In his appeal to the omnipresent audience he is prepared to be governed by its human desires, its capacity for shock, its cruelty (from which he himself is not free), and the limits of its intelligence. But to men's illusions about themselves, to false images of immutable virtue, to hopes for permanent happiness or nobility, in short, to the sources of men's pride, he will make not the slightest concession. His own conception of man's state forbids his affirming the value of "higher" principles or suggesting, either in his substance or his method, that beauty is more than skin deep. Thus, for Swift, pretensions to lyricism are impossible; Fancy is only the enemy of Reason; Inspiration, in even its broadest sense, is bogus and subversive.

The final truth, as Swift seems to have expressed it, is both so simple and so devastating that it is disclosed only once or twice in the course of a literary lifetime. Beyond this, it takes no direct literary form. But because it is the truth for Swift, it dictates the austere path which all of his literary undertakings must follow. It is a path which allows him little chance to appear lovable, affirmatively dedicated, or constructive. Yet it offers, nonetheless, a particular kind of freedom. For it liberates him from the claims of false benevolence, false eloquence, false hope, false wisdom. Thus free, he can preach, with total conviction, the doctrine of duty to those for whom duty is the necessary substitute for understanding. He can wage exuberant warfare against bogus prophets and savants. He can devote his greatest powers to the practice of that savage but useful art whose glory is not to proclaim truth but to destroy falsehood.

Index